Level 1

BENCHMARK SERIES

Microsoft® Word

365

2019 Edition

Nita Rutkosky | **Audrey Roggenkamp** | **Ian Rutkosky**
Pierce College Puyallup | Pierce College Puyallup
Puyallup, Washington | Puyallup, Washington

PARADIGM
EDUCATION SOLUTIONS

St. Paul

Vice President, Content and Digital Solutions: Christine Hurney
Director of Content Development, Computer Technology: Cheryl Drivdahl
Developmental Editor: Jennifer Joline Anderson
Director of Production: Timothy W. Larson
Production Editor/Project Manager: Jen Weaverling
Senior Design and Production Specialist: Jack Ross
Cover and Interior Design: Valerie King
Copy Editor: Communicáto, Ltd
Testers: Janet Blum, Traci Post
Indexer: Terry Casey
Vice President, Director of Digital Products: Chuck Bratton
Digital Projects Manager: Tom Modl
Digital Solutions Manager: Gerry Yumul
Senior Director of Digital Products and Onboarding: Christopher Johnson
Supervisor of Digital Products and Onboarding: Ryan Isdahl
Vice President, Marketing: Lara Weber McLellan
Marketing and Communications Manager: Selena Hicks

ISBN 978-0-76388-716-2 (print)
ISBN 978-0-76388-708-7 (digital)

© 2020 by Paradigm Publishing, LLC
875 Montreal Way
St. Paul, MN 55102
Email: CustomerService@ParadigmEducation.com
Website: ParadigmEducation.com

Brief Contents

Contents

Achieving Proficiency in Word

The Benchmark Series, *Microsoft® Word 365*, 2019 Edition, is designed for students who want to learn how to use Microsoft's powerful word processing program to create professional-looking documents for school, work, and personal communication needs. No prior knowledge of word processing is required. After successfully completing a course using this courseware, students will be able to do the following:

- Create and edit memos, letters, flyers, announcements, and reports of varying complexity.
- Apply appropriate formatting elements and styles to a range of document types.
- Add graphics and other visual elements to enhance written communication.
- Plan, research, write, revise, design, and publish documents to meet specific information needs.
- Given a workplace scenario requiring a written solution, assess the communication purpose and then prepare materials that achieve the goal efficiently and effectively.

Well-designed pedagogy is important, but students learn technology skills through practice and problem solving. Technology provides opportunities for interactive learning as well as excellent ways to quickly and accurately assess student performance. To this end, this course is supported with Cirrus, Paradigm's cloud-based training and assessment learning management system. Details about Cirrus as well as its integrated student courseware and instructor resources can be found on page xii.

Proven Instructional Design

The Benchmark Series has long served as a standard of excellence in software instruction. Elements of the series function individually and collectively to create an inviting, comprehensive learning environment that leads to full proficiency in computer applications. The following visual tour highlights the structure and features that comprise the highly popular Benchmark model.

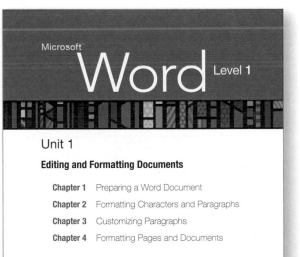

Unit Openers display the unit's four chapter titles. Each level of the course contains two units with four chapters each.

Chapter Openers Present Learning Objectives

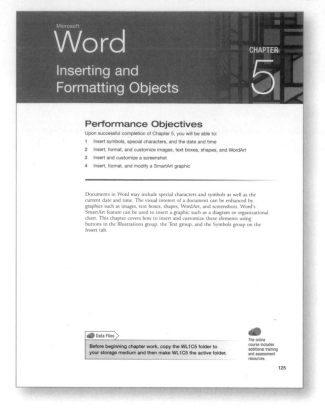

Chapter Openers present the performance objectives and an overview of the skills taught.

Data Files are provided for each chapter. A prominent note reminds students to copy the appropriate chapter data folder and make it active.

Activities Build Skill Mastery within Realistic Context

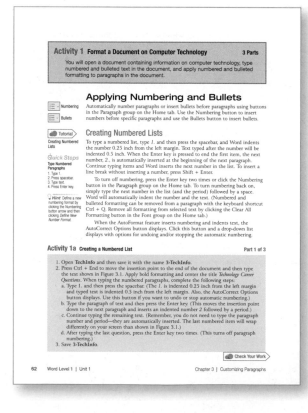

Multipart Activities provide a framework for instruction and practice on software features. An activity overview identifies tasks to accomplish and key features to use in completing the work.

Typically, a file remains open throughout all parts of the activity. Students save their work incrementally. At the end of the activity, students save, print, and then close the file.

Tutorials provide interactive, guided training and measured practice.

Quick Steps in the margins allow fast reference and review.

Hints offer useful tips on how to use software features efficiently and effectively.

Step-by-Step Instructions guide students to the desired outcome for each activity part. Screen captures illustrate what the screen should look like at key points.

Between activity parts, the text presents instruction on the features and skills necessary to accomplish the next portion of the activity.

Magenta Text identifies material to type.

Check Your Work model answer images are available in the online course, and students can use those images to confirm they have completed the activity correctly.

Chapter Review Tools Reinforce Learning

A **Chapter Summary** reviews the purpose and execution of key features.

A **Commands Review** summarizes visually the major software features and alternative methods of access.

The Cirrus Solution
Elevating student success and instructor efficiency

Powered by Paradigm, Cirrus is the next-generation learning solution for developing skills in Microsoft Office. Cirrus seamlessly delivers complete course content in a cloud-based learning environment that puts students on the fast track to success. Students can access their content from any device anywhere, through a live internet connection; plus, Cirrus is platform independent, ensuring that students get the same learning experience whether they are using PCs, Macs, or Chromebook computers.

Cirrus provides Benchmark Series content in a series of scheduled assignments that report to a grade book to track student progress and achievement. Assignments are grouped in modules, providing many options for customizing instruction.

Dynamic Training

The online Benchmark Series courses include interactive resources to support learning.

Watch and Learn Lessons include a video demonstrating how to perform the chapter activity, a reading to provide background and context, and a short quiz to check understanding of concepts and skills.

Guide and Practice Tutorials provide interactive, guided training and measured practice.

Hands On Activities enable students to complete chapter activities, compare their solutions against a Check Your Work model answer image, and submit their work for instructor review.

Chapter Review and Assessment

Review and assessment activities for each chapter are available for completion in Cirrus.

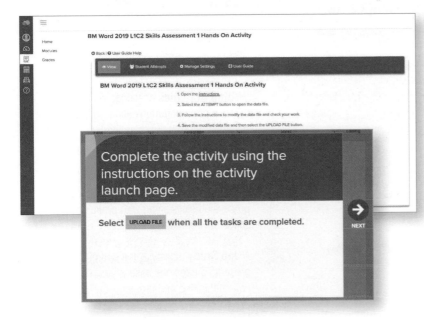

Concepts Check completion exercises assess their comprehension and recall of application features and functions as well as key terminology.

Skills Assessment Hands On Activity exercises evaluate the ability to apply chapter skills and concepts in solving realistic problems. Each is completed live in Word and is uploaded through Cirrus for instructor evaluation.

Visual Benchmark assessments test problem-solving skills and mastery of application features.

A **Case Study** requires analyzing a workplace scenario and then planning and executing a multipart project. Students search the web and/or use the program's Help feature to locate additional information required to complete the Case Study.

Exercises and **Projects** provide opportunities to develop and demonstrate skills learned in each chapter. Each is completed live in the Office application and is automatically scored by Cirrus. Detailed feedback and how-to videos help students evaluate and improve their performance.

Skills Check Exams evaluate students' ability to complete specific tasks. Skills Check Exams are completed live in the Office application and are scored automatically. Detailed feedback and instructor-controlled how-to videos help student evaluate and improve their performance.

Multiple-choice **Concepts Exams** assess understanding of key commands and concepts presented in each chapter.

Unit Review and Assessment

Review and assessment activities for each unit of each Benchmark course are also available for completion in Cirrus.

Assessing Proficiency exercises check mastery of software application functions and features.

Writing Activities challenge students to use written communication skills while demonstrating their understanding of important software features and functions.

Internet Research assignments reinforce the importance of research and information processing skills along with proficiency in the Office environment.

A **Job Study** activity at the end of Unit 2 presents a capstone assessment requiring critical thinking and problem solving.

Unit-Level Projects allow students to practice skills learned in the unit. Each is completed live in the Office application and automatically scored by Cirrus. Detailed feedback and how-to videos help students evaluate and improve their performance.

Student eBook

The Student eBook, accessed through the Cirrus online course, can be downloaded to any device (desktop, laptop, tablet, or smartphone) to make Benchmark Series content available anywhere students wish to study.

Instructor eResources

Cirrus tracks students' step-by-step interactions as they move through each activity, giving instructors visibility into their progress and missteps. With Exam Watch, instructors can observe students in a virtual, live, skills-based exam and join remotely as needed—a helpful option for struggling students who need one-to-one coaching, or for distance learners. In addition to these Cirrus-specific tools, the Instructor eResources for the Benchmark Series include the following support:

- Planning resources, such as lesson plans, teaching hints, and sample course syllabi
- Delivery resources, such as discussion questions and online images and templates
- Assessment resources, including live and annotated PDF model answers for chapter work and review and assessment activities, rubrics for evaluating student work, and chapter-based exam banks in RTF format

About the Authors

Nita Rutkosky began her career teaching business education at Pierce College in Puyallup, Washington, in 1978 and holds a master's degree in occupational education. In her years as an instructor, she taught many courses in software applications to students in postsecondary information technology certificate and degree programs. Since 1987, Nita has been a leading author of courseware for computer applications training and instruction. Her current titles include Paradigm's popular Benchmark Series, Marquee Series, and Signature Series. She is a contributor to the Cirrus online content for Office application courses and has also written textbooks for keyboarding, desktop publishing, computing in the medical office, and essential skills for digital literacy.

Audrey Roggenkamp holds a master's degree in adult education and curriculum and has been an adjunct instructor in the Business Information Technology department at Pierce College in Puyallup, Washington, since 2005. Audrey has also been a content provider for Paradigm Education Solutions since 2005. In addition to contributing to the Cirrus online content for Office application courses, Audrey co-authors Paradigm's Benchmark Series, Marquee Series, and Signature Series. Her other available titles include *Keyboarding & Applications I* and *II* and *Using Computers in the Medical Office: Word, PowerPoint, and Excel.*

Ian Rutkosky has a master's degree in business administration and has been an adjunct instructor in the Business Information Technology department at Pierce College in Puyallup, Washington, since 2010. In addition to joining the author team for the Benchmark Series and Marquee Series, he has co-authored titles on medical office computing and digital literacy and has served as a co-author and consultant for Paradigm's Cirrus training and assessment software.

Microsoft® Office

Getting Started in Office 365

Microsoft Office is a suite of applications for personal computers and other devices. These programs, known as *software*, include Word, a word processor; Excel, a spreadsheet editor; Access, a database management system; and PowerPoint, a presentation program used to design and present slideshows. Microsoft Office 365 is a subscription service that delivers continually updated versions of those applications. Specific features and functionality of Microsoft Office vary depending on the user's account, computer setup, and other factors. The Benchmark courseware was developed using features available in Office 365. You may find that with your computer and version of Office, the appearance of the software and the steps needed to complete an activity vary slightly from what is presented in the courseware.

Identifying Computer Hardware

The Microsoft Office suite can run on several types of computer equipment, referred to as *hardware*. You will need access to a laptop or a desktop computer system that includes a PC/tower, monitor, keyboard, printer, drives, and mouse. If you are not sure what equipment you will be operating, check with your instructor. The computer system shown in Figure G.1 consists of six components. Each component is discussed separately in the material that follows.

Figure G.1 Computer System

USB drive

PC/tower

monitor

printer

keyboard

mouse

Figure G.2 System Unit Ports

Ethernet port | USB ports | microphone connection | speaker connection | video port

System Unit (PC/Tower)

Traditional desktop computing systems include a system unit known as the *PC (personal computer)* or *tower*. This is the brain of the computer, where all processing occurs. It contains a Central Processing Unit (CPU), hard drives, and video cards plugged into a motherboard. Input and output ports are used for attaching peripheral equipment such as a keyboard, monitor, printer, and so on, as shown in Figure G.2. When a user provides input, the PC computes it and outputs the results.

Monitor

💡 *Hint* Monitor size is measured diagonally and is generally the distance from the bottom left corner to the top right corner of the monitor.

A computer monitor looks like a television screen. It displays the visual information output by the computer. Monitor size can vary, and the quality of display for monitors varies depending on the type of monitor and the level of resolution.

Keyboard

The keyboard is used to input information into the computer. The number and location of the keys on a keyboard can vary. In addition to letters, numbers, and symbols, most computer keyboards contain function keys, arrow keys, and a numeric keypad. Figure G.3 shows a typical keyboard.

The 12 keys at the top of the keyboard, labeled with the letter *F* followed by a number, are called *function keys*. Use these keys to perform functions within each of the Office applications. To the right of the regular keys is a group of special or dedicated keys. These keys are labeled with specific functions that will be performed when you press the key. Below the special keys are arrow keys. Use these keys to move the insertion point in the document screen.

Some keyboards include mode indicator lights to indicate that a particular mode, such as Caps Lock or Num Lock, has been turned on. Pressing the Caps Lock key disables the lowercase alphabet so that text is typed in all caps, while pressing the Num Lock key disables the special functions on the numeric keypad so that numbers can be typed using the keypad. When you select these modes, a light appears on the keyboard.

Figure G.3 Keyboard

function keys

mode indicator lights

alphanumeric keys

arrow keys or insertion point control keys

numeric, insertion point control, and special keys

Drives and Ports

An internal hard drive is a disk drive that is located inside the PC and that stores data. External hard drives may be connected via USB ports for additional storage. Ports are the "plugs" on the PC, and are used to connect devices to the computer, such as the keyboard and mouse, the monitor, speakers, USB flash drives and so on. Most PCs will have a few USB ports, at least one display port, audio ports, and possibly an ethernet port (used to physically connect to the internet or a network).

Printer

An electronic version of a file is known as a *soft copy*. If you want to create a hard copy of a file, you need to print it. To print documents, you will need to access a printer, which will probably be either a laser printer or an ink-jet printer. A laser printer uses a laser beam combined with heat and pressure to print documents, while an ink-jet printer prints a document by spraying a fine mist of ink on the page.

Mouse

Most functions and commands in the Microsoft Office suite are designed to be performed using a mouse or a similar pointing device. A mouse is an input device that sits on a flat surface next to the computer. You can operate a mouse with your left or right hand. Moving the mouse on the flat surface causes a corresponding pointer to move on the screen, and clicking the left or right mouse buttons allows you to select various objects and commands.

Using the Mouse The applications in the Microsoft Office suite can be operated with the keyboard and a mouse. The mouse generally has two buttons on top, which you press to execute specific functions and commands. A mouse may also contain a wheel, which can be used to scroll in a window or as a third button. To use the mouse, rest it on a flat surface or a mouse pad. Put your hand over it with your palm resting on top of the mouse and your index finger resting on the left mouse button. As you move your hand, and thus the mouse, a corresponding pointer moves on the screen.

When using the mouse, you should understand four terms — *point, click, double-click*, and *drag*. To *point* means to position the mouse pointer on a desired item, such as an option, button, or icon. With the mouse pointer positioned on the item, *click* the left mouse button once to select the item. (In some cases you may *right-click*, which means to click the right mouse button, but generally, *click* refers to the left button.) To complete two steps at one time, such as choosing and then executing a function, *double-click* the left mouse button by tapping it twice in quick succession. The term *drag* means to click and hold down the left mouse button, move the mouse pointer to a specific location, and then release the button. Clicking and dragging is used, for instance, when moving a file from one location to another.

Using the Mouse Pointer The mouse pointer will look different depending on where you have positioned it and what function you are performing. The following are some of the ways the mouse pointer can appear when you are working in the Office suite:

- The mouse pointer appears as an I-beam (called the *I-beam pointer*) when you are inserting text in a file. The I-beam pointer can be used to move the insertion point or to select text.
- The mouse pointer appears as an arrow pointing up and to the left (called the *arrow pointer*) when it is moved to the Title bar, Quick Access Toolbar, ribbon, or an option in a dialog box, among other locations.
- The mouse pointer becomes a double-headed arrow (either pointing left and right, pointing up and down, or pointing diagonally) when you perform certain functions such as changing the size of an object.
- In certain situations, such as when you move an object or image, the mouse pointer displays with a four-headed arrow attached. The four-headed arrow means that you can move the object left, right, up, or down.
- When a request is being processed or when an application is being loaded, the mouse pointer may appear as a moving circle. The moving circle means "please wait." When the process is completed, the circle is replaced with a normal mouse pointer.
- When the mouse pointer displays as a hand with a pointing index finger, it indicates that more information is available about an item. The mouse pointer also displays as a hand with a pointing index finger when you hover over a hyperlink.

Touchpad

If you are working on a laptop computer, you may be using a touchpad instead of a mouse. A *touchpad* allows you to move the mouse pointer by moving your finger across a surface at the base of the keyboard (as shown in Figure G.4). You click and right-click by using your thumb to press the buttons located at the bottom of the touchpad. Some touchpads have special features such as scrolling or clicking something by tapping the surface of the touchpad instead of pressing a button with a thumb.

Figure G.4 Touchpad

Touchscreen

Smartphones, tablets, and touch monitors all use touchscreen technology (as shown in Figure G.5), which allows users to directly interact with the objects on the screen by touching them with fingers, thumbs, or a stylus. Multiple fingers or both thumbs can be used on most touchscreens, giving users the ability to zoom, rotate, and manipulate items on the screen. While many activities in this textbook can be completed using a device with a touchscreen, a mouse or touchpad might be required to complete a few activities.

Figure G.5 Touchscreen

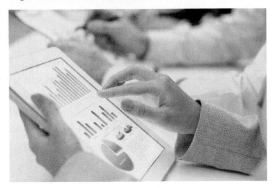

Choosing Commands

A *command* is an instruction that tells an application to complete a certain task. When an application such as Word or PowerPoint is open, the *ribbon* at the top of the window displays buttons and options for commands. To select a command with the mouse, point to it and then click the left mouse button.

Notice that the ribbon is organized into tabs, including File, Home, Insert, and so on. When the File tab is clicked, a *backstage area* opens with options such as opening or saving a file. Clicking any of the other tabs will display a variety of commands and options on the ribbon. Above the ribbon, buttons on the Quick Access Toolbar provide fast access to frequently used commands such as saving a file and undoing or redoing an action.

Using Keyboard Shortcuts and Accelerator Keys

As an alternative to using the mouse, keyboard shortcuts can be used for many commands. Shortcuts generally require two or more keys. For instance, in Word, press and hold down the Ctrl key while pressing P to display the Print backstage area, or press Ctrl + O to display the Open backstage area. A complete list of keyboard shortcuts can be found by searching the Help files in any Office application.

Office also provides shortcuts known as *accelerator keys* for every command or action on the ribbon. These accelerator keys are especially helpful for users with motor or visual disabilities or for power users who find it faster to use the keyboard than click with the mouse. To identify accelerator keys, press the Alt key on the keyboard. KeyTips display on the ribbon, as shown in Figure G.6. Press the keys indicated to execute the desired command. For example, to begin checking

Figure G.6 Word Home Tab KeyTips

the spelling and grammar in a document, press the Alt key, press the R key on the keyboard to display the Review tab, and then press the letter C and the number 1 on the keyboard to open the Editor task pane.

Choosing Commands from a Drop-Down List

Some buttons include arrows that can be clicked to display a drop-down list of options. Point and click with the mouse to choose an option from the list. Some options in a drop-down list may have a letter that is underlined. This indicates that typing the letter will select the option. For instance, to select the option *Insert Table*, type the letter I on the keyboard.

If an option in a drop-down list is not available to be selected, it will appear gray or dimmed. If an option is preceded by a check mark, it is currently active. If it is followed by an ellipsis (…), clicking the option will open a dialog box.

Choosing Options from a Dialog Box or Task Pane

Some buttons and options open a *dialog box* or a task pane containing options for applying formatting or otherwise modifying the data in a file. For example, the Font dialog box shown in Figure G.7 contains options for modifying the font and adding effects. The dialog box contains two tabs—the Font tab and the Advanced tab. The tab that displays in the front is the active tab. Click a tab to make it active or press Ctrl + Tab on the keyboard. Alternately, press the Alt key and then type the letter that is underlined in the tab name.

Figure G.7 Word Font Dialog Box

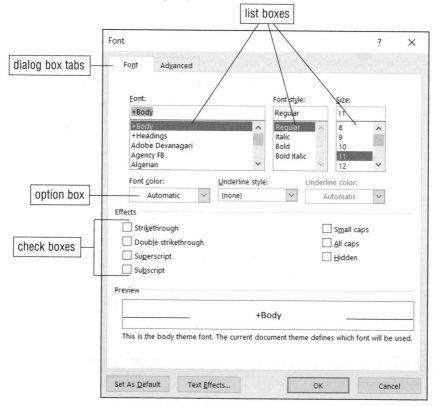

To choose an option from a dialog box using the mouse, position the arrow pointer on the option and then click the left mouse button. To move forward from option to option using the keyboard, you can press the Tab key. Press Shift + Tab to move back to a previous option. If the option displays with an underlined letter, you can choose it by pressing the Alt key and the underlined letter. When an option is selected, it is highlighted in blue or surrounded by a dotted or dashed box called a *marquee*. A dialog box contains one or more of the following elements: list boxes, option boxes, check boxes, text boxes, command buttons, radio buttons, and measurement boxes.

List Boxes and Option Boxes The fonts available in the Font dialog box, shown in Figure G.7 (on the previous page), are contained in a *list box*. Click an option in the list to select it. If the list is long, click the up or down arrows in the *scroll bar* at the right side of the box to scroll through all the options. Alternately, press the up or down arrow keys on the keyboard to move through the list, and press the Enter key when the desired option is selected.

Option boxes contain a drop-down list or gallery of options that opens when the arrow in the box is clicked. An example is the *Font color* option box in Figure G.8. To display the different color options, click the arrow at the right side of the box. If you are using the keyboard, press Alt + C.

Check Boxes Some options can be selected using a check box, such as the effect options in the dialog box in Figure G.7. If a check mark appears in the box, the option is active (turned on). If the check box does not contain a check mark, the option is inactive (turned off). Click a check box to make the option active or inactive. If you are using the keyboard, press Alt + the underlined letter of the option.

Text Boxes Some options in a dialog box require you to enter text. For example, see the Find and Replace dialog box shown in Figure G.8. In a text box, type or edit text with the keyboard, using the left and right arrow keys to move the insertion point without deleting text and use the Delete key or Backspace key to delete text.

Command Buttons The buttons at the bottom of the dialog box shown in Figure G.8 are called *command buttons*. Use a command button to execute or cancel a command. Some command buttons display with an ellipsis (...), which means another dialog box will open if you click that button. To choose a command button, click with the mouse or press the Tab key until the command button is surrounded by a marquee and then press the Enter key.

Figure G.8 Excel Find and Replace Dialog Box

Figure G.9 Word Insert Table Dialog Box

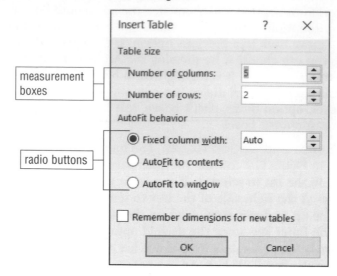

Radio Buttons The Insert Table dialog box shown in Figure G.9 contains an example of *radio buttons*. Only one radio button can be selected at any time. When the button is selected, it is filled with a dark circle. Click a button to select it, or press and hold down the Alt key, press the underlined letter of the option, and then release the Alt key.

Measurement Boxes A *measurement box* contains an amount that can be increased or decreased. An example is shown in Figure G.9. To increase or decrease the number in a measurement box, click the up or down arrow at the right side of the box. Using the keyboard, press and hold down the Alt key and then press the underlined letter for the option, press the Up Arrow key to increase the number or the Down Arrow key to decrease the number, and then release the Alt key.

Choosing Commands with Shortcut Menus

The Office applications include shortcut menus that contain commands related to different items. To display a shortcut menu, point to the item for which you want to view more options with the mouse pointer and then click the right mouse button, or press Shift + F10. The shortcut menu will appear wherever the insertion point is positioned. In some cases, the Mini toolbar will also appear with the shortcut menu. For example, if the insertion point is positioned in a paragraph of text in a Word document, clicking the right mouse button or pressing Shift + F10 will display the shortcut menu and Mini toolbar, as shown in Figure G.10.

To select an option from a shortcut menu with the mouse, click the option. If you are using the keyboard, press the Up or Down Arrow key until the option is selected and then press the Enter key. To close a shortcut menu without choosing an option, click outside the menu or press the Esc key.

Figure G.10 Shortcut Menu and Mini Toolbar

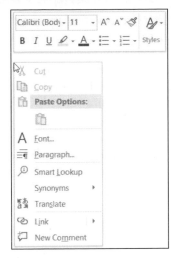

Working with Multiple Applications

As you learn the various applications in the Microsoft Office suite, you will notice many similarities between them. For example, the steps to save, close, and print are virtually the same whether you are working in Word, Excel, or PowerPoint. This consistency greatly enhances your ability to transfer knowledge learned in one application to another within the suite. Another benefit to using Microsoft Office is the ability to have more than one application open at the same time and to integrate content from one program with another. For example, you can open Word and create a document, open Excel and create a worksheet, and then copy a worksheet from the workbook into Word.

The Windows taskbar at the bottom of the screen displays buttons representing all the programs that are currently open. For example, Figure G.11 shows the taskbar with Word, Excel, Access, and PowerPoint open. To move from one program to another, click the taskbar button representing the desired application.

Maintaining Files and Folders

Windows includes a program named File Explorer that can be used to maintain files and folders. To open File Explorer, click the folder icon on the Windows taskbar. Use File Explorer to complete tasks such as copying, moving, renaming, and deleting files and folders and creating new folders. Some file management tasks can also be completed within Word, Excel, PowerPoint, or Access by clicking File and then *Open* or *Save As* and then clicking the *Browse* option to browse folders and files in a dialog box.

Directions and activities in this course assume that you are managing files and folders stored on a USB flash drive or on your computer's hard drive. If you are using your OneDrive account or another cloud-based storage service, some of the file and folder management tasks may vary.

Figure G.11 Windows Taskbar with Word, Excel, Access, and PowerPoint Open

Creating and Naming a Folder

Files (such as Word documents, Excel workbooks, PowerPoint presentations, and Access databases) are easier to find again when they are grouped logically in folders. In File Explorer and in the Open or Save As dialog box, the names of files and folders are displayed in the Content pane. Each file has an icon showing what type of file it is, while folders are identified with the icon of a folder. See Figure G.12 for an example of the File Explorer window.

Create a new folder by clicking the New folder button at the top of the File Explorer window or in the dialog box. A new folder displays with the name *New folder* highlighted. Type a name for the folder to replace the highlighted text, and then press the Enter key. Folder names can include numbers, spaces, and some symbols.

Selecting and Opening Files and Folders

Select files or folders in the window to be managed. To select one file or folder, simply click on it. To select several adjacent files or folders, click the first file or folder, hold down the Shift key, and then click the last file or folder. To select files or folders that are not adjacent, click the first file or folder, hold down the Ctrl key, click any other files or folders, and then release the Ctrl key. To deselect, click anywhere in the window or dialog box.

When a file or folder is selected, the path to the folder displays in the Address bar. If the folder is located on an external storage device, the drive letter and name may display in the path. A right-pointing arrow displays to the right of each folder name in the Address bar. Click the arrow to view a list of subfolders within a folder.

Double-click a file or folder in the Content pane to open it. You can also select one or more files or folders, right-click, and then click the *Open* option in the shortcut menu.

Figure G.12 File Explorer Window

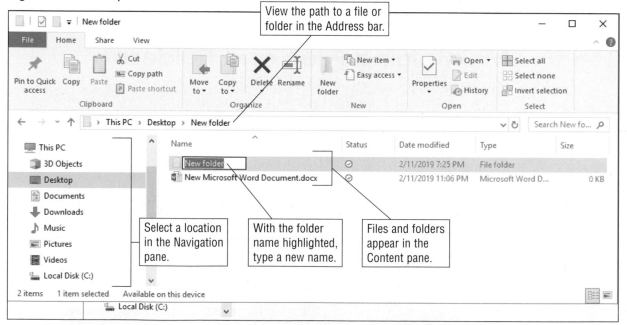

Deleting Files and Folders

Deleting files and folders is part of file maintenance. To delete a file or folder, select it and then press the Delete key. Alternatively, use the Delete button on the Home tab of the File Explorer window, or click the Organize button and then *Delete* in the dialog box. You can also right-click a file or folder and then choose the *Delete* option in the shortcut menu.

Files and folders deleted from the hard drive of the computer are automatically sent to the Recycle Bin, where they can easily be restored if necessary. If a file or folder is stored in another location, such as an external drive or online location, it may be permanently deleted. In this case, a message may appear asking for confirmation. To confirm that the file or folder should be deleted, click Yes.

To view the contents of the Recycle Bin, display the Windows desktop and then double-click the *Recycle Bin* icon. Deleted items in the Recycle Bin can be restored to their original locations, or the Recycle Bin can be emptied to free up space on the hard drive.

Moving and Copying Files and Folders

A file or folder may need to be moved or copied to another location. In File Explorer, select the file or folder and then click the Copy button at the top of the window, use the keyboard shortcut Ctrl + C, or right-click the file and select *Copy* in the shortcut menu. Navigate to the destination folder and then click the Paste button, use the keyboard shortcut Ctrl + P, or right-click and select *Paste*. If a copy is pasted to the same folder as the original, it will appear with the word *Copy* added to its name. To copy files in the Open or Save As dialog box, use the Organize button drop-down list or right-click to access the shortcut menu.

To move a file or folder, follow the same steps, but select *Cut* instead of *Copy* or press Ctrl + X instead of Ctrl + C. Files can also be dragged from one location to another. To do this, open two File Explorer windows. Click a file or folder and drag it to the other window while holding down the left mouse button.

Renaming Files and Folders

To rename a file or folder in File Explorer, click its name to highlight it and then type a new name, or right-click the file or folder and then select *Rename* at the shortcut menu. You can also select the file or folder and then click the Rename button on the Home tab of the File Explorer window or click *Rename* from the Organize button drop-down list at the Open or Save As dialog box. Type in a new name and then press the Enter key.

Viewing Files and Folders

Change how files and folders display in the Content pane in File Explorer by clicking the View tab and then clicking one of the view options in the Layout group. View files and folders as large, medium, or small icons; as tiles; in a list; or with details or information about the file or folder content. At the Open or Save As dialog box, click the Change your view button arrow and a list displays with similar options for viewing folders and files. Click to select an option in the list or click the Change your view button to see different views.

Displaying File Extensions Each file has a file extension that identifies the program and what type of file it is. Excel files have the extension *.xlsx;* Word files end with *.docx,* and so on. By default, file extensions are turned off. To view file extensions, open File Explorer, click the View tab, and then click the *File name extensions* check box to insert a check mark. Click the check box again to remove the check mark and stop viewing file extensions.

Displaying All Files The Open or Save As dialog box in an Office application may display only files specific to that application. For example, the Open or Save As dialog box in Word may only display Word documents. Viewing all files at the Open dialog box can be helpful in determining what files are available. Turn on the display of all files at the Open dialog box by clicking the file type button arrow at the right side of the *File Name* text box and then clicking *All Files* at the drop-down list.

Managing Files at the Info Backstage Area

The Info backstage area in Word, Excel, and PowerPoint provide buttons for managing files such as uploading and sharing a file, copying a path, and opening File Explorer with the current folder active. To use the buttons at the Info backstage area, open Word, Excel, or PowerPoint and then open a file. Click the File tab and then click the *Info* option. If a file is opened from the computer's hard drive or an external drive, four buttons display near the top of the Info backstage area as shown in Figure G.13.

Click the Upload button to upload the open file to a shared location such as a OneDrive account. Click the Share button and a window displays indicating that the file must be saved to OneDrive before it can be shared and provides an option that, when clicked, will save the file to OneDrive. Click the Copy Path button and a copy of the path for the current file is saved in a temporary location. This path can be pasted into another file, an email, or any other location where you want to keep track of the file's path. Click the Open file location button and File Explorer opens with the current folder active.

Figure G.13 Info Backstage Buttons

If you open Word, Excel, or PowerPoint and then open a file from OneDrive, only two buttons display—Share and Open file location. Click the Share button to display a window with options for sharing the file with others and specifying whether the file can be viewed and edited, or only viewed. Click the Open file location button to open File Explorer with the current folder active.

Customizing Settings

Before beginning computer activities in this textbook, you may need to customize your monitor's settings and change the DPI display setting. Activities in the course assume that the monitor display is set at 1920×1080 pixels and the DPI set at 125%. If you are unable to make changes to the monitor's resolution or the DPI settings, the activities can still be completed successfully. Some references in the text might not perfectly match what you see on your screen, so you may not be able to perform certain steps exactly as written. For example, an item in a drop-down gallery might appear in a different column or row than what is indicated in the step instructions.

Before you begin learning the applications in the Microsoft Office suite, take a moment to check the display settings on the computer you are using. Your monitor's display settings are important because the ribbon in the Microsoft Office suite adjusts to the screen resolution setting of your computer monitor. A computer monitor set at a high resolution will have the ability to show more buttons in the ribbon than will a monitor set to a low resolution. The illustrations in this textbook were created with a screen resolution display set at 1920×1080 pixels, as shown in Figure G.14.

Figure G.14 Word Ribbon Set at 1920 x 1080 Screen Resolution

Activity 1 Adjusting Monitor Display

Note: The resolution settings may be locked on lab computers. Also, some laptop screens and small monitors may not be able to display in a 1920 × 1080 resolution or change the DPI setting.

1. At the Windows desktop, right-click in a blank area of the screen.
2. In the shortcut menu, click the *Display settings* option.

3. At the Settings window with the *Display* option selected, scroll down and look at the current setting displayed in the *Resolution* option box. If your screen is already set to 1920 × 1080, skip ahead to Step 6.

Scale and layout

Change the size of text, apps, and other items

125%

Advanced scaling settings

Resolution

1920 × 1080 (Recommended)

③

4. Click the Resolution option box and then click the *1920 × 1080* option. **Note: Depending on the privileges you are given on a school machine, you may not be able to complete Steps 4–5. If necessary, check with your instructor for alternative instructions**.

Change the size of text, apps, and other items

125%

1920 × 1080 (Recommended)

④

1680 × 1050

1600 × 900

1440 × 900

1280 × 1024

5. Click the Keep Changes button.
6. At the Settings window, take note of the current DPI percentage next to the text *Change the size of text, apps, and other items*. If the percentage is already set to 125%, skip to Step 8.
7. Click the option box below the text *Change the size of text, apps, and other items,* and then click the *125%* option in the drop-down list

Scale and layout

100% (Recommended)   ems

125%

⑦

150%

175%

8. Click the Close button to close the Settings window.

GS-14   Office 365 | Getting Started

Retrieving and Copying Data Files

While working through the activities in this course, you will often be using data files as starting points. These files are provided through your Cirrus online course, and your instructor may post them in another location such as your school's network drive. You can download all the files at once (described in the activity below), or download only the files needed for a specific chapter.

Activity 2 **Downloading Files to a USB Flash Drive**

Note: In this activity, you will download data files from your Cirrus online course. Make sure you have an active internet connection before starting this activity. Check with your instructor if you do not have access to your Cirrus online course.

1. Insert your USB flash drive into an available USB port.
2. Navigate to the Course Resources section of your Cirrus online course. *Note: The steps in this activity assume you are using the Chrome browser. If you are using a different browser, the following steps may vary.*
3. Click the Student Data Files link in the Course Resources section. A zip file containing the student data files will automatically begin downloading from the Cirrus website.
4. Click the button in the lower left corner of the screen once the files have finished downloading.

5. Right-click the *StudentDataFiles* folder in the Content pane.
6. Click the *Copy* option in the shortcut menu.
7. Click the USB flash drive that displays in the Navigation pane at the left side of the File Explorer window.
8. Click the Home tab in the File Explorer window.
9. Click the Paste button in the Clipboard group.

10. Close the File Explorer window by clicking the Close button in the upper right corner of the window.

Microsoft® Word Level 1

Unit 1

Editing and Formatting Documents

Microsoft® Word

Preparing a Word Document

CHAPTER 1

Performance Objectives

Upon successful completion of Chapter 1, you will be able to:

1. Open Microsoft Word
2. Create, save, name, print, open, and close a Word document
3. Close Word
4. Open a document from and pin/unpin a document at the *Recent* Option list
5. Edit a document
6. Move the insertion point within a document
7. Scroll within a document
8. Select text
9. Use the Undo and Redo buttons
10. Check spelling and grammar
11. Use the Tell Me and Help features

In this chapter, you will learn to create, save, name, print, open, close, and edit a Word document as well as complete a spelling and grammar check. You will also learn about the Tell Me feature, which provides information and guidance on how to complete a function, and the Help feature, an on-screen reference manual that provides information on features and commands for each program in the Microsoft Office suite. Before continuing, make sure you read the *Getting Started* section presented at the beginning of this book. It contains information about computer hardware and software, using the mouse, executing commands, and managing files.

 Data Files

Before beginning chapter work, copy the WL1C1 folder to your storage medium and then make WL1C1 the active folder.

The online course includes additional training and assessment resources.

3

Activity 1 Prepare a Word Document
2 Parts

You will create a short document containing information on resumes and then save, print, and close the document.

Opening a Blank
Document

Opening Microsoft Word

Microsoft Office contains a word processing program named Word that can be used to create, save, edit, and print documents. The steps to open Word may vary but generally include clicking the Start button on the Windows desktop and then clicking the Word tile at the Start menu. At the Word opening screen, click the *Blank document* template.

Exploring the Word
Screen

Quick Steps

**Open Word and Open
Blank Document**
1. Click Word tile at
   Windows Start
   menu.
2. Click *Blank
   document* template.

Creating, Saving, Printing, and Closing a Document

When the *Blank document* template is clicked, a blank document displays on the screen, as shown in Figure 1.1. The features of the document screen are described in Table 1.1.

At a blank document, type information to create a document. A document is a record containing information, such as a letter, report, term paper, or table. To create a new document, begin typing in the blank page. Here are some things to consider when typing text:

- **Word wrap:** As text is typed in the document, Word wraps text to the next line, so the Enter key does not need to be pressed at the end of each line. A word is wrapped to the next line if it continues past the right margin. The only times the Enter key needs to be pressed are to end a paragraph, create a blank line, or to end a short line.

- **AutoCorrect:** Word contains a feature that automatically corrects certain words as they are typed. For example, if *adn* is typed instead of *and*, Word automatically corrects it when the spacebar is pressed after typing the word. AutoCorrect will also format as superscript the letters that follow an ordinal number (a number indicating a position in a series). For example, type *2nd* and then press the spacebar or Enter key, and Word will convert this ordinal number to 2nd.

- **Automatic spelling checker:** Word contains an Editor that checks the spelling and grammar in a document. By default, words that are not found in the Spelling dictionary are underlined with a wavy red line. These may include misspelled words, proper names, some terminology, and some foreign words. If a typed word is not recognized by the Spelling dictionary, leave it as written if the word is spelled correctly. However, if the spelling is incorrect, retype the word or position the I-beam pointer on the word, click the right mouse button, and then click the correct spelling at the shortcut menu.

- **Automatic grammar checker:** Word's Editor includes an automatic grammar checker. If the grammar checker detects a sentence containing a possible grammatical error, the error will be underlined with a double blue line. The sentence can be left as written or corrected. To correct the sentence, position the I-beam pointer on the error, click the right mouse button, and choose from the shortcut menu of possible corrections.

Hint The Status bar includes a book icon. A check mark on the book indicates no spelling errors have been detected by the spelling checker, while an X on the book indicates errors. Click the book icon to display the Editor task pane. If the book icon is not visible, right-click the Status bar and then click the *Spelling and Grammar Check* option at the shortcut menu.

Figure 1.1 Blank Document

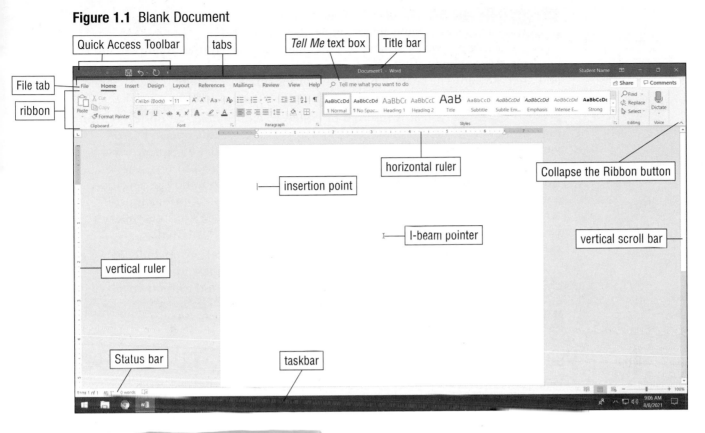

Labels on the figure: Quick Access Toolbar · tabs · *Tell Me* text box · Title bar · File tab · ribbon · horizontal ruler · Collapse the Ribbon button · insertion point · I-beam pointer · vertical scroll bar · vertical ruler · Status bar · taskbar

Table 1.1 Microsoft Word Screen Features

Feature	Description
Collapse the Ribbon button	when clicked, removes the ribbon from the screen
File tab	when clicked, displays the backstage area, which contains options for working with and managing documents
horizontal ruler	used to set margins, indents, and tabs
I-beam pointer	used to move the insertion point or to select text
insertion point	indicates the location of the next character entered at the keyboard
Quick Access Toolbar	contains buttons for commonly used commands
ribbon	area containing tabs with options and buttons divided into groups
Status bar	on the left, indicates the number of pages and words in the document; on the right, includes view buttons and Zoom slider bar
tabs	contain commands and features organized into groups
taskbar	contains icons for launching programs, buttons for active tasks, and a notification area
Tell Me text box	provides information and guidance on how to complete functions
Title bar	shows the document name followed by the program name
vertical ruler	used to set the top and bottom margins
vertical scroll bar	used to move the viewing area up or down through the document

- **Spacing punctuation:** The default typeface in Word is Calibri, which is a proportional typeface. (You will learn more about typefaces in Chapter 2.) When typing text in a proportional typeface, use only one space (rather than two) after end-of-sentence punctuation such as a period, question mark, or exclamation point and after a colon. The characters in a proportional typeface are set closer together, and extra white space at the end of a sentence or after a colon is not needed.

- **Option buttons:** As text is inserted or edited in a document, an option button may display near the text. The name and appearance of this option button varies depending on the action. If a typed word is corrected by AutoCorrect, if an automatic list is created, or if autoformatting is applied to text, the AutoCorrect Options button appears. Click this button to undo the specific automatic action. If text is pasted in a document, the Paste Options button appears near the text. Click this button to display the Paste Options gallery, which has buttons for controlling how the pasted text is formatted.

- **AutoComplete:** Microsoft Word and other Office applications include an AutoComplete feature that inserts an entire item when a few identifying characters are typed. For example, type the letters *Mond* and *Monday* displays in a ScreenTip above the letters. Press the Enter key or press the F3 function key and Word inserts *Monday* in the document.

Entering Text

Using the New Line Command

A Word document is based on a template that applies default formatting. Some basic formatting includes 1.08 line spacing and 8 points of spacing after a paragraph. Each time the Enter key is pressed, a new paragraph begins and 8 points of spacing is inserted after the paragraph. To move the insertion point down to the next line without including the additional 8 points of spacing, use the New Line command, Shift + Enter.

Activity 1a Creating a Document   Part 1 of 2

1. Open Word by clicking the Word tile at the Windows Start menu.
2. At the Word opening screen, click the *Blank document* template. (These steps may vary. Check with your instructor for specific instructions.)
3. At a blank document, type the information shown in Figure 1.2 with the following specifications:
   a. Correct any spelling or grammatical errors identified by the Editor as they occur.
   b. Press the spacebar once after end-of-sentence punctuation.
   c. After typing *Created:* press Shift + Enter to move the insertion point to the next line without adding 8 points of additional spacing.
   d. To insert the word *Thursday* at the end of the document, type Thur and then press the F3 function key. (This is an example of the AutoComplete feature.)
   e. To insert the word *December*, type Dece and then press the Enter key. (This is another example of the AutoComplete feature.)
   f. Press Shift + Enter after typing *December 9, 2021.*
   g. When typing the last line (the line containing the ordinal numbers), type the ordinal number text and AutoCorrect will automatically convert the letters in the ordinal number to a superscript.
4. When you are finished typing the text, press the Enter key. (Keep the document open for the next activity.)

Check Your Work

Figure 1.2 Activity 1a

The traditional chronological resume lists your work experience in reverse-chronological order (starting with your current or most recent position). The functional style deemphasizes the "where" and "when" of your career and instead groups similar experiences, talents, and qualifications regardless of when they occurred.

Like the chronological resume, the hybrid resume includes specifics about where you worked, when you worked there, and what your job titles were. Like a functional resume, a hybrid resume emphasizes your most relevant qualifications in an expanded summary section, in several "career highlights" bullet points at the top of your resume, or in activity summaries.

Created:
Thursday, December 9, 2021
Note: The two paragraphs will become the 2nd and 3rd paragraphs in the 5th section.

Tutorial

Saving with a New Name

Save

Quick Steps

Save Document
1. Click File tab.
2. Click *Save As* option.
3. Click *Browse* option.
4. Type document name in *File name* text box.
5. Press Enter key.

Hint Save a document approximately every 15 minutes or when interrupted.

Saving a Document

If a document will be used in the future, it must be saved. To save a new document, click the File tab and then click the *Save* or the *Save As* option. The Save As backstage area displays, as shown in Figure 1.3. Click the *Browse* option to open the Save As dialog box, shown in Figure 1.4. (Pressing the F12 function key will also open this dialog box.) At the dialog box, navigate to the location where the file is to be saved, type a file name, and then press the Enter key or click the Save button. Continue saving periodically whenever edits are made by clicking the Save button on the Quick Access Toolbar or with the keyboard shortcut Ctrl + S.

To save a new version of a document while keeping the original, click the File tab and then click the *Save As* option to display the Save As backstage area. (Do not click *Save*, or changes will be saved to the existing file.) At the Save As backstage area, click the *Browse* option to display the Save As dialog box. Type a new name for the document, select a location where the document is to be saved, and then press the Enter key or click the Save button.

Figure 1.3 Save As Backstage Area

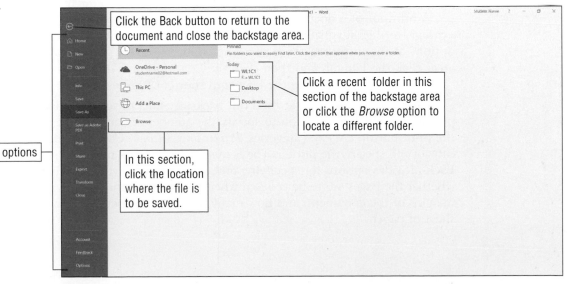

Click the Back button to return to the document and close the backstage area.

Click a recent folder in this section of the backstage area or click the *Browse* option to locate a different folder.

In this section, click the location where the file is to be saved.

options

Figure 1.4 Save As Dialog Box

Address bar

toolbar

Navigation pane

Content pane

Type the document name in this text box.

Details pane

Naming a Document

Hint Word will not allow you to save two documents with the same name in the same folder. This is true even if you make one name uppercase and one lowercase.

Document names created in Word and other applications in the Microsoft Office suite can be up to 255 characters in length, including the drive letter and any folder names, and they may include spaces. File names cannot include any of the following characters:

forward slash (/)	less-than symbol (<)	quotation marks (" ")
backslash (\)	asterisk (*)	colon (:)
greater-than symbol (>)	question mark (?)	pipe symbol (|)

Printing a Document

Tutorial

Printing a Document

Quick Steps
Print Document
1. Click File tab.
2. Click *Print* option.
3. Click Print button.

Click the File tab and the backstage area displays. The buttons and options at the backstage area change depending on the option selected at the left side of the backstage area. To leave the backstage area without completing an action, click the Back button in the upper left corner of the backstage area, or press the Esc key on the keyboard.

A printout of a document on paper is known as a *hard copy*, as opposed to the *soft copy*, or digital version, which displays on the screen. Print a document with options at the Print backstage area, shown in Figure 1.5. To display this backstage area, click the File tab and then click the *Print* option. The Print backstage area can also be displayed using the keyboard shortcut Ctrl + P.

Click the Print button at the Print backstage area to send the document to the printer. Use the *Copies* option to specify the number of copies to be printed. Below the Print button are two categories: *Printer* and *Settings*. Use the gallery in the *Printer* category to specify the printer. The *Settings* category contains a number of galleries. Each provides options for specifying how the document will print, including whether the pages are to be collated when printed; the orientation, page size, and margins of the document; and how many pages of the document are to print on a sheet of paper.

Figure 1.5 Print Backstage Area

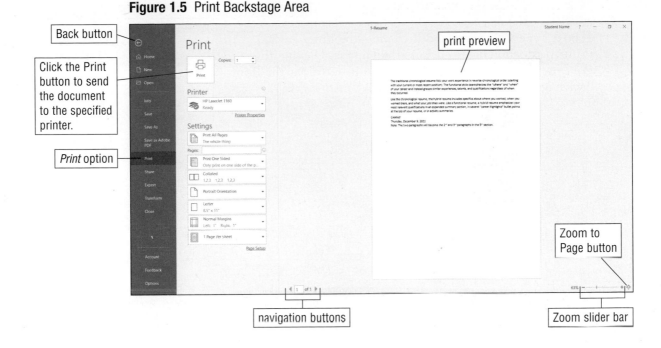

Back button

Click the Print button to send the document to the specified printer.

Print option

print preview

Zoom to Page button

navigation buttons

Zoom slider bar

Quick Print

Quick Steps

Close Document
1. Click File tab.
2. Click *Close* option.

Close Word
Click Close button.

Another method for printing a document is to insert the Quick Print button on the Quick Access Toolbar and then click the button. This sends the document directly to the printer without displaying the Print backstage area. To insert the button on the Quick Access Toolbar, click the Customize Quick Access Toolbar button at the right side of the toolbar and then click *Quick Print* at the drop-down list. To remove the Quick Print button from the Quick Access Toolbar, right-click the button and then click the *Remove from Quick Access Toolbar* option at the shortcut menu.

Tutorial

Closing a Document and Closing Word

Close

Closing a Document and Closing Word

When a document is saved, it is saved to the specified location and also remains on the screen. To remove the document from the screen, click the File tab and then click the *Close* option or use the keyboard shortcut Ctrl + F4. When a document is closed, it is removed and a blank screen displays. At this screen, open a previously saved document, create a new document, or close Word. To close Word, click the Close button in the upper right corner of the screen. The keyboard shortcut Alt + F4 also closes Word.

Activity 1b Saving, Printing, and Closing a Document and Closing Word
Part 2 of 2

1. Save the document you created for Activity 1a and name it **1-Resume** (*1-* for Chapter 1 and *Resume* because the document is about resumes) by completing the following steps:
   a. Click the File tab.
   b. Click the *Save As* option.
   c. At the Save As backstage area, click the *Browse* option.
   d. At the Save As dialog box, if necessary, navigate to the WL1C1 folder on your storage medium.

1a

e. Click in the *File name* text box (this selects any text in the box), type 1-Resume, and then press the Enter key.

2. Print the document by clicking the File tab, clicking the *Print* option, and then clicking the Print button at the Print backstage area.

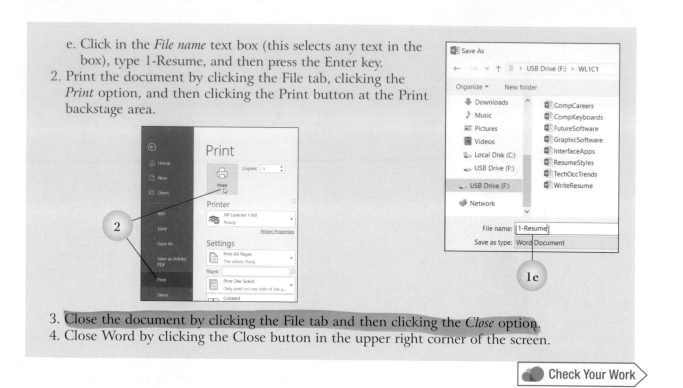

3. Close the document by clicking the File tab and then clicking the *Close* option.
4. Close Word by clicking the Close button in the upper right corner of the screen.

Check Your Work

Activity 2 **Save a Document with a New Name and the Same Name** **2 Parts**

You will open a document in the WL1C1 folder on your storage medium, save the document with a new name, add text, and then save the document with the same name. You will also print and then close the document.

Creating a New Document

Quick Steps

Create New Document
1. Click File tab.
2. Click *Blank document* template.

When a document is closed, a blank screen displays. To create a new document, click the File tab, click the *New* option, and then click the *Blank document* template. A new document can also be opened with the keyboard shortcut Ctrl + N or with the New button on the Quick Access Toolbar. To insert the button on the Quick Access Toolbar, click the Customize Quick Access Toolbar button at the right of the toolbar and then click *New* at the drop-down list.

Additional templates can be found by clicking the File tab and then clicking the *Home* or the *New* option. Double-click the *Single spaced (blank)* template to open a new document with single spacing and no added space after paragraphs.

 Tutorial

Opening a Document from a Removable Disk

Opening a Document

After a document is saved and closed, it can be opened at the Open dialog box, shown in Figure 1.6. Display the dialog box by clicking the File tab, clicking the *Open* option, and then clicking the *Browse* option at the backstage area. Other methods for displaying the Open backstage area include using the keyboard shortcut Ctrl + O, inserting an Open button on the Quick Access Toolbar, and clicking the <u>More documents</u> hyperlink in the lower right corner of the Word opening screen and the Home backstage area.

Figure 1.6 Open Dialog Box

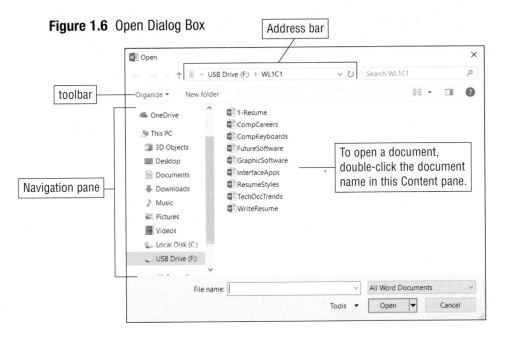

At the Open backstage area, click the *Browse* option and the Open dialog box displays. Go directly to the Open dialog box without displaying the Open backstage area by pressing Ctrl + F12. At the Open dialog box, navigate to the desired location (such as the drive containing your storage medium), open the folder containing the document, and then double-click the document name in the Content pane.

Quick Steps

Open Document
1. Click File tab.
2. Click *Open* option.
3. Click *Browse* option.
4. Double-click document name.

Tutorial

Opening a Document from the *Recent* Option List

Opening a Document from the *Recent* Option List

At the Open backstage area with the *Recent* option selected, the names of the most recently opened documents are listed. By default, Word lists the names of the 50 most recently opened documents and groups them into categories such as *Today*, *Yesterday*, and perhaps another category such as *This Week*. To open a document from the *Recent* option list, scroll down the list and then click the document name. The Word opening screen and the Home backstage area also provide a list of the names of the most recently opened documents. Click a document name in the Recent list to open the document.

Tutorial

Pinning and Unpinning a Document at the *Recent* Option List

Pinning and Unpinning Documents and Folders

If a document is opened on a regular basis, consider pinning it so it can be found more easily. At the Open backstage area, hover the mouse pointer over the document name in the *Recent* option list and then click the push pin icon that appears. The document will now appear at the top of the list in the *Pinned* category, with the push pin icon pointing down. A document can also be pinned at the Home backstage area. Click the push pin icon next to a document name, and the document will display in the *Pinned* tab.

To "unpin" a document from the *Recent* option list at the Open backstage area or the Pinned list at the Home backstage area, click the push pin icon to the right of the document name. More than one document can be pinned to a list.

Another method for pinning and unpinning documents is to use the shortcut menu. Right-click a document name and then click the *Pin to list* or *Unpin from list* option. The shortcut menu also includes the *Remove from list* option, which removes a document from the *Recent* option list and the Recent list. Right-click a pinned document in the *Recent* option list at the Open backstage area and the shortcut menu includes the option *Clear unpinned Documents*, which removes all unpinned documents from the *Recent* option list.

In addition to documents, folders can be pinned for easier access. To pin a frequently-used folder, display the Open backstage area and then click the *Folders* option. Recently opened folders are listed and grouped into categories such as *Today*, *Yesterday*, and *Last Week* to reflect the time they were last accessed. Click the push pin icon to the right of a folder and it will be pinned to the top of the list.

Activity 2a Opening, Pinning, Unpinning, and Saving a Document   Part 1 of 2

1. Open Word and then open **CompCareers** by completing the following steps:
   a. At the Word opening screen, click the <u>More documents</u> hyperlink in the lower right corner of the screen. (You may need to scroll down the screen to display this hyperlink.)
   b. At the Open backstage area, click the *Browse* option.
   c. At the Open dialog box, navigate to the external drive containing your storage medium.
   d. Double-click the **WL1C1** folder in the Content pane.
   e. Double-click **CompCareers** in the Content pane.
2. Close **CompCareers**.
3. Press Ctrl + F12 to display the Open dialog box and then double-click **FutureSoftware** in the Content pane to open the document.
4. Close **FutureSoftware**.
5. Pin **CompCareers** to the *Recent* option list by completing the following steps:
   a. Click the File tab and then click the *Open* option.
   b. At the Open backstage area, hover the mouse pointer over **CompCareers** in the *Recent* option list and then click the left-pointing push pin icon to the right of the document. (The **CompCareers** file will now appear in the *Pinned* category at the top of the list, and the push pin icon will be pointing downward.)

6. Click **CompCareers** in the *Pinned* category at the top of the *Recent* option list to open the document.
7. Unpin **CompCareers** from the *Recent* option list by completing the following steps:
   a. Click the File tab and then click the *Open* option.
   b. At the Open backstage area, click the down-pointing push pin icon to the right of **CompCareers** in the *Pinned* category in the *Recent* option list. (This removes the file from the *Pinned* category and changes the pin to a left-pointing push pin.)
   c. Click the Back button to return to the document.

8. With **CompCareers** open, save the document with a new name by completing the following steps:
   a. Click the File tab and then click the *Save As* option.
   b. At the Save As backstage area, click the *Browse* option.
   c. At the Save As dialog box, if necessary, navigate to the WL1C1 folder on your storage medium.
   d. Press the Home key on your keyboard to move the insertion point to the beginning of the file name and then type 1-.
   e. Press the Enter key.

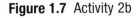 **Tutorial**

Saving with the Same Name

Saving Changes to a Document

After making changes to a document, save the changes before closing the file. Consider saving on a periodic basis to ensure that no changes are lost if the application crashes or freezes or if power is interrupted. Unless keeping an older version of the document is important, changes can be saved using the same file name. Save a document with the same name using the Save button on the Quick Access Toolbar, the *Save* option at the backstage area, or with the keyboard shortcut Ctrl + S.

Note: If a document is stored in a cloud location such as Microsoft OneDrive or SharePoint Online, any changes to it will be saved automatically with the AutoSave feature. AutoSave can be turned on or off by clicking the toggle switch in the upper left corner of the Word screen.

Quick Steps

Save Document with Same Name
Click Save button on Quick Access Toolbar.
OR
1. Click File tab.
2. Click *Save* option.

Activity 2b Saving a Document with the Same Name   Part 2 of 2

1. With **1-CompCareers** open and the insertion point positioned at the beginning of the document, type the text shown in Figure 1.7.
2. Save the changes you just made by clicking the Save button on the Quick Access Toolbar.
3. Print the document by clicking the File tab, clicking the *Print* option, and then clicking the Print button at the Print backstage area. (If your Quick Access Toolbar contains the Quick Print button, you can click the button to send the document directly to the printer.)
4. Close the document by pressing Ctrl + F4.

Check Your Work

Figure 1.7 Activity 2b

The majority of new jobs being created in the United States today involve daily work with computers. Computer-related careers include technical support jobs, sales and training, programming and applications development, network and database administration, and computer engineering.

You will open a previously created document, save it with a new name, and then use scrolling and browsing techniques to move the insertion point to specific locations in the document.

Scrolling

Editing a Document

When a document is being edited, text may need to be inserted or deleted. To edit a document, use the mouse, the keyboard, or a combination of the two to move the insertion point to specific locations in the document. To move the insertion point using the mouse, position the I-beam pointer where the insertion point is to be positioned and then click the left mouse button.

Scrolling in a document changes the text display but does not move the insertion point. Use the mouse with the vertical scroll bar, at the right side of the screen, to scroll through text in a document. Click the up scroll arrow at the top of the vertical scroll bar to scroll up through the document, and click the down scroll arrow to scroll down through the document.

The scroll bar contains a scroll box that indicates the location of the text in the document screen in relation to the remainder of the document. To scroll up one screen at a time, position the mouse pointer above the scroll box (but below the up scroll arrow) and then click the left mouse button. Position the mouse pointer below the scroll box and click the left button to scroll down a screen. Click and hold down the left mouse button and the action becomes continuous.

Another method for scrolling is to position the mouse pointer on the scroll box, click and hold down the left mouse button, and then drag the scroll box along the scroll bar to reposition text in the document screen. As the scroll box is dragged along the vertical scroll bar in a longer document, page numbers are shown in a box at the right side of the document screen.

Activity 3a Scrolling in a Document   Part 1 of 2

1. Open **InterfaceApps** (from the WL1C1 folder you copied to your storage medium).
2. Save the document with the new name **1-InterfaceApps** to your WL1C1 folder.
3. Position the I-beam pointer at the beginning of the first paragraph and then click the left mouse button.
4. Click the down scroll arrow on the vertical scroll bar several times. (This scrolls down lines of text in the document.) With the mouse pointer on the down scroll arrow, click and hold down the left mouse button and keep it down until you reach the end of the document.
5. Position the mouse pointer on the up scroll arrow and then click and hold down the left mouse button until you reach the beginning of the document.
6. Position the mouse pointer below the scroll box and then click the left mouse button. Continue clicking the mouse button (with the mouse pointer positioned below the scroll box) until you reach the end of the document.
7. Position the mouse pointer on the scroll box in the vertical scroll bar. Click and hold down the left mouse button, drag the scroll box to the top of the vertical scroll bar, and then release the mouse button. (Notice that the document page numbers are shown in a box at the right side of the document screen.)
8. Click in the title at the beginning of the document. (This moves the insertion point to the location of the mouse pointer.)

Moving the Insertion Point to a Specific Line or Page

Find

Word includes a Go To feature that moves the insertion point to a specific location in a document, such as a line or page. To use the feature, click the Find button arrow in the Editing group on the Home tab and then click *Go To* at the drop-down list. At the Find and Replace dialog box with the Go To tab selected, move the insertion point to a specific page by typing the page number in the *Enter page number* text box and then pressing the Enter key. Move to a specific line by clicking the *Line* option in the *Go to what* list box, typing the line number in the *Enter line number* text box, and then pressing the Enter key. Click the Close button to close the dialog box.

Moving the Insertion Point with the Keyboard

Tutorial

Moving the
Insertion Point
and Inserting and
Deleting Text

To move the insertion point with the keyboard, use the arrow keys to the right of the regular keyboard or use the arrow keys on the numeric keypad. When using the arrow keys on the numeric keypad, make sure Num Lock is off. Use the arrow keys together with other keys to move the insertion point to various locations in the document, as shown in Table 1.2.

When moving the insertion point, Word considers a word to be any series of characters between spaces. A paragraph is any text that is followed by a single press of the Enter key. A page is text that is separated by a soft or hard page break.

Table 1.2 Insertion Point Movement Commands

To move insertion point	Press
one character left	Left Arrow
one character right	Right Arrow
one line up	Up Arrow
one line down	Down Arrow
one word left	Ctrl + Left Arrow
one word right	Ctrl + Right Arrow
to beginning of line	Home
to end of line	End
to beginning of current paragraph	Ctrl + Up Arrow
to beginning of next paragraph	Ctrl + Down Arrow
up one screen	Page Up
down one screen	Page Down
to top of previous page	Ctrl + Page Up
to top of next page	Ctrl + Page Down
to beginning of document	Ctrl + Home
to end of document	Ctrl + End

Resuming Reading or Editing in a Document

If a previously saved document is opened, pressing Shift + F5 will move the insertion point to the position it was last located when the document was closed.

When a multiple-page document is reopened, Word remembers the page where the insertion point was last positioned. A "Welcome back!" message appears at the right side of the screen near the vertical scroll bar, identifying the page where the insertion point was last located. Click the message and the insertion point is positioned at the top of that page.

Activity 3b Moving the Insertion Point in a Document

Part 2 of 2

1. With **1-InterfaceApps** open, move the insertion point to line 15 and then to page 3 by completing the following steps:
   a. Click the Find button arrow in the Editing group on the Home tab and then click *Go To* at the drop-down list.
   b. At the Find and Replace dialog box with the Go To tab selected, click *Line* in the *Go to what* list box.
   c. Click in the *Enter line number* text box, type 15, and then press the Enter key.
   d. Click *Page* in the *Go to what* list box.
   e. Click in the *Enter page number* text box, type 3, and then press the Enter key.
   f. Click the Close button to close the Find and Replace dialog box.
2. Close the document.
3. Open the document by clicking the File tab and then clicking the document name *1-InterfaceApps* in the Recent list.
4. Move the mouse pointer to the right side of the screen to display the "Welcome back!" message. Hover the mouse pointer over the message and then click the left mouse button. (This positions the insertion point at the top of the third page—the page the insertion point was positioned when you closed the document.)
5. Press Ctrl + Home to move the insertion point to the beginning of the document.
6. Practice using the keyboard commands shown in Table 1.2 to move the insertion point within the document.
7. Close **1-InterfaceApps**.

Activity 4 Insert and Delete Text   2 Parts

You will open a previously created document, save it with a new name, and then make editing changes to the document. The editing changes will include selecting, inserting, and deleting text and undoing and redoing edits.

Inserting and Deleting Text

Editing a document may include inserting and/or deleting text. To insert text in a document, position the insertion point at the location text is to be typed and then type the text. Existing characters move to the right as text is typed. A number of options are available for deleting text. Some deletion commands are shown in Table 1.3.

Tutorial

Selecting, Replacing, and Deleting Text

Selecting Text

Use the mouse and/or keyboard to select a specific amount of text. Selected text can be deleted or other Word functions can be performed on it. When text is selected, it displays with a gray background, as shown in Figure 1.8, and the Mini toolbar displays. The Mini toolbar contains buttons for common tasks. (You will learn more about the Mini toolbar in Chapter 2.)

Table 1.3 Deletion Commands

To delete	Press
character right of insertion point	Delete key
character left of insertion point	Backspace key
text from insertion point to beginning of word	Ctrl + Backspace
text from insertion point to end of word	Ctrl + Delete

Figure 1.8 Selected Text and Mini Toolbar

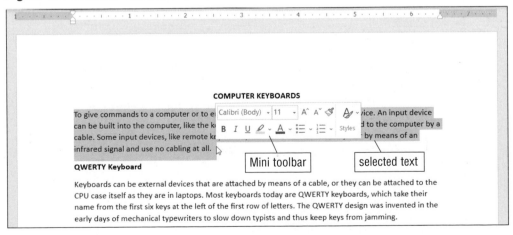

Selecting Text with the Mouse Use the mouse to select a word, line, sentence, paragraph, or entire document. Table 1.4 indicates the steps to follow to select various amounts of text.

One way to select text is by clicking in the selection bar. The selection bar is the space at the left side of the document screen between the left edge of the page and the text. When the mouse pointer is positioned in the selection bar, the pointer turns into an arrow pointing up and to the right (instead of to the left). Click once to select a line of text, twice to select a paragraph, and three times to select all the text in the document.

Another way to select text is by using the I-beam pointer. Position the pointer on the first character of the text to be selected, click and hold down the left mouse button, drag the I-beam pointer to the last character of the text to be selected, and then release the mouse button. Alternately, position the insertion point where the selection is to begin, press and hold down the Shift key, click the I-beam pointer at the end of the selection, and then release the Shift key. To cancel a selection, simply click in the document screen.

Select text vertically in a document by pressing and holding down the Alt key while dragging with the mouse. This is especially useful when selecting a group of text, such as text set in columns.

Selecting Text with the Keyboard To select text using the keyboard, turn on the Selection mode by pressing the F8 function key. With the Selection mode activated, use the arrow keys to select text. To cancel the selection, press the Esc key and then press any arrow key. The Status bar can be customized to indicate that the Selection mode is activated. To do this, right-click on the Status bar and then click *Selection Mode* at the pop-up list. When the F8 function key is pressed to turn on the Selection mode, the words *Extend Selection* display on the Status bar. Text can also be selected with the commands shown in Table 1.5.

Table 1.4 Selecting Text with the Mouse

To select	Complete these steps using the mouse
a word	Double-click the word.
a line of text	Click in the selection bar to the left of the line.
multiple lines of text	Drag in the selection bar to the left of the lines.
a sentence	Press and hold down the Ctrl key and then click in the sentence.
a paragraph	Double-click in the selection bar next to the paragraph, or triple-click in the paragraph.
multiple paragraphs	Drag in the selection bar.
an entire document	Triple-click in the selection bar, or click the Select button in Editing group and then click *Select All*.

Table 1.5 Selecting Text with the Keyboard

To select	Press
one character to right	Shift + Right Arrow
one character to left	Shift + Left Arrow
to end of word	Ctrl + Shift + Right Arrow
to beginning of word	Ctrl + Shift + Left Arrow
to end of line	Shift + End
to beginning of line	Shift + Home
one line up	Shift + Up Arrow
one line down	Shift + Down Arrow
to beginning of paragraph	Ctrl + Shift + Up Arrow
to end of paragraph	Ctrl + Shift + Down Arrow
one screen up	Shift + Page Up
one screen down	Shift + Page Down
to end of document	Ctrl + Shift + End
to beginning of document	Ctrl + Shift + Home
entire document	Ctrl + A

Activity 4a Editing a Document

1. Open **CompKeyboards**. (This document is in the WL1C1 folder you copied to your storage medium.)
2. Save the document with the new name **1-CompKeyboards**.
3. Change the word *give* in the first sentence of the first paragraph to *enter* by double-clicking *give* and then typing enter.
4. Change the second *to* in the first sentence to *into* by double-clicking *to* and then typing into.
5. Select the words *means of* in the first sentence in the *QWERTY Keyboard* section and then press the Delete key to delete the selected text.
6. At the end of the last sentence of the first paragraph, select the words *and use no cabling at all* and the period that follows, being careful not to select the space following the period. Press the Delete key to delete the selected text.
7. Insert a period immediately following the word *signal*.

8. Delete the heading *QWERTY Keyboard* using the Selection mode by completing the following steps:

   a. Position the insertion point immediately left of the *Q* in *QWERTY*.

   b. Press the F8 function key to turn on the Selection mode.

   c. Press the Down Arrow key.

   d. Press the Delete key.

9. Complete steps similar to those in Step 8 to delete the heading *DVORAK Keyboard.*

10. Begin a new paragraph with the sentence that reads *Keyboards have different physical appearances* by completing the following steps:

   a. Position the insertion point immediately left of the *K* in *Keyboards* (the first word of the fifth sentence in the last paragraph).

   b. Press the Enter key.

11. Save **1-CompKeyboards**.

8a-8c

> To enter commands into a co
> device can be built into the c
> computer by a cable. Some i
> means of an infrared signal.
>
> **QWERTY Keyboard**
>
> Keyboards can be external d
> itself as they are in laptops. I
> the first six keys at the left of
> of mechanical typewriters to

10a-10b

> To enter commands into a computer
> device can be built into the compute
> computer by a cable. Some input dev
> means of an infrared signal.
>
> Keyboards can be external devices th
> itself as they are in laptops. Most key
> the first six keys at the left of the firs
> of mechanical typewriters to slow do
>
> The DVORAK keyboard is an alternati
> commonly used keys are placed close
> install software on a QWERTY keyboa
> keyboards is convenient especially w
>
> Keyboards have different physical ap
> that of a calculator, containing numb
> "broken" into two pieces to reduce s
> change the symbol or character ente

> Check Your Work

Using the Undo and Redo Buttons

> Tutorial

Using Undo and Redo

 Undo

 Redo

💡 *Hint* You cannot undo a save.

💡 *Hint* Use the keyboard shortcut Ctrl + Z to undo an action.

💡 *Hint* Use the keyboard shortcut Ctrl + Y to redo an action.

Undo typing, formatting, or another action by clicking the Undo button on the Quick Access Toolbar. For example, type text and then click the Undo button and the text is removed. Or apply formatting to text and then click the Undo button and the formatting is removed.

Click the Redo button on the Quick Access Toolbar to reverse the original action. For example, apply formatting such as underlining to text and then click the Undo button and the underlining is removed. Click the Redo button and the underlining formatting is reapplied to the text. Many Word actions can be undone or redone. Some actions, however, such as printing and saving, cannot be undone or redone.

Word maintains actions in temporary memory. To undo an action performed earlier, click the Undo button arrow. This causes a drop-down list to display. To make a selection from this drop-down list, click the desired action; the action, along with any actions listed above it in the drop-down list, is undone.

1. With **1-CompKeyboards** open, delete the last sentence in the last paragraph using the mouse by completing the following steps:
   a. Hover the I-beam pointer anywhere over the sentence that begins *All keyboards have modifier keys*.
   b. Press and hold down the Ctrl key, click the left mouse button, and then release the Ctrl key.

> install software on a QWERTY keyboard that emulates a DVORAK keyboard. The ability to emulate other keyboards is convenient especially when working with foreign languages.
>
> Keyboards have different physical appearances. Many keyboards have a separate numeric keypad, like that of a calculator, containing numbers and mathematical operators. Some keyboards are sloped and "broken" into two pieces to reduce strain. All keyboards have modifier keys that enable the user to change the symbol or character entered when a given key is pressed.

1a-1b

   c. Press the Delete key.
2. Delete the last paragraph by completing the following steps:
   a. Position the I-beam pointer anywhere in the last paragraph (the paragraph that begins *Keyboards have different physical appearances*).
   b. Triple-click the left mouse button.
   c. Press the Delete key.
3. Undo the deletion by clicking the Undo button on the Quick Access Toolbar.
4. Redo the deletion by clicking the Redo button on the Quick Access Toolbar.
5. Select the first sentence in the second paragraph and then delete it.
6. Select the first paragraph in the document and then delete it.
7. Undo the two deletions by completing the following steps:
   a. Click the Undo button arrow.
   b. Click the second *Clear* listed in the drop-down list. (This will redisplay the first paragraph and the first sentence in the second paragraph. The sentence will be selected.)

7a   7b

8. Click outside the sentence to deselect it.
9. Save, print, and then close **1-CompKeyboards**.

Check Your Work

Activity 5 Complete a Spelling and Grammar Check   1 Part

You will open a previously created document, save it with a new name, and then check the spelling and grammar in the document.

Tutorial

Checking Spelling and Grammar

Quick Steps

Check Spelling and Grammar

1. Click Review tab.
2. Click Check Document button.
3. Click the Results button.
4. Change or ignore errors.
5. Click OK.

abc ✓ Check Document

Checking the Spelling and Grammar in a Document

Thoughtful and well-written documents are free of errors in spelling and grammar. Word contains an Editor that checks for spelling and grammar errors in documents and offers suggested corrections. It may also suggest refinements for clarity and conciseness. The Editor's spell checking feature can find and correct misspelled words, duplicate words, and irregular capitalizations. To check spelling, it compares the words in the document with the words in its dictionary. If it finds a match, it passes over the word. If the word is not found in its dictionary, it offers possible corrections. The grammar checker searches a document for errors in grammar, punctuation, and word usage. There are some types of errors that the Editor cannot find, however. Using the Editor does not eliminate the need for proofreading.

To complete a spelling and grammar check, click the Review tab and then click the Check Document button in the Proofing group or press the F7 function key. The Editor task pane opens at the right side of the screen and contains a Results button indicating the number of possible spelling and grammar errors. The task pane also contains options in the *Corrections* section identifying the number of possible spelling errors and grammar errors and a *Refinements* section identifying the number of areas that may need editing. Click the Results button to search and display spelling and grammar errors as they are encountered. Click the *Spelling* option in the *Corrections* section to review all possible spelling errors and click the *Grammar* option to review all possible grammar errors.

Click the Results button at the Editor task pane and the first spelling or grammar error is selected. The *Suggestions* list box contains one or more possible corrections. Click a suggestion to make the correction in the document. Or, click the arrow to the right of a suggestion for more options, as described in Table 1.6. If none of the suggestions seems right and the word is correct as typed, use the other options in the task pane to ignore the error or add the word to the spell checker's dictionary. Refer to Table 1.7 for descriptions of the options in the Editor task pane.

If Word detects a grammar error, the text containing the error is selected and possible corrections are provided in the Editor task pane *Suggestions* list box. Depending on the error, some of the options described in Table 1.7 may be available and a grammar rule will be provided near the top of the task pane. Click the down arrow at the right of the grammar rule and information about the grammar rule displays along with suggestions on how to correct the error.

When checking the spelling and grammar in a document, temporarily leave the Editor task pane by clicking in the document. To resume the spelling and grammar check, click the Resume button in the task pane.

Table 1.6 Suggestion Drop-Down List Options

Option	Function
Read Aloud	reads the suggested correction aloud (speaker necessary)
Spell Out	spells the suggested correction aloud (speaker necessary)
Change All	changes all instances of the error to the suggested correction
Add to AutoCorrect	makes a suggested correction automatic by adding it as an option in AutoCorrect

Table 1.7 Editor Task Pane Options

Option	Function
Ignore Once	ignores the selected error
Ignore All	ignores the error and all other occurrences of it in the document
Add to Dictionary	adds the word to the spelling checker dictionary
Delete Repeated Word	deletes one of two repeated words
Don't check for this issue	ignores a suspected grammar error and no longer checks for this type of error in the document

Activity 5 Checking the Spelling and Grammar in a Document   Part 1 of 1

1. Open **TechOccTrends** and save it with the name **1-TechOccTrends**.
2. Click the Review tab and then click the Check Document button in the Proofing group.

3. The Editor task pane opens and identifies the total number of possible spelling and grammar errors along with information in the *Corrections* section. Click the Results button (displays as *6 Results*) to display the first possible error.

4. The spelling checker selects the word *tecnology* in the document and provides the correct spelling in the *Suggestions* list box in the Editor task pane. Click *technology* in the *Suggestions* list box to change the word to the correct spelling.
5. The grammar checker selects the word *too* in the document and provides the word *to* in the *Suggestions* list box of the Editor task pane. Click the down arrow to the right of the text *Possible Word Choice Error* near the top of the task pane, read the information provided about a possible word choice error, and then click the up arrow to remove the information.

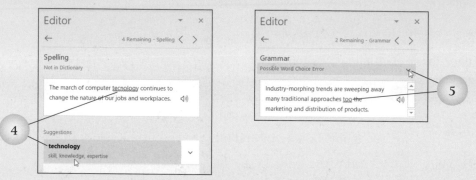

6. Click *to* in the *Suggestions* list box to correct the grammar error.
7. The grammar checker selects the words *downloaded* and *versus*, noting that two spaces appear between the words. The *Suggestions* list box in the Editor task pane provides an option with the words *downloaded versus* with only one space between the words. Click the option in the *Suggestions* list box to correct the error.
8. The spelling checker selects the word *sucessful* in the document and provides *successful* in the Editor task pane *Suggestions* list box. Since this word is misspelled in another location in the document, click the arrow at the right of the *successful* option in the *Suggestions* list box and then click *Change All* at the drop-down list.
9. The spelling checker selects the word *are*, which is used two times in a row. Click the *Delete Repeated Word* option in the Editor task pane to delete the second *are*.

10. When the message indicating the spelling and grammar check is complete, click OK.
11. Close the Editor task pane by clicking the Close button in the upper right corner of the task pane.
12. Save, print, and then close **1-TechOccTrends**.

Check Your Work

Using the Tell Me Feature

Using the Tell Me Feature

Word includes a Tell Me feature that provides information and guidance on how to use various functions in the program. To get help finding or using a function in Word, click in the *Tell Me* text box on the ribbon (or press Alt + Q) and then type the function. A drop-down list displays with options for completing the function. The drop-down list will also include links to find more information online or through the Help feature.

Click the last option in the Tell Me drop-down list to search for more results. A Smart Lookup task pane will open at the right of the screen, providing information from various sources on the internet. The Smart Lookup task pane can also be displayed by clicking the Smart Lookup button in the Research group on the References tab or by selecting text, right-clicking the selected text, and then clicking *Smart Lookup* at the shortcut menu.

Activity 6a Using the Tell Me Feature   Part 1 of 2

1. Open **GraphicSoftware** and then save it with the name **1-GraphicSoftware**.
2. Press Ctrl + A to select all text in the document.
3. Use the Tell Me feature to learn how to double-space the text in the document by completing the following steps:
   a. Click in the *Tell Me* text box on the ribbon.
   b. Type double space.
   c. Hover the mouse pointer over the *Line and Paragraph Spacing* option.
   d. At the side menu, click the *2.0* option. (This double-spaces the selected text in the document.)

   e. Click in the document to deselect the text.

4. Use the Tell Me feature to display help information on AutoCorrect by completing the following steps:
   a. Click in the *Tell Me* text box.
   b. Type autocorrect.
   c. Hover the mouse pointer over the *Get Help on "autocorrect"* option.
   d. At the side menu, click the first option (an article on AutoCorrect). This displays the Help task pane with the article information.

   e. Read the information in the Help task pane and then close the task pane by clicking the the Close button in the upper right corner of the task pane.
5. Display information on scrolling in the Smart Lookup task pane by completing the following steps:
   a. Click in the *Tell Me* text box.
   b. Type scrolling.
   c. Click the *See more search results for "scrolling"* option. (The option may display as *Smart Lookup on "scrolling."*)
   d. Look at the information on scrolling in the Smart Lookup task pane.
   e. Close the Smart Lookup task pane by clicking the task pane Close button.
6. Save, print, and then close **1-GraphicSoftware**.

> Check Your Work

 Tutorial

Using the Help Feature

(?) Help

Using the Help Feature

The Help feature is an on-screen reference manual containing information about Word features and commands. The Help feature in Word is similar to the Help features in Excel, PowerPoint, and Access. Get help by using the Tell Me feature, at the Help task pane, or at the Microsoft Office support website. Display the Help task pane by pressing the F1 function key or clicking the Help tab and then clicking the Help button.

At the Help task pane, type a topic, feature, or question in the search text box and then press the Enter key. Articles related to the search text are shown in the task pane. Click an article to display the article information in the task pane.

Getting Help from a ScreenTip

Hover the mouse pointer over a certain button, such as the Format Painter button or Font Color button, and the ScreenTip displays with a Help icon and the <u>Tell me more</u> hyperlinked text. Click <u>Tell me more</u> or press the F1 function key and the Help task pane displays with information about the button feature.

Getting Help at the Backstage Area

Click the File tab in Word to display the backstage area. A Microsoft Word Help button, labeled with a question mark (?), appears in the upper right corner of the backstage area. The Help button is also available at many of the other backstage areas. Click the Help button and the Microsoft Office support website opens in a browser window with information about the backstage area. After reading the information, close the browser window and return to Word.

Getting Help in a Dialog Box

Some dialog boxes contain a Help button. Open a dialog box and then click the Help button and the Microsoft Office support website opens in a browser window with information about the dialog box. After reading the information, close the browser window.

Activity 6b Using the Help Feature   Part 2 of 2

1. Open a new blank document by completing the following steps:
   a. Click the File tab.
   b. At the Home backstage area, double-click the *Single spaced (blank)* template. (For Word 2019, click the File tab, click the *New* option, and then double-click the *Single spaced (blank)* template.)

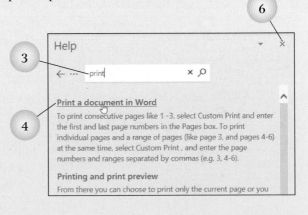

2. Press the F1 function key to display the Help task pane.
3. Type print in the task pane search text box and then press the Enter key.
4. When the list of articles displays, click the Print a document in Word hyperlinked article. (You may need to scroll down the task pane to find this article.)
5. Read the information in the task pane about printing a document.
6. Click the Close button to close the Help task pane.
7. Hover the mouse pointer over the Format Painter button in the Clipboard group on the Home tab.

8. Click the <u>Tell me more</u> hyperlinked text at the bottom of the ScreenTip.
9. Read the information in the Help task pane about the Format Painter feature.
10. Click the Help task pane Close button.
11. Click the File tab.
12. Click the Microsoft Word Help button in the upper right corner of the backstage area.

13. Look at the information on the Microsoft Office support website and then close the browser window.
14. Click the Back button to return to the document.
15. Close the blank document.

Chapter Summary

- Refer to Figure 1.1 and Table 1.1 (on page 5) for an example and a list, respectively, of key Word screen features.
- Click the File tab and the backstage area displays, containing options for working with and managing documents.
- Document names can contain a maximum of 255 characters, including the drive letter and folder names, and they may include spaces.
- The Quick Access Toolbar contains buttons for commonly used commands.
- The ribbon contains tabs with options and buttons divided into groups.
- The insertion point displays as a blinking vertical line and indicates the position of the next character to be entered in the document.
- Print a hard copy of a document by clicking the File tab, clicking the *Print* option, and then clicking the Print button.
- Close a document by clicking the File tab and then clicking the *Close* option or with the keyboard shortcut Ctrl + F4.
- Close Word by clicking the Close button in the upper right corner of the screen or with the keyboard shortcut Alt + F4.
- Create a new document by clicking the File tab, clicking the *Home* or *New* option as needed, and then clicking the *Blank document* template or by using the keyboard shortcut Ctrl + N.
- Create a new single-spaced document by clicking the File tab, clicking the *Home* or *New* option, and then clicking the *Single spaced (blank)* template.
- Display the Open backstage area by clicking the File tab and then clicking the *Open* option; by using the keyboard shortcut Ctrl + O; or by clicking the <u>More documents</u> hyperlink at the Home backstage area or the Word opening screen.
- Display the Open dialog box by clicking the *Browse* option at the Open backstage area or with the keyboard shortcut Ctrl + F12.

- At the Open backstage area with the *Recent* option selected, 50 of the most recently opened documents display.

- Pin a frequently-used document or folder to the *Recent* option list at the Open backstage area or pin a document at the Home backstage area by clicking the push pin icon to the right of the document or folder name. Pinned documents and folders appear in the *Pinned* category. Click the push pin icon again to unpin a document or folder from the list.

- Save a document with the same name by clicking the Save button on the Quick Access Toolbar, with the *Save* option at the backstage area, or with the keyboard shortcut Ctrl + S.

- The scroll box on the vertical scroll bar indicates the location of the text in the document screen in relation to the remainder of the document.

- The insertion point can be moved throughout the document using the mouse, the keyboard, or a combination of the two.

- The insertion point can be moved by character, word, screen, or page and from the first to the last character in a document. Refer to Table 1.2 (on page 7) for keyboard insertion point movement commands.

- Delete text by character, word, line, several lines, or partial page using specific keys or by selecting text using the mouse or the keyboard. Refer to Table 1.3 (on page 17) for deletion commands.

- A specific amount of text can be selected using the mouse and/or the keyboard. Refer to Table 1.4 (on page 18) for information on selecting with the mouse, and refer to Table 1.5 (on page 19) for information on selecting with the keyboard.

- Use the Undo button on the Quick Access Toolbar to undo an action such as typing, deleting, or formatting text. Use the Redo button to redo something that has been undone with the Undo button.

- Word contains an Editor that checks for spelling and grammar errors in the document. Corrections are suggested in the Editor task pane. Refer to Table 1.6 and Table 1.7 (on page 23) for a description of options at the Editor task pane.

- The Tell Me feature provides information and guidance on how to complete a function. The *Tell Me* text box is on the ribbon.

- Word's Help feature is an on-screen reference manual containing information about Word features and commands. Press the F1 function key to display the Help task pane or click the Help tab and then click the Help button.

- Hover the mouse pointer over a certain button and the ScreenTip displays with a Help icon and the <u>Tell me more</u> hyperlinked text. Click this hyperlinked text to display the Help task pane, which contains information about the button feature.

- Some dialog boxes and the backstage area contain a Help button that links to the Microsoft Office support website to provide more information about available functions and features.

Commands Review

FEATURE	RIBBON TAB, GROUP/OPTION	BUTTON, OPTION	KEYBOARD SHORTCUT
AutoComplete entry			F3
close document	File, *Close*		Ctrl + F4
close Word		✕	Alt + F4
Go To feature	Home, Editing	🔍, *Go To*	Ctrl + G
Help task pane	Help, Help	⑦	F1
leave backstage area		←	Esc
move insertion point to previous location when document was closed			Shift + F5
new blank document	File, *New* OR File, *Home*	*Blank document*	Ctrl + N
New Line command			Shift + Enter
Open backstage area	File, *Open*		Ctrl + O
Open dialog box	File, *Open*	*Browse*	Ctrl + F12
Print backstage area	File, *Print*		Ctrl + P
redo action		↪	Ctrl + Y
save	File, *Save*	💾	Ctrl + S
Save As backstage area	File, *Save As*		
Save As dialog box	File, *Save As*	*Browse*	F12
Selection mode			F8
spelling and grammar check	Review, Proofing	abc✓	F7
Tell Me feature			Alt + Q
undo action		↩ˇ	Ctrl + Z

Microsoft®

Word

Formatting Characters and Paragraphs

Performance Objectives

Upon successful completion of Chapter 2, you will be able to:

1 Change the font and font size and choose font effects

2 Format selected text with buttons on the Mini toolbar

3 Apply styles from style sets

4 Apply themes

5 Customize styles and themes

6 Change the alignment of text in paragraphs

7 Indent text in paragraphs

8 Increase and decrease spacing before and after paragraphs

9 Repeat the last action

10 Automate formatting with Format Painter

11 Change line spacing

12 Reveal and compare formatting

The appearance of a document on the screen and when printed is called the *format*. A Word document is based on a template that applies default formatting. Some of the default formats include 11-point Calibri font, line spacing of 1.08, 8 points of spacing after each paragraph, and left-aligned text. In this chapter, you will learn about changing the typeface, type size, and typestyle as well as applying font effects such as bold and italic. You will also learn to format paragraphs by changing text alignment and line spacing, indenting text, and applying formatting with Format Painter.

 Data Files

Before beginning chapter work, copy the WL1C2 folder to your storage medium and then make WL1C2 the active folder.

The online course includes additional training and assessment resources.

You will open a document containing a glossary of terms and then format the document by changing the font and the font size; adding bold, italics, and underlining; and applying font effects.

 Tutorial

Applying Font
Formatting Using
the Font Group

Applying Font Formatting

One of the most visible aspects of a document's format is the font. Font formatting can be applied to the individual characters of text, including letters, numbers, and symbols. A font consists of three elements: typeface, type size, and typestyle. By default, a Word document is formatted with the Calibri typeface in 11-point size. The typestyle is roman type; that is, regular and not bold or italic. This default may need to be changed to another font for such reasons as altering the mood of the document, enhancing its visual appeal, and increasing its readability.

💡 **Hint** Change
the default font by
selecting the font at
the Font dialog box and
then clicking the Set As
Default button.

The Font group on the Home tab, shown in Figure 2.1, contains a number of options and buttons for applying font formatting to characters in a document. The top row contains options for changing the font and font size as well as buttons for increasing and decreasing the size of the font and changing the text case. The bottom row contains buttons for applying typestyles such as bold, italic, and underline and for applying text effects, highlighting, and color. Also notice the Clear All Formatting button in the top row of the Font group. Use this button to remove all formatting applied to characters and paragraphs in the text. To remove only character formatting, select text and then use the keyboard shortcut Ctrl + spacebar.

💡 **Hint** Use a serif
typeface for text-
intensive documents.

A typeface is a set of characters with a common design and shape and can be decorative or plain and either monospaced or proportional. Word refers to a typeface as a *font*. A monospaced typeface allots the same amount of horizontal space for each character, while a proportional typeface allots varying amounts of space for different characters. Typefaces are divided into two main categories: serif and sans serif. A serif is a small line at the end of a character stroke. Consider using a serif typeface for text-intensive documents because the serifs help move the reader's eyes across the page. Use a sans serif typeface for headings, headlines, and advertisements. Some popular typefaces are shown in Table 2.1.

Figure 2.1 Font Group Option Boxes and Buttons

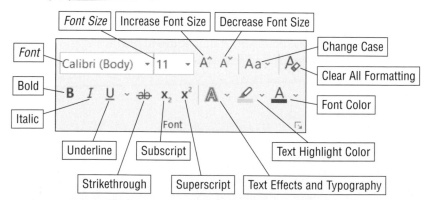

Table 2.1 Categories of Typefaces

Serif Typefaces	Sans Serif Typefaces	Monospaced Typefaces
Cambria	Calibri	Consolas
Constantia	Candara	Courier New
Times New Roman	Corbel	Lucida Console
Bookman Old Style	Arial	MS Gothic

💡 **Hint** Press Ctrl +] to increase font size by 1 point and press Ctrl + [to decrease font size by 1 point.

Type is generally set in proportional size. The size of proportional type is measured vertically in units called *points*. A point is approximately $\frac{1}{72}$ of an inch—the higher the point size, the larger the characters. Within a typeface, characters may have varying styles, including regular, bold, italic, bold italic, and underlined.

Use the *Font* option box in the Font group to change the font. Select the text in the document, click the *Font* option box arrow, and then click a font option at the drop-down gallery. Another method for changing the font is to click the current font name in the *Font* option box to select it and then type the new font name. Change the font size by clicking the *Font Size* option box arrow and then clicking the font size at the drop-down gallery. Or, click the current font size in the *Font Size* option box to select it and then type the new font size number.

To see a live preview of the text in different fonts and sizes before changing the formatting in the document, select the text and open the *Font* or *Font Size* drop-down gallery. Hover the mouse pointer over different font options to see how the selected text displays in each font or size.

Activity 1a Changing the Font and Font Size   Part 1 of 4

1. Open **CompTerms** and then save it with the name **2-CompTerms**.
2. Change the typeface to Cambria by completing the following steps:
   a. Select all text in the document by pressing Ctrl + A. (You can also do this by clicking the Select button in the Editing group and then clicking *Select All* at the drop-down list.)
   b. Click the *Font* option box arrow, scroll down the drop-down gallery until *Cambria* displays, and then hover the mouse pointer over *Cambria*. This displays a live preview of the text set in Cambria.
   c. Click the *Cambria* option.

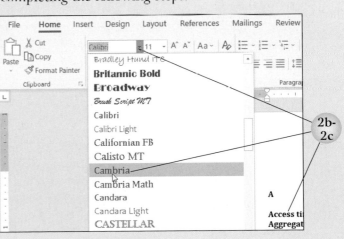

3. Change the type size to 14 points by completing the following steps:
   a. With the text in the document still selected, click the *Font Size* option box arrow.
   b. At the drop-down gallery, hover the mouse pointer over *14* and look at the live preview of the text with 14 points applied.
   c. Click the *14* option.

4. Change the type size and typeface by completing the following steps:
   a. Click the Decrease Font Size button in the Font group three times. (This decreases the size to 10 points.)
   b. Click the Increase Font Size button two times. (This increases the size to 12 points.)
   c. Click the *Font* option box arrow, scroll down the drop-down gallery, and then click *Constantia*. (The most recently used fonts are listed at the beginning of the gallery, followed by a listing of all fonts.)

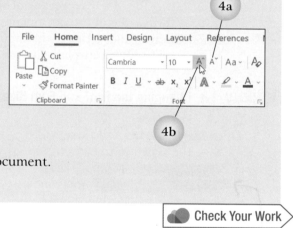

5. Deselect the text by clicking anywhere in the document.
6. Save **2-CompTerms**.

> **Check Your Work**

Choosing a Typestyle

B Bold

I Italic

<u>U</u> ▾ Underline

Apply a typestyle to emphasize text using the Bold, Italic, and Underline buttons in the bottom row in the Font group on the Home tab. More than one typestyle can be applied to text. For example, a word may be set as bold italic and also underlined. Click the Underline button arrow and a drop-down gallery displays with underlining options such as a double line, dashed line, and thicker underline. Click the *Underline Color* option at the Underline button drop-down gallery and a side menu displays with color options.

1. With **2-CompTerms** open, press Ctrl + Home to move the insertion point to the beginning of the document.
2. Type a heading for the document by completing the following steps:
   a. Click the Bold button in the Font group. (This turns on bold formatting.)
   b. Click the Underline button in the Font group. (This turns on underline formatting.)
   c. Type Glossary of Terms.

3. Press Ctrl + End to move the insertion point to the end of the document.
4. Type the text shown in Figure 2.2 with the following specifications:
   a. While typing, make the appropriate text bold, as shown in the figure, by completing the following steps:
      1) Click the Bold button. (This turns on bold formatting.)
      2) Type the text.
      3) Click the Bold button. (This turns off bold formatting.)
   b. Press the Enter key two times after typing the C heading.
   c. While typing, italicize the appropriate text, as shown in the figure, by completing the following steps:
      1) Click the Italic button in the Font group.
      2) Type the text.
      3) Click the Italic button.
5. After typing the text, press the Enter key two times and then press Ctrl + Home to move the insertion point to the beginning of the document.
6. Change the underlining below the title by completing the following steps:
   a. Select the title *Glossary of Terms*.
   b. Click the Underline button arrow and then click the third underline option from the top of the drop-down gallery (*Thick underline*).

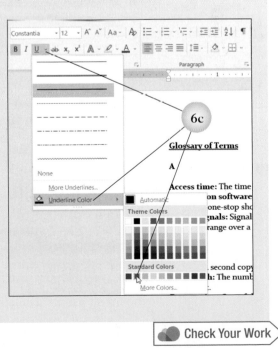

   c. Click the Underline button arrow, point to the *Underline Color* option, and then click the *Red* option (second color option in the *Standard Colors* section).
7. With the title still selected, change the font size to 14 points.
8. Save **2-CompTerms**.

Check Your Work

Figure 2.2 Activity 1b

> **C**
>
> **Chip:** A thin wafer of *silicon* containing electronic circuitry that performs various functions, such as mathematical calculations, storage, and controlling computer devices.
>
> **Cluster:** A group of two or more *sectors* on a disk; a cluster is the smallest unit of storage space used to store data.
>
> **Coding:** A term used by programmers to refer to the act of writing source code.
>
> **Crackers:** A term coined by computer hackers for those who intentionally enter (or hack) computer systems to damage them.

 Tutorial

Highlighting Text

 Clear All Formatting

 Change Case

 Strikethrough

 Subscript

x² Superscript

Text Effects and Typography

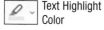 Text Highlight Color

Font Color

Choosing a Font Effect

Apply font effects with buttons in the top and bottom rows in the Font group on the Home tab, or clear all formatting from selected text with the Clear All Formatting button. Change the case of text with the Change Case button drop-down list. Click the Change Case button in the top row in the Font group and then click one of the options in the drop-down list: *Sentence case, lowercase., UPPERCASE, Capitalize Each Word,* and *tOGGLE cASE.* The case of selected text can also be changed with the keyboard shortcut Shift + F3. Each time Shift + F3 is pressed, the selected text displays in the next case option in the list.

The bottom row in the Font group contains buttons for applying font effects. Use the Strikethrough button to draw a line through selected text. This has a practical application in some legal documents in which deleted text must be retained in the document. Use the Subscript button to create text that is lowered slightly below the line, as in the chemical formula H_2O. Use the Superscript button to create text that is raised slightly above the text line, as in the mathematical equation four to the third power (written as 4^3).

Click the Text Effects and Typography button in the bottom row and a drop-down gallery displays with effect options. The Text Highlight Color and Font Color buttons are used to highlight text or change the color of the font. To apply highlighting, select text and then click the Text Highlight Color button. The default color is yellow; other colors can be selected from the drop-down list. Or, click the button to make the I-beam pointer display with a highlighter pen attached, and then select text with the mouse pointer to highlight it. Click the button again to turn off highlighting. To change font color, select text, click the Font Color button arrow, and then click a color at the drop-down gallery.

Applying Formatting Using Keyboard Shortcuts

Several of the options and buttons in the Font group have keyboard shortcuts. For example, press Ctrl + B to turn bold formatting on or off and press Ctrl + I to turn italic formatting on or off. Position the mouse pointer on an option or button and an enhanced ScreenTip displays with the name and description of the option or button and the keyboard shortcut, if it has one. Table 2.2 identifies the keyboard shortcuts available for options and buttons in the Font group.

Table 2.2 Font Group Option and Button Keyboard Shortcuts

Font Group Option/Button	Keyboard Shortcut
Font	Ctrl + Shift + F
Font Size	Ctrl + Shift + P
Increase Font Size	Ctrl + Shift + > OR Ctrl +]
Decrease Font Size	Ctrl + Shift + < OR Ctrl + [
Bold	Ctrl + B
Italic	Ctrl + I
Underline	Ctrl + U
Subscript	Ctrl + =
Superscript	Ctrl + Shift + +
Change Case	Shift + F3

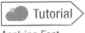

Applying Font
Formatting Using
the Mini Toolbar

Formatting with the Mini Toolbar

When text is selected, the Mini toolbar displays above the selected text, as shown in Figure 2.3. Click a button on the Mini toolbar to apply formatting to the selected text. When the mouse pointer is moved away from the Mini toolbar, the toolbar disappears.

Figure 2.3 Mini Toolbar

Activity 1c Applying Font Effects

Part 3 of 4

1. With **2-CompTerms** open, move the insertion point to the beginning of the term *Chip*, press the Enter key, and then press the Up Arrow key.
2. Type the text shown in Figure 2.4. Create each superscript number by clicking the Superscript button, typing the number, and then clicking the Superscript button.

3. Remove underlining and change the case of the text in the title by completing the following steps:
   a. Select the title *Glossary of Terms*.
   b. Remove all formatting from the title by clicking the Clear All Formatting button in the Font group.
   c. Click the Change Case button in the Font group and then click *UPPERCASE* at the drop-down list.

   d. Click the Text Effects and Typography button in the Font group and then click the option in the second column, second row (the option with blue gradient fill and reflection).

   e. Change the font size to 14 points.
4. Strike through text by completing the following steps:
   a. In the *Crackers* definition, select the phrase *or hack* and the parentheses around it.
   b. Click the Strikethrough button in the Font group.

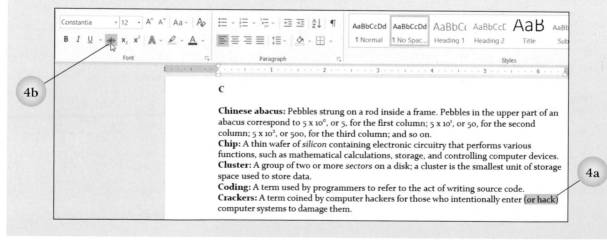

5. Change the font color by completing the following steps:
   a. Press Ctrl + A to select the entire document.
   b. Click the Font Color button arrow.
   c. Click the *Dark Red* option (first color option in the *Standard Colors* section) at the drop-down gallery.
   d. Click in the document to deselect text.
6. Highlight text in the document by completing the following steps:
   a. Select the term *Beta-testing* and the definition that follows.
   b. Click the Text Highlight Color button in the Font group. (This applies yellow text highlighting color to the selected text.)
   c. Click the Text Highlight Color button arrow and then click the *Turquoise* color (third column, first row) at the drop-down palette. (This turns on highlighting and the mouse pointer displays as an I-beam pointer with a highlighter pen attached.)
   d. Select the term *Cluster* and the definition that follows.
   e. Click the Text Highlight Color button arrow and then click the *Yellow* color (first column, first row) at the drop-down gallery.
   f. Click the Text Highlight Color button to turn off highlighting.
7. Apply italic formatting using the Mini toolbar by completing the following steps:
   a. In the definition for *Aggregation software*, select the phrase *one-stop shopping* (When you select the text, the Mini toolbar displays.)
   b. Click the Italic button on the Mini toolbar.
   c. In the definition for *Bandwidth*, select the word *bits* and then click the Italic button on the Mini toolbar.
8. Save **2-CompTerms**.

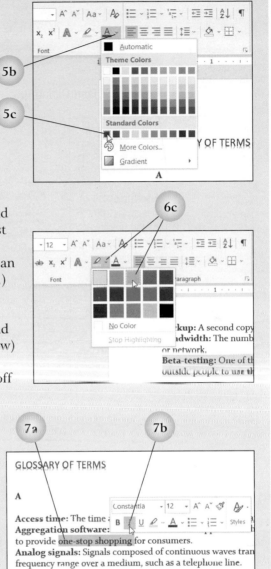

Check Your Work

Figure 2.4 Activity 1c

Chinese abacus: Pebbles strung on a rod inside a frame. Pebbles in the upper part of an abacus correspond to 5×10^0, or 5, for the first column; 5×10^1, or 50, for the second column; 5×10^2, or 500, for the third column; and so on.

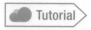

Applying Font Formatting Using the Font Dialog Box

Quick Steps

**Change Font at
Font Dialog Box**
1. Select text.
2. Click Font group
   dialog box launcher.
3. Choose options at
   dialog box.
4. Click OK.

In addition to options and buttons in the Font group, options at the Font dialog box, shown in Figure 2.5, can be used to change the typeface, type size, and typestyle of text as well as apply font effects. Display the Font dialog box by clicking the Font group dialog box launcher. The dialog box launcher is a small icon with a diagonal-pointing arrow in the lower right corner of the Font group.

Figure 2.5 Font Dialog Box

Choose a typeface in this list box. Use the scroll bar at the right of the box to view available typefaces.

Choose a typestyle in this list box. The options in the box may vary depending on the selected typeface.

Choose a type size in this list box, or select the current size in the option box and then type the desired size.

Apply a font effect to text by clicking the check box next to the desired effect.

See a preview of the text with the selected formatting applied.

Click this button to change the default font.

Click this button to display the Format Text Effects dialog box, which contains options with special text effects.

Activity 1d Changing the Font at the Font Dialog Box

Part 4 of 4

1. With **2-CompTerms** open, press Ctrl + End to move the insertion point to the end of the document. (Make sure the insertion point is positioned a double space below the last line of text.)
2. Type Created by Susan Ashby and then press the Enter key.
3. Type Wednesday, February 24, 2021.
4. Change the font to 13-point Candara and the color to standard dark blue for the entire document by completing the following steps:
   a. Press Ctrl + A to select the entire document.
   b. Click the Font group dialog box launcher.

c. At the Font dialog box, type can in the *Font* option box (this displays fonts that begin with *can*) and then click *Candara* in the *Font* list box.

d. Click in the *Size* option box and then type 13.

e. Click the *Font color* option box arrow and then click the *Dark Blue* option (ninth option in the *Standard Colors* section).

f. Click OK to close the dialog box.

5. Double-underline text by completing the following steps:

a. Select *Wednesday, February 24, 2021*.

b. Click the Font group dialog box launcher.

c. At the Font dialog box, click the *Underline style* option box arrow and then click the double-line option at the drop-down list.

d. Click OK to close the dialog box.

6. Change text to small caps by completing the following steps:

a. Select the text *Created by Susan Ashby* and *Wednesday, February 24, 2021*.

b. Display the Font dialog box.

c. Click the *Small caps* check box in the *Effects* section. (This inserts a check mark in the check box.)

d. Click OK to close the dialog box.

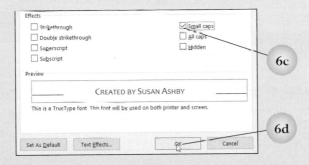

7. Save, print, and then close **2-CompTerms**.

Check Your Work

Activity 2 Apply Styles and Themes   3 Parts

You will open a document containing information on the life cycle of software, apply styles to text, and then change the style set. You will also apply a theme and then change the theme colors, fonts, and paragraph spacing.

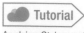
Tutorial

Applying Styles and Style Sets

Applying Styles from a Style Set

Make a document look more polished and professional by applying different styles to the title, headings, and body paragraphs. Word provides a set of predesigned styles in the Styles group on the Home tab. Each style is a different combination of font style, color, and size. Click the More Styles button (the arrow button at the right side of the gallery) to display all the style options. Position the insertion point in the text and then hover the mouse pointer over the options in the gallery to see how the text will look in various styles. Click a style to apply it.

Quick Steps

Apply Style
1. Position insertion point in text.
2. Click More Styles button in Styles group.
3. Click style.

If a heading style (such as Heading 1, Heading 2, and so on) is applied to text, the text below the heading can be collapsed and expanded. Hover the mouse pointer over text with a heading style applied and a collapse triangle (solid, right- and down-pointing triangle) displays to the left of the heading. Click this collapse triangle and any text below the heading collapses (is hidden). Redisplay the text below a heading by hovering the mouse pointer over the heading text until an expand triangle displays (hollow, right-pointing triangle) and then click the expand triangle. This expands (redisplays) the text below the heading.

Removing Default Formatting

The default formatting for a Word document includes 8 points of spacing after paragraphs and line spacing of 1.08. (You will learn more about these formatting options later in this chapter.) This default formatting, as well as any character formatting applied to text in the document, can be removed by applying the No Spacing style to the text. This style is in the styles gallery in the Styles group.

Changing the Style Set

Quick Steps

Change Style Set
1. Click Design tab.
2. Click style set.

To quickly change the look of an entire document, choose a new style set. Style sets can be found in a gallery on the Design tab in the Document Formatting group. Each set contains a different combination of title, heading, and paragraph styles. To apply a new style set, click the Design tab and then click the style set in the style sets gallery in the Document Formatting group.

Activity 2a Applying Styles and Changing the Style Set   Part 1 of 3

1. Open **SoftwareCycle** and then save it with the name **2-SoftwareCycle**.
2. Position the insertion point anywhere in the title *COMMERCIAL LIFE CYCLE* and then click the *Heading 1* style in the Styles group.

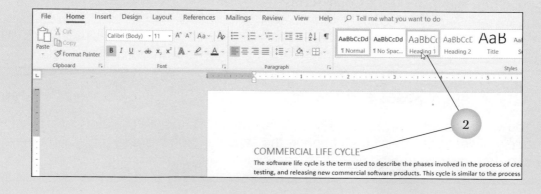

3. Position the insertion point anywhere in the heading *Proposal and Planning* and then click the *Heading 2* style in the styles gallery.

4. Position the insertion point anywhere in the heading *Design* and then click the *Heading 2* style in the styles gallery.

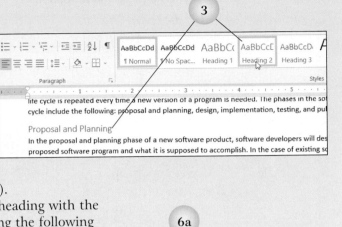

5. Apply the Heading 2 style to the remaining headings (*Implementation*, *Testing*, and *Public Release and Support*).

6. Collapse and expand text below the heading with the Heading 1 style applied by completing the following steps:

   a. Hover the mouse pointer over the heading *COMMERCIAL LIFE CYCLE* until a collapse triangle displays at the left of the heading and then click the triangle. (This collapses all the text below the heading.)

   b. Click the expand triangle at the left of the heading *COMMERCIAL LIFE CYCLE*. (This redisplays the text in the document.)

7. Click the Design tab.

8. Click the *Casual* style set in the style sets gallery in the Document Formatting group (the ninth option in the style set). (Notice how the Heading 1 and Heading 2 formatting changes.)

9. Save and then print **2-SoftwareCycle**.

Check Your Work

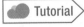 Tutorial

Applying and Modifying a Theme

Applying a Theme

 Themes

Quick Steps

Apply Theme
1. Click Design tab.
2. Click Themes button.
3. Click theme.

Word provides a number of themes for formatting text in a document. A theme is a set of formatting choices that includes a color theme (a set of colors), a font theme (a set of heading and body text fonts), and an effects theme (a set of line and fill effects). To apply a theme, click the Design tab, click the Themes button in the Document Formatting group, and then click the theme at the drop-down gallery. Hover the mouse pointer over a theme and the live preview feature displays the document with the theme formatting applied. Applying a theme is an easy way to give a document a professional look.

1. With **2-SoftwareCycle** open, click the Themes button in the Document Formatting group on the Design tab.
2. At the drop-down gallery, hover your mouse pointer over several different themes and notice how the text formatting changes in your document.
3. Click the *Organic* theme.

4. Save and then print **2-SoftwareCycle**.

Check Your Work

Modifying a Theme

Quick Steps
Change Theme Color
1. Click Design tab.
2. Click Colors button.
3. Click theme color option.
Change Theme Fonts
1. Click Design tab.
2. Click Fonts button.
3. Click theme font option.
Change Paragraph Spacing
1. Click Design tab.
2. Click Paragraph Spacing button.
3. Click paragraph spacing option.

 Theme Colors

A Theme Fonts

Theme Effects

 Paragraph Spacing

The color and font of a style or theme can be modified using buttons in the Document Formatting group on the Design tab. Click the Colors button and a drop-down gallery displays with various color schemes. Click the Fonts button in this group and a drop-down gallery displays with font choices. Each font group in the drop-down gallery contains two choices. The first choice is the font that is applied to headings, and the second choice is applied to body text in the document. If a document contains graphics with lines and fills, a specific theme effect can be applied with options at the Effects button drop-down gallery.

The buttons in the Document Formatting group provide a visual representation of the current theme. If the theme colors are changed, the small color squares in the Themes button and the larger squares in the Colors button reflect the change. Change the theme fonts and the *As* on the Themes button and the upper-case *A* on the Fonts button reflect the change. If the theme effects are changed, the circle in the Effects button reflects the change.

The Paragraph Spacing button in the Document Formatting group on the Design tab contains predesigned paragraph spacing options. To change paragraph spacing, click the Paragraph Spacing button and then click an option at the drop-down gallery. Hover the mouse pointer over an option at the drop-down gallery and after a moment a ScreenTip displays with information about the formatting applied by the option. For example, hover the mouse pointer over the *Compact* option at the side menu and a ScreenTip displays indicating that selecting the *Compact* option will change the spacing before paragraphs to 0 points, the spacing after paragraphs to 4 points, and the line spacing to single line spacing.

1. With **2-SoftwareCycle** open, click the Colors button in the Document Formatting group on the Design tab and then click *Red Orange* at the drop-down gallery. (Notice how the colors in the title and headings change.)
2. Click the Fonts button and then click the *Corbel* option. (Notice how the document text font changes.)
3. Click the Paragraph Spacing button and then, one at a time, hover the mouse pointer over each paragraph spacing option, beginning with *Compact*. For each option, read the ScreenTip that explains the paragraph spacing applied by the option.
4. Click the *Double* option.
5. Scroll through the document and notice the paragraph spacing.
6. Change the paragraph spacing by clicking the Paragraph Spacing button and then clicking *Compact*.
7. Save, print, and then close **2-SoftwareCycle**.

Check Your Work

Activity 3 Apply Paragraph Formatting and Use Format Painter   6 Parts

You will open a report on intellectual property and fair use issues and then format the report by changing the alignment and indent of text in paragraphs, changing spacing before and after paragraphs of text, and repeating the last formatting command. You will also format headings using Format Painter and change the line spacing of text.

Tutorial

Changing Paragraph Alignment

Changing Paragraph Alignment

By default, paragraphs in a Word document are aligned at the left margin and are ragged at the right margin. Change this default alignment with buttons in the Paragraph group on the Home tab or with keyboard shortcuts, as shown in Table 2.3. The alignment of text in paragraphs can be changed before text is typed, or the alignment of existing text can be changed.

Table 2.3 Paragraph Alignment Buttons and Keyboard Shortcuts

To align text	Paragraph Group Button	Keyboard Shortcut
At the left margin		Ctrl + L
Between margins		Ctrl + E
At the right margin		Ctrl + R
At the left and right margins		Ctrl + J

Changing Paragraph Alignment as Text Is Typed

Center

Show/Hide ¶

Align Right

Align Left

If the alignment is changed before text is typed, the alignment formatting is inserted in the paragraph mark. Type text and press the Enter key and the paragraph formatting is continued. For example, click the Center button in the Paragraph group on the Home tab, type text for the first paragraph, and then press the Enter key; the center alignment formatting is still active and the insertion point is centered between the left and right margins. To display the paragraph symbols in a document, click the Show/Hide ¶ button in the Paragraph group. With the Show/Hide ¶ button active (displays with a gray background), nonprinting formatting symbols display, such as the paragraph symbol ¶, indicating a press of the Enter key, or a dot, indicating a press of the spacebar.

In addition to paragraph symbols, other formatting or formatting symbols display when the Show/Hide ¶ button is active. For example, hide text in a document using the *Hidden* option at the Font dialog box and the hidden text displays when the Show/Hide ¶ button is active.

Changing Paragraph Alignment of Existing Text

Hint Align text to help the reader follow the message of a document and to make the layout look appealing.

To change the alignment of existing text in a paragraph, position the insertion point anywhere within the paragraph. The entire paragraph does not need to be selected. To change the alignment of several adjacent paragraphs in a document, select a portion of the first paragraph through a portion of the last paragraph. All the text in the paragraphs does not need to be selected.

To return paragraph alignment to the default (left-aligned), click the Align Left button in the Paragraph group. All paragraph formatting can also be returned to the default with the keyboard shortcut Ctrl + Q. This keyboard shortcut removes paragraph formatting from selected text. To remove all formatting from selected text, including character and paragraph formatting, click the Clear All Formatting button in the Font group.

1. Open **IntelProp**. (Some of the default formatting in this document has been changed.)
2. Save the document with the name **2-IntelProp**.
3. Click the Show/Hide ¶ button in the Paragraph group on the Home tab to turn on the display of nonprinting characters.

4. Press Ctrl + A to select the entire document and then change the paragraph alignment to justified alignment by clicking the Justify button in the Paragraph group.
5. Press Ctrl + End to move the insertion point to the end of the document.
6. Press the Enter key.
7. Press Ctrl + E to move the insertion point to the middle of the page.
8. Type Prepared by Clarissa Markham.
9. Press Shift + Enter and then type Edited by Joshua Streeter.

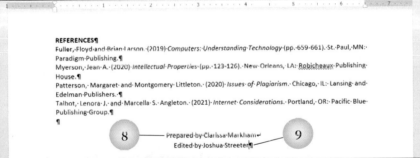

10. Select the two lines of text you just typed and then hide the text by completing the following steps:
    a. Click the Font group dialog box launcher.
    b. Click the *Hidden* check box to insert a check mark.
    c. Click OK to close the dialog box. (Since the Show/Hide ¶ button is active, the two lines of text display with a dotted underline.)
11. Click the Show/Hide ¶ button in the Paragraph group to turn off the display of nonprinting characters. (Notice that the two lines of text you identified as hidden are no longer visible.)
12. Specify that the two lines of text should not be hidden by completing the following steps:
    a. Click the Show/Hide ¶ button.
    b. Select the two lines of text.
    c. Click the Font group dialog box launcher.
    d. Click the *Hidden* check box to remove the check mark.
    e. Click OK.
    f. Click the Show/Hide ¶ button to turn off the display of nonprinting characters.
13. Save **2-IntelProp**.

Check Your Work

Changing Alignment at the Paragraph Dialog Box

Along with buttons in the Paragraph group on the Home tab and keyboard shortcuts, options in the *Alignment* option box at the Paragraph dialog box, shown in Figure 2.6, can be used to change paragraph alignment. Display this dialog box by clicking the Paragraph group dialog box launcher. At the Paragraph dialog box, click the *Alignment* option box arrow. At the drop-down list, click the alignment option and then click OK to close the dialog box.

Figure 2.6 Paragraph Dialog Box with the Indents and Spacing Tab Selected

Change paragraph alignment by clicking the *Alignment* option box arrow and then clicking the alignment option at the drop-down list.

Use these options to adjust spacing before and after paragraphs.

Activity 3b Changing Paragraph Alignment at the Paragraph Dialog Box

Part 2 of 6

1. With **2-IntelProp** open, change the paragraph alignment by completing the following steps:
   a. Select the entire document.
   b. Click the Paragraph group dialog box launcher.
   c. At the Paragraph dialog box with the Indents and Spacing tab selected, click the *Alignment* option box arrow and then click the *Left* option at the drop-down list.
   d. Click OK to close the dialog box.
   e. Deselect the text.
2. Change the paragraph alignment by completing the following steps:
   a. Press Ctrl + End to move the insertion point to the end of the document if necessary.
   b. Position the insertion point anywhere in the text *Prepared by Clarissa Markham*.

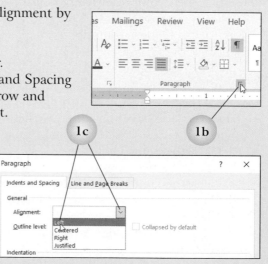

c. Click the Paragraph group dialog box launcher.

d. At the Paragraph dialog box with the Indents and Spacing tab selected, click the *Alignment* option box arrow and then click the *Right* option at the drop-down list.

e. Click OK to close the dialog box. (The line of text containing the name *Clarissa Markham* and the line of text containing the name *Joshua Streeter* are both aligned at the right since you used the New Line command, Shift + Enter, to separate the lines of text without creating a new paragraph.)

3. Save and then print **2-IntelProp**.

 Check Your Work

Tutorial

Indenting Text

Indenting Text in Paragraphs

The first line of a paragraph is commonly indented to show paragraph breaks in a document. Paragraphs may also be indented from the left and right margins to set them off from the rest of the text. For instance, a long quotation or a bulleted or numbered list may be indented in this manner.

To indent text from the left margin, the right margin, or both margins, use the indent buttons in the Paragraph group on the Layout tab, keyboard shortcuts, options from the Paragraph dialog box, markers on the horizontal ruler, or the Alignment button above the vertical ruler. Figure 2.7 identifies indent markers on the horizontal ruler as well as the Alignment button. Refer to Table 2.4 for methods for indenting text in a document. If the horizontal ruler is not visible, display the ruler by clicking the View tab and then clicking the *Ruler* check box in the Show group to insert a check mark.

Quick Steps

Indent Text

Drag indent marker(s) on horizontal ruler.
OR
Press keyboard shortcut keys.
OR
1. Click Paragraph group dialog box launcher.
2. Insert measurement in *Left, Right,* and/or *By* measurement box.
3. Click OK.

Figure 2.7 Horizontal Ruler and Indent Markers

Alignment button | First Line Indent marker
Left Indent marker | Hanging Indent marker | Right Indent marker

Table 2.4 Methods for Indenting Text

Indent	Methods for Indenting
First line of paragraph	• Press the Tab key.
	• Display the Paragraph dialog box, click the *Special* option box arrow, click *First line*, and then click OK.
	• Drag the First Line Indent marker on the horizontal ruler.
	• Click the Alignment button above the vertical ruler until the First Line Indent symbol displays and then click the horizontal ruler at the desired location.

continues

Table 2.4 Methods for Indenting Text—*continued*

Indent	Methods for Indenting
Text from left margin	• Click the Increase Indent button in the Paragraph group on the Home tab to increase the indent or click the Decrease Indent button to decrease the indent. • Insert a measurement in the *Indent Left* measurement box in the Paragraph group on the Layout tab. • Press Ctrl + M to increase the indent or press Ctrl + Shift + M to decrease the indent. • Display the Paragraph dialog box, type the indent measurement in the *Left* measurement box, and then click OK. • Drag the Left Indent marker on the horizontal ruler.
Text from right margin	• Insert a measurement in the *Indent Right* measurement box in the Paragraph group on the Layout tab. • Display the Paragraph dialog box, type the indent measurement in the *Right* measurement box, and then click OK. • Drag the Right Indent marker on the horizontal ruler.
All lines of text except first (called a *hanging indent*)	• Press Ctrl + T. (Press Ctrl + Shift + T to remove a hanging indent.) • Display the Paragraph dialog box, click the *Special* option box arrow, click *Hanging*, and then click OK. • Click the Alignment button, left of the horizontal ruler and above the vertical ruler, until the Hanging Indent symbol displays and then click the horizontal ruler at the desired location. • Drag the Hanging Indent marker on the horizontal ruler.
Text from both left and right margins	• Display the Paragraph dialog box, type the indent measurement in the *Left* measurement box, type the indent measurement in the *Right* measurement box, and then click OK. • Insert measurements in the *Indent Right* and *Indent Left* measurement boxes in the Paragraph group on the Layout tab. • Drag the Left Indent marker on the horizontal ruler and then drag the Right Indent marker on the horizontal ruler.

Activity 3c Indenting Text

1. With **2-IntelProp** open, indent the first line of text in each paragraph by completing the following steps:
   a. Select the first two paragraphs of text in the document (the text after the title *PROPERTY PROTECTION ISSUES* and before the heading *Intellectual Property*).
   b. Make sure the horizontal ruler is visible. (If it is not, click the View tab and then click the *Ruler* check box in the Show group to insert a check mark.)
   c. Position the mouse pointer on the First Line Indent marker on the horizontal ruler, click and hold down the left mouse button, drag the marker to the 0.5-inch mark, and then release the mouse button.

d. Select the paragraphs of text in the *Intellectual Property* section and then drag the First Line Indent marker on the horizontal ruler to the 0.5-inch mark.

e. Select the paragraphs of text in the *Fair Use* section, click the Alignment button above the vertical ruler until the First Line Indent symbol displays, and then click the horizontal ruler at the 0.5-inch mark.

f. Position the insertion point anywhere in the paragraph of text below the heading *Intellectual Property Protection*, make sure the First Line Indent symbol displays on the Alignment button, and then click the 0.5-inch mark on the horizontal ruler.

2. Since the text in the second paragraph in the *Fair Use* section is a quote, indent the text from the left and right margins by completing the following steps:

a. Position the insertion point anywhere in the second paragraph in the *Fair Use* section (the paragraph that begins *[A] copyrighted work, including such*).

b. Click the Paragraph group dialog box launcher.

c. At the Paragraph dialog box with the Indents and Spacing tab selected, select the current measurement in the *Left* measurement box and then type 0.5.

d. Select the current measurement in the *Right* measurement box and then type 0.5.

e. Click the *Special* option box arrow and then click *(none)* at the drop-down list.

f. Click OK.

3. Create a hanging indent for the first paragraph in the *REFERENCES* section by positioning the insertion point anywhere in the first paragraph below the heading *REFERENCES* (on the third page) and then pressing Ctrl + T.

4. Create a hanging indent for the second paragraph in the *REFERENCES* section by completing the following steps:

a. Position the insertion point anywhere in the second paragraph in the *REFERENCES* section.

b. Click the Alignment button until the Hanging Indent symbol displays.

c. Click the 0.5-inch mark on the horizontal ruler.

5. Create a hanging indent for the third and fourth paragraphs by completing the following steps:
   a. Select a portion of the third and fourth paragraphs.
   b. Click the Paragraph group dialog box launcher.
   c. At the Paragraph dialog box with the Indents and Spacing tab selected, click the *Special* option box arrow and then click *Hanging* at the drop-down list.
   d. Click OK or press the Enter key.
6. Save **2-IntelProp**.

> Check Your Work

Check Your Work

Tutorial

Changing Spacing Before and After Paragraphs

Hint Line spacing determines the amount of vertical space between lines, while paragraph spacing determines the amount of space above or below paragraphs of text.

Spacing Before and After Paragraphs

By default, Word applies 8 points of additional spacing after a paragraph. This spacing can be removed or it can be increased or decreased, and spacing can be inserted above the paragraph. To change spacing before or after a paragraph, use the *Before* and *After* measurement boxes in the Paragraph group on the Layout tab, or use the *Before* and *After* measurement boxes at the Paragraph dialog box with the Indents and Spacing tab selected. Spacing can also be added before and after paragraphs with options at the Line and Paragraph Spacing button drop-down list in the Paragraph group on the Home tab.

Spacing before or after a paragraph is part of the paragraph and will be moved, copied, or deleted with the paragraph. If a paragraph, such as a heading, contains spacing before it and the paragraph falls at the top of a page, Word ignores the spacing.

Spacing before and after paragraphs is added in points. One vertical inch is equivalent to approximately 72 points. To add spacing before or after a paragraph, click the Layout tab, select the current measurement in the *Before* or *After* measurement box, and then type the number of points. The up or down arrows at the *Before* and *After* measurement boxes can also be clicked to increase or decrease the amount of spacing.

Automating Formatting

Applying consistent formatting in a document, especially a multiple-page document, can be time consuming. Word provides options for applying formatting automatically. Use the Repeat command to repeat the last action, such as applying formatting, or the Format Painter to apply formatting to multiple locations in a document.

Tutorial

Repeating the Last Command

Quick Steps

Repeat Last Action
Press F4.
OR
Press Ctrl + Y.

Repeating the Last Command

Formatting applied to text can be applied to other text in the document using the Repeat command. To use this command, apply the formatting, move the insertion point to the next location the formatting is to be applied, and then press the F4 function key or the keyboard shortcut Ctrl + Y. The Repeat command will repeat only the last command executed.

Activity 3d Changing Spacing Before and After Paragraphs and Repeating
the Last Command

1. With **2-IntelProp** open, add 6 points of
spacing before and after each paragraph in the
document by completing the following steps:
    a. Select the entire document.
    b. Click the Layout tab.
    c. Click the *Before* measurement box up arrow in
    the Paragraph group. (This inserts *6 pt* in the
    box.)
    d. Click the *After* measurement box up arrow
    two times. (This inserts *6 pt* in the box.)

2. Add an additional 6 points of spacing above the headings by completing the following steps:
    a. Position the insertion point anywhere in the heading *Intellectual Property* and then click
    the *Before* measurement box up arrow. (This changes the measurement to *12 pt*.)

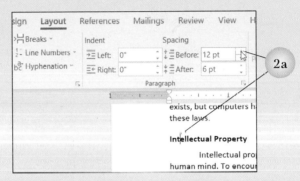

    b. Position the insertion point anywhere in the heading *Fair Use* and then press the F4
    function key. (F4 is the Repeat command.)
    c. Position the insertion point anywhere in the heading *Intellectual Property Protection* and
    then press the F4 function key.
    d. Position the insertion point anywhere in the heading *REFERENCES* and then press
    Ctrl + Y. (Ctrl + Y is also the Repeat command.) (When a heading displays at the
    beginning of a page, the spacing above is ignored.)
3. Save **2-IntelProp**.

> Check Your Work

 Tutorial

Formatting with
Format Painter

 Format Painter

Quick Steps
**Format with Format
Painter**
1. Click in formatted
text.
2. Click Format Painter
button.
3. Select text.

Formatting with Format Painter

The Home tab contains a button for copying formatting, which displays in the
Clipboard group with a paintbrush. To use this button, called Format Painter,
position the insertion point anywhere in text containing the desired formatting,
click the Format Painter button, and then select the text to which the formatting
is to be applied. When the Format Painter button is clicked, the I-beam pointer
displays with a paintbrush attached. To apply the formatting a single time, click
the Format Painter button. To apply the formatting in more than one location in
the document, double-click the Format Painter button and then select the text to
which the formatting is to be applied. When finished, click the Format Painter
button to turn it off. The Format Painter button can also be turned off by pressing
the Esc key.

1. With **2-IntelProp** open, click the Home tab.
2. Select the entire document and then change the font to 12-point Cambria.
3. Select the title *PROPERTY PROTECTION ISSUES*, click the Center button in the Paragraph group, and then change the font to 16-point Candara.
4. Apply 16-point Candara and center-alignment formatting to the heading *REFERENCES* by completing the following steps:
   a. Click in the title *PROPERTY PROTECTION ISSUES*.
   b. Click the Format Painter button in the Clipboard group.

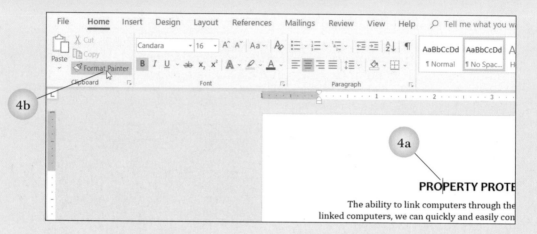

   c. Press Ctrl + End to move the insertion point to the end of the document and then click in the heading *REFERENCES*. (This applies the 16-point Candara formatting and centers the text.)
5. Select the heading *Intellectual Property* and then change the font to 14-point Candara.
6. Use the Format Painter button to apply 14-point Candara formatting to the other headings by completing the following steps:
   a. Position the insertion point anywhere in the heading *Intellectual Property*.
   b. Double-click the Format Painter button in the Clipboard group.
   c. Using the mouse, select the heading *Fair Use*.
   d. Using the mouse, select the heading *Intellectual Property Protection*.
   e. Click the Format Painter button in the Clipboard group. (This turns off the feature and deactivates the button.)
   f. Deselect the heading.
7. Save **2-IntelProp**.

> **Check Your Work** >

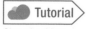

Tutorial >

Changing Line
Spacing

Line and
Paragraph
Spacing

Changing Line Spacing

The default line spacing for a document is 1.08. (The line spacing for the IntelProp file, which you opened at the beginning of Activity 3, had been changed to single line spacing.) In certain situations, Word automatically adjusts the line spacing. For example, if a large character or object, such as a graphic, is inserted into a line, Word increases the line spacing of that line. The line spacing for a section or an entire document can also be changed.

Quick Steps

Change Line Spacing
1. Click Line and Paragraph Spacing button.
2. Click option.
OR
Press keyboard shortcut command.
OR
1. Click Paragraph group dialog box launcher.
2. Click *Line spacing* option box arrow.
3. Click line spacing option.
4. Click OK.
OR
1. Click Paragraph group dialog box launcher.
2. Type line measurement in *At* measurement box.
3. Click OK.

Change line spacing using the Line and Paragraph Spacing button in the Paragraph group on the Home tab, keyboard shortcuts, or options in the Paragraph dialog box. Table 2.5 shows the keyboard shortcuts to change line spacing.

Line spacing can also be changed at the Paragraph dialog box with the *Line spacing* option or the *At* measurement box. Click the *Line spacing* option box arrow and a drop-down list displays with a variety of spacing options, such as *Single*, *1.5 lines*, and *Double*. A specific line spacing measurement can be entered in the *At* measurement box. For example, to change the line spacing to 1.75 lines, type *1.75* in the *At* measurement box.

Table 2.5 Line Spacing Keyboard Shortcuts

Press	To change line spacing to
Ctrl + 1	single line spacing (1.0)
Ctrl + 2	double line spacing (2.0)
Ctrl + 5	1.5 line spacing

Activity 3f Changing Line Spacing

Part 6 of 6

1. With **2-IntelProp** open, change the line spacing for all paragraphs to double spacing by completing the following steps:
   a. Select the entire document.
   b. Click the Line and Paragraph Spacing button in the Paragraph group on the Home tab.
   c. Click *2.0* at the drop-down list.
2. With the entire document still selected, press Ctrl + 5. (This changes the line spacing to 1.5 lines.)
3. Change the line spacing to 1.2 lines at the Paragraph dialog box by completing the following steps:
   a. With the entire document still selected, click the Paragraph group dialog box launcher.
   b. At the Paragraph dialog box, make sure the Indents and Spacing tab is selected, click in the *At* measurement box, and then type *1.2*. (This measurement box is to the right of the *Line spacing* option box.)
   c. Click OK or press the Enter key.
   d. Deselect the text.
4. Save, print, and then close **2-IntelProp**.

Check Your Work

You will open a document containing two computer-related problems to solve, reveal the formatting, compare the formatting, and make formatting changes.

Revealing and Comparing Formatting

Display formatting applied to specific text in a document at the Reveal Formatting task pane, shown in Figure 2.8. The Reveal Formatting task pane displays font, paragraph, and section formatting applied to text where the insertion point is positioned or to selected text. Display the Reveal Formatting task pane with the keyboard shortcut Shift + F1. Generally, a collapse triangle (a solid right-and-down-pointing triangle) precedes *Font* and *Paragraph* and an expand triangle (a hollow right-pointing triangle) precedes *Section* in the *Formatting of selected text* list box in the Reveal Formatting task pane. Click the collapse triangle to hide any items below a heading and click the expand triangle to reveal items. Some of the items below headings in the *Formatting of selected text* list box are hyperlinks. Click a hyperlink and a dialog box displays with the specific option.

Figure 2.8 Reveal Formatting Task Pane

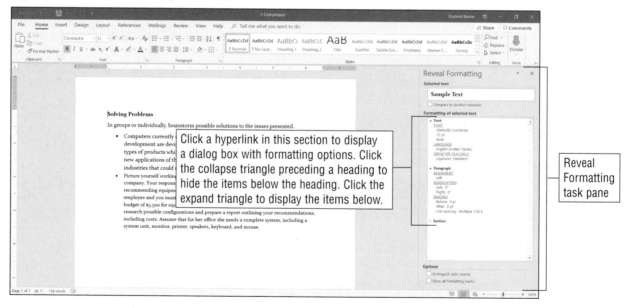

Activity 4a **Revealing Formatting** Part 1 of 2

1. Open **CompIssues** and then save it with the name **2-CompIssues**.
2. Press Shift + F1 to display the Reveal Formatting task pane.
3. Click in the heading *Solving Problems* and then notice the formatting information in the Reveal Formatting task pane.
4. Click in the bulleted paragraph and then notice the formatting information in the Reveal Formatting task pane.
5. Leave **2-CompIssues** open for the next activity.

Quick Steps

Compare Formatting
1. Press Shift + F1 to display Reveal Formatting task pane.
2. Click or select text.
3. Click *Compare to another selection* check box.
4. Click or select text.

Along with displaying formatting applied to text, the Reveal Formatting task pane can be used to compare formatting in two text selections to determine what is different. To compare formatting, select the first instance of formatting to be compared, click the *Compare to another selection* check box, and then select the second instance of formatting to be compared. Any differences between the two selections display in the *Formatting differences* list box.

Activity 4b Comparing Formatting   Part 2 of 2

1. With **2-CompIssues** open, make sure the Reveal Formatting task pane is visible. If it is not, turn it on by pressing Shift + F1.
2. Select the first bulleted paragraph (the paragraph that begins *Computers currently offer both*).
3. Click the *Compare to another selection* check box to insert a check mark.
4. Select the second bulleted paragraph (the paragraph that begins *Picture yourself working in the*).
5. Determine the formatting differences by reading the information in the *Formatting differences* list box. (The list box shows *12 pt -> 11 pt* below the FONT hyperlink, indicating that the difference is point size.)
6. Format the second bulleted paragraph so it is set in 12-point size.
7. Click the *Compare to another selection* check box to remove the check mark.
8. Select the word *visual*, which is used in the first sentence in the first bulleted paragraph.
9. Click the *Compare to another selection* check box to insert a check mark.
10. Select the word *audio*, which is used in the first sentence of the first bulleted paragraph.
11. Determine the formatting differences by reading the information in the *Formatting differences* list box.
12. Format the word *audio* so it matches the formatting of the word *visual*.
13. Click the *Compare to another selection* check box to remove the check mark.
14. Close the Reveal Formatting task pane by clicking the Close button in the upper right corner of the task pane.
15. Save, print, and then close **2-CompIssues**.

Check Your Work

Chapter Summary

- A font consists of three elements: typeface, type size, and typestyle.

- A typeface (font) is a set of characters with a common design and shape. Typefaces are monospaced, allotting the same amount of horizontal space for each character, or proportional, allotting varying amounts of space for different characters. Typefaces are divided into two main categories: serif and sans serif.

- Type size is measured in points; the higher the point size, the larger the characters.

- A typestyle is a variation of style within a certain typeface, such as bold, italic, or underline. Apply typestyles with buttons in the Font group on the Home tab.

- Apply font effects such as superscript, subscript, and strikethrough formatting with buttons in the second row in the Font group on the Home tab.

- The Mini toolbar automatically displays above selected text. Use options and buttons on this toolbar to apply formatting to the selected text.

- Use options at the Font dialog box to change the typeface, type size, and typestyle and to apply specific font effects. Display this dialog box by clicking the Font group dialog box launcher in the Font group on the Home tab.

- A Word document contains a number of predesigned formats grouped into style sets. Change to a different style set by clicking the Design tab and then clicking the style set in the styles set gallery in the Document Formatting group.

- Apply a theme and change theme colors, fonts, and effects with buttons in the Document Formatting group on the Design tab.

- Click the Paragraph Spacing button in the Document Formatting group on the Design tab to apply a predesigned paragraph spacing option to text.

- By default, paragraphs in a Word document are aligned at the left margin and ragged at the right margin. Change this default alignment with buttons in the Paragraph group on the Home tab, at the Paragraph dialog box, or with keyboard shortcuts.

- To turn on or off the display of nonprinting characters, such as paragraph symbols, click the Show/Hide ¶ button in the Paragraph group on the Home tab.

- Indent text in paragraphs with indent buttons in the Paragraph group on the Home tab, buttons in the Paragraph group on the Layout tab, keyboard shortcuts, options from the Paragraph dialog box, markers on the horizontal ruler, or the Alignment button above the vertical ruler.

- Increase and/or decrease spacing before and after paragraphs using the *Before* and *After* measurement boxes in the Paragraph group on the Layout tab or using the *Before* and/or *After* options at the Paragraph dialog box.

- Repeat the last command by pressing the F4 function key or the keyboard shortcut Ctrl + Y.

- Use the Format Painter button in the Clipboard group on the Home tab to copy formatting already applied to text to different locations in the document.

- Change line spacing with the Line and Paragraph Spacing button in the Paragraph group on the Home tab, keyboard shortcuts, or options at the Paragraph dialog box.

- Display the Reveal Formatting task pane with the keyboard shortcut Shift + F1. Use the *Compare to another selection* option in the task pane to compare formatting of two text selections to determine what is different.

Commands Review

FEATURE	RIBBON TAB, GROUP	BUTTON	KEYBOARD SHORTCUT
bold text	Home, Font	B	Ctrl + B
center-align text	Home, Paragraph		Ctrl + E
change case of text	Home, Font	Aa⌄	Shift + F3
clear all formatting	Home, Font	A⌀	
clear character formatting			Ctrl + spacebar
clear paragraph formatting			Ctrl + Q
decrease font size	Home, Font	A⌄	Ctrl + Shift + < OR Ctrl + [
decrease indent	Home, Paragraph		
display or hide nonprinting characters	Home, Paragraph	¶	Ctrl + Shift + *
font	Home, Font		Ctrl + Shift + F
font color	Home, Font	A⌄	
Font dialog box	Home, Font		Ctrl + Shift + F
font size	Home, Font		Ctrl + Shift + P
Format Painter	Home, Clipboard		Ctrl + Shift + C
highlight text	Home, Font		
increase font size	Home, Font	A^	Ctrl + Shift + > OR Ctrl +]
increase indent	Home, Paragraph		
italicize text	Home, Font	I	Ctrl + I
justify text	Home, Paragraph		Ctrl + J
left-align text	Home, Paragraph		Ctrl + L
line spacing	Home, Paragraph		Ctrl + 1 (single) Ctrl + 2 (double) Ctrl + 5 (1.5)

FEATURE	RIBBON TAB, GROUP	BUTTON	KEYBOARD SHORTCUT
Paragraph dialog box	Home, Paragraph		
paragraph spacing	Design, Document Formatting		
repeat last action			F4 or Ctrl + Y
Reveal Formatting task pane			Shift + F1
right-align text	Home, Paragraph		Ctrl + R
spacing after paragraph	Layout, Paragraph		
spacing before paragraph	Layout, Paragraph		
strikethrough text	Home, Font		
subscript text	Home, Font		Ctrl + =
superscript text	Home, Font		Ctrl + Shift + +
text effects and typography	Home, Font		
theme colors	Design, Document Formatting		
theme effects	Design, Document Formatting		
theme fonts	Design, Document Formatting		
themes	Design, Document Formatting		
underline text	Home, Font		Ctrl + U

Microsoft®
Word

CHAPTER
3

Customizing Paragraphs

Performance Objectives

Upon successful completion of Chapter 3, you will be able to:

1 Apply numbered and bulleted formatting to text

2 Apply paragraph borders and shading

3 Sort paragraphs of text

4 Set, clear, and move tabs on the horizontal ruler and at the Tabs dialog box

5 Cut, copy, and paste text in a document

6 Use the Paste Options button to specify how text is pasted in a document

7 Use the Clipboard task pane to copy and paste text within and between documents

As you learned in Chapter 2, Word contains a variety of options for formatting text in paragraphs. In this chapter, you will learn how to apply numbered and bulleted formatting as well as borders and shading. You will also learn how to sort paragraphs of text in alphabetical, numerical, and date order and to set and modify tabs on the horizontal ruler and at the Tabs dialog box. Editing some documents might include selecting and then deleting, moving, or copying text. You can perform these types of editing tasks with buttons in the Clipboard group on the Home tab or with keyboard shortcuts.

 Data Files

Before beginning chapter work, copy the WL1C3 folder to your storage medium and then make WL1C3 the active folder.

The online course includes additional training and assessment resources.

You will open a document containing information on computer technology, type numbered and bulleted text in the document, and apply numbered and bulleted formatting to paragraphs in the document.

Applying Numbering and Bullets

 Numbering

Bullets

Automatically number paragraphs or insert bullets before paragraphs using buttons in the Paragraph group on the Home tab. Use the Numbering button to insert numbers before specific paragraphs and use the Bullets button to insert bullets.

Tutorial

Creating Numbered Lists

Creating Numbered Lists

To type a numbered list, type *1.* and then press the spacebar, and Word indents the number 0.25 inch from the left margin. Text typed after the number will be indented 0.5 inch. When the Enter key is pressed to end the first item, the next number, *2.*, is automatically inserted at the beginning of the next paragraph. Continue typing items and Word inserts the next number in the list. To insert a line break without inserting a number, press Shift + Enter.

Quick Steps

Type Numbered Paragraphs
1. Type 1.
2. Press spacebar.
3. Type text.
4. Press Enter key.

Hint Define a new numbering format by clicking the Numbering button arrow and then clicking *Define New Number Format*.

To turn off numbering, press the Enter key two times or click the Numbering button in the Paragraph group on the Home tab. To turn numbering back on, simply type the next number in the list (and the period) followed by a space. Word will automatically indent the number and the text. (Numbered and bulleted formatting can be removed from a paragraph with the keyboard shortcut Ctrl + Q. Remove all formatting from selected text by clicking the Clear All Formatting button in the Font group on the Home tab.)

When the AutoFormat feature inserts numbering and indents text, the AutoCorrect Options button displays. Click this button and a drop-down list displays with options for undoing and/or stopping the automatic numbering.

Activity 1a **Creating a Numbered List** **Part 1 of 3**

1. Open **TechInfo** and then save it with the name **3-TechInfo**.
2. Press Ctrl + End to move the insertion point to the end of the document and then type the text shown in Figure 3.1. Apply bold formatting and center the title *Technology Career Questions*. When typing the numbered paragraphs, complete the following steps:
   a. Type *1.* and then press the spacebar. (The *1.* is indented 0.25 inch from the left margin and typed text is indented 0.5 inch from the left margin. Also, the AutoCorrect Options button displays. Use this button if you want to undo or stop automatic numbering.)
   b. Type the paragraph of text and then press the Enter key. (This moves the insertion point down to the next paragraph and inserts an indented number *2* followed by a period.)
   c. Continue typing the remaining text. (Remember, you do not need to type the paragraph number and period—they are automatically inserted. The last numbered item will wrap differently on your screen than shown in Figure 3.1.)
   d. After typing the last question, press the Enter key two times. (This turns off paragraph numbering.)
3. Save **3-TechInfo**.

Check Your Work

Figure 3.1 Activity 1a

Technology Career Questions

1. What is your ideal technical job?
2. Which job suits your personality?
3. Which is your first-choice certificate?
4. How does the technical job market look in your state right now? Is the job market wide open or are the information technology career positions limited?

Automatic numbering is turned on by default. Turn off automatic numbering at the AutoCorrect dialog box with the AutoFormat As You Type tab selected, as shown in Figure 3.2. To display this dialog box, click the File tab and then click *Options*. At the Word Options dialog box, click the *Proofing* option in the left panel and then click the AutoCorrect Options button in the *AutoCorrect options* section of the dialog box. At the AutoCorrect dialog box, click the AutoFormat As You Type tab and then click the *Automatic numbered lists* check box to remove the check mark. Click OK to close the AutoCorrect dialog box and then click OK to close the Word Options dialog box.

Quick Steps

Create Numbered List
1. Select text.
2. Click Numbering button.

To create a numbered list, click the Numbering button in the Paragraph group on the Home tab. Type text and it will be formatted as a numbered list. Click the button again to turn off numbering, or select existing text and then click the Numbering button to apply numbered formatting.

Figure 3.2 AutoCorrect Dialog Box with the AutoFormat As You Type Tab Selected

1. With **3-TechInfo** open, apply numbers to paragraphs by completing the following steps:
   a. Select the five paragraphs of text in the *Technology Information Questions* section.
   b. Click the Numbering button in the Paragraph group on the Home tab.

2. Add text between paragraphs 4 and 5 in the *Technology Information Questions* section by completing the following steps:
   a. Position the insertion point immediately right of the question mark at the end of the fourth paragraph.
   b. Press the Enter key.
   c. Type What kinds of networks are used in your local area?

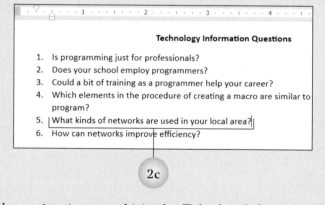

3. Delete the second question (paragraph) in the *Technology Information Questions* section by completing the following steps:
   a. Select the text of the second paragraph. (You will not be able to select the number.)
   b. Press the Delete key.
4. Save **3-TechInfo**.

Check Your Work

Creating Bulleted Lists

In addition to automatically numbering paragraphs, Word's AutoFormat feature creates bulleted lists. A bulleted list with a hanging indent is automatically created when a paragraph begins with the symbol *, >, or -. Type one of the symbols and then press the spacebar and the AutoFormat feature inserts a bullet 0.25 inch from the left margin and indents the text following the bullet another 0.25 inch. Change the indent of bulleted text by pressing the Tab key to demote text or pressing Shift + Tab to promote text. Word uses different bullets for demoted text.

Bulleted formatting can be turned on or applied to existing text with the Bullets button in the Paragraph group on the Home tab. Click the Bullets button to turn on bulleting, type text, and then click the button again to turn off bulleting. Or select existing text and then click the Bullets button to apply bulleted formatting. When the AutoFormat feature inserts bullets and indents text, the AutoCorrect Options button displays. This button contains options for undoing and/or stopping the automatic bulleting. The automatic bulleting feature can be turned off at the AutoCorrect dialog box with the AutoFormat As You Type tab selected.

Quick Steps

Type Bulleted List
1. Type *, >, or - symbol.
2. Press spacebar.
3. Type text.
4. Press Enter key.

Create Bulleted List
1. Select text.
2. Click Bullets button.

Activity 1c Creating a Bulleted List and Applying Bulleted Formatting   Part 3 of 3

1. With **3-TechInfo** open, press Ctrl + End to move the insertion point to the end of the document.
2. Type Technology Timeline: Computer Design and apply bold formatting and center alignment, as shown in Figure 3.3, and then press the Enter key.
3. Turn off bold formatting and change to left alignment.
4. Type a greater-than symbol (>), press the spacebar, type the text of the first bulleted paragraph in Figure 3.3, and then press the Enter key.
5. Press the Tab key (which demotes the bullet to a hollow circle) and then type the bulleted text.
6. Press the Enter key (which displays another hollow circle bullet), type the bulleted text, and then press the Enter key.
7. Press Shift + Tab (which promotes the bullet to an arrow), type the bulleted text, and then press the Enter key two times (which turns off bulleting).
8. Promote bulleted text by positioning the insertion point at the beginning of the text *1958: Jack Kilby, an engineer* and then pressing Shift + Tab. Promote the other hollow circle bullet to an arrow. (The four paragraphs of text should be preceded by arrow bullets.)
9. Format the paragraphs of text in the *Technology Timeline: Computers in the Workplace* section as a bulleted list by completing the following steps:
    a. Select the paragraphs of text in the *Technology Timeline: Computers in the Workplace* section.
    b. Click the Bullets button in the Paragraph group. (Word will insert the same arrow bullets that you inserted in Step 4. Word keeps the same bullet formatting until you choose a different bullet style.)
10. Save, print, and then close **3-TechInfo**.

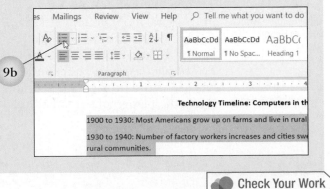

<Check Your Work

Figure 3.3 Activity 1c

Technology Timeline: Computer Design

➤ 1937: Dr. John Atanasoff and Clifford Berry design and build the first electronic digital computer.
  ○ 1958: Jack Kilby, an engineer at Texas Instruments, invents the integrated circuit, thereby laying the foundation for fast computers and large-capacity memory.
  ○ 1981: IBM enters the personal computer field by introducing the IBM-PC.
➤ 2004: Wireless computer devices, including keyboards, mice, and wireless home networks, become widely accepted among users.

Activity 2 **Customize a Document on Chapter Questions**　　　**3 Parts**

You will open a document containing chapter questions and then apply border and shading formatting to text.

Adding Emphasis to Paragraphs

To call attention to or to highlight specific text in a document, consider adding emphasis to the text by applying paragraph borders and/or shading. Apply borders with the Borders button in the Paragraph group on the Home tab and shading with the Shading button. Additional border and shading options are available at the Borders and Shading dialog box.

Applying Borders

　Borders

Applying Paragraph Borders

Every paragraph in a Word document contains an invisible frame, and a border can be applied to the frame around the paragraph. Apply a border to specific sides of the paragraph frame or to all sides. Add borders to paragraphs using the Borders button in the Paragraph group on the Home tab or using options at the Borders and Shading dialog box.

When a border is added to a paragraph of text, the border expands and contracts as text is inserted or deleted from the paragraph. Insert a border around the active paragraph or around selected paragraphs.

One method for inserting a border is to use options from the Borders button in the Paragraph group. Click the Borders button arrow and a drop-down gallery displays. At the drop-down gallery, click the option that will insert the desired border. For example, to insert a border at the bottom of the paragraph, click the *Bottom Border* option. Clicking an option will add the border to the paragraph where the insertion point is located. To add a border to more than one paragraph, select the paragraphs first and then click the option.

Quick Steps
Apply Borders with Borders Button
1. Select text.
2. Click Borders button arrow.
3. Click border option at drop-down gallery.

1. Open **Questions** and then save it with the name **3-Questions**.
2. Insert an outside border to specific text by completing the following steps:
   a. Select text from the heading *Chapter 1 Questions* through the four bulleted paragraphs.
   b. In the Paragraph group on the Home tab, click the Borders button arrow.
   c. Click the *Outside Borders* option at the drop-down gallery.
3. Select text from the heading *Chapter 2 Questions* through the five bulleted paragraphs and then click the Borders button (The button will apply the border option that was previously selected.)
4. Save **3-Questions**.

Check Your Work

Quick Steps

Apply Borders at Borders and Shading Dialog Box
1. Select text.
2. Click Borders button arrow.
3. Click *Borders and Shading* option.
4. Choose options in dialog box.
5. Click OK.

To further customize paragraph borders, use options at the Borders and Shading dialog box, as shown in Figure 3.4. Display this dialog box by clicking the Borders button arrow and then clicking *Borders and Shading* at the drop-down list. At the Borders and Shading dialog box, specify the border setting, style, color, and width.

Figure 3.4 Borders and Shading Dialog Box with the Borders Tab Selected

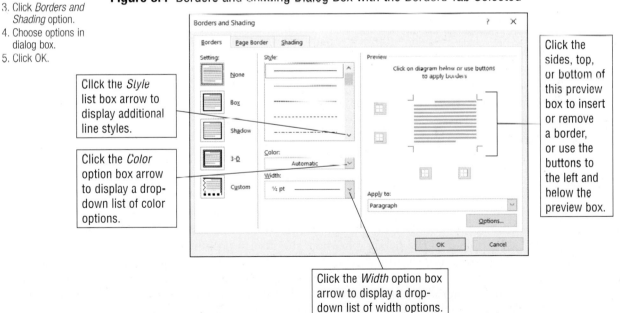

Click the *Style* list box arrow to display additional line styles.

Click the *Color* option box arrow to display a drop-down list of color options.

Click the sides, top, or bottom of this preview box to insert or remove a border, or use the buttons to the left and below the preview box.

Click the *Width* option box arrow to display a drop-down list of width options.

1. With **3-Questions** open, remove the paragraph borders around the heading *Chapter 1 Questions* by completing the following steps:
   a. Position the insertion point anywhere in the heading *Chapter 1 Questions*.
   b. Click the Borders button arrow and then click *No Border* at the drop-down gallery.
2. Apply a bottom border to the heading *Chapter 1 Questions* by completing the following steps:
   a. Click the Borders button arrow.
   b. Click the *Borders and Shading* option.
   c. At the Borders and Shading dialog box, click the *Style* list box down arrow two times. (This displays a double-line option.)
   d. Click the double-line option.
   e. Click the *Color* option box arrow.
   f. Click the *Blue* option (eighth color option in the *Standard Colors* section).
   g. Click the *Width* option box arrow.
   h. Click the *3/4 pt* option at the drop-down list.
   i. Click the *None* option in the *Setting* section.
   j. Click the bottom border of the box in the *Preview* section.
   k. Click OK to close the dialog box and apply the border.
3. Apply the same border to the other heading by completing the following steps:
   a. With the insertion point positioned in the heading *Chapter 1 Questions*, click the Format Painter button.
   b. Click in the heading *Chapter 2 Questions*.
4. Save **3-Questions**.

> Check Your Work

Tutorial

Applying Shading

 Shading

Quick Steps

Apply Shading
1. Select text.
2. Click Shading button.
OR
1. Click Borders button arrow.
2. Click *Borders and Shading* option.
3. Click Shading tab.
4. Choose options in dialog box.
5. Click OK.

Applying Shading

Apply shading to selected text or paragraphs in a document with the Shading button in the Paragraph group on the Home tab. If no text is selected, shading is applied to the paragraph where the insertion point is positioned. Select text or paragraphs and then click the Shading button arrow, and a drop-down gallery displays. Shading colors are presented in themes in the drop-down gallery. Use one of the theme colors or click one of the standard colors at the bottom of the gallery. Click the *More Colors* option and the Colors dialog box displays. At the Colors dialog box with the Standard tab selected, click a color or click the Custom tab and then specify a custom color.

Shading can also be applied using options at the Borders and Shading dialog box. Display this dialog box by clicking the Borders button arrow and then clicking the *Borders and Shading* option. At the Borders and Shading dialog box, click the Shading tab. Use options in the dialog box to specify a fill color, choose a pattern style, and specify a color for the dots that make up the pattern.

1. With **3-Questions** open, apply shading to the paragraph containing the heading *Chapter 1 Questions* by completing the following steps:
   a. Click in the heading *Chapter 1 Questions*.
   b. Click the Shading button arrow.
   c. Click the *Blue, Accent 5, Lighter 80%* option (ninth column, second row in the *Theme Colors* section).

2. Apply the same blue shading to the other heading by completing the following steps:
   a. With the insertion point positioned in the heading *Chapter 1 Questions*, click the Format Painter button.
   b. Click in the heading *Chapter 2 Questions*.
3. Apply shading to selected paragraphs with options at the Borders and Shading dialog box by completing the following steps:
   a. Select the four bulleted paragraphs below the heading *Chapter 1 Questions*.
   b. Click the Borders button arrow.
   c. Click the *Borders and Shading* option.
   d. At the Borders and Shading dialog box, click the Shading tab.
   e. Click the *Fill* option box arrow.
   f. Click the *Gold, Accent 4, Lighter 80%* option (eighth column, second row in the *Theme Colors* section).
   g. Click the *Style* option box arrow.
   h. Click the *5%* option.
   i. Click the *Color* option box arrow.
   j. Click the *Blue, Accent 5, Lighter 60%* color option (ninth column, third row in the *Theme Colors* section).
   k. Click OK to close the dialog box.
4. Apply the same shading to the bulleted paragraphs below the heading *Chapter 2 Questions* by completing the following steps:
   a. Click in the bulleted paragraphs below the heading *Chapter 1 Questions*.
   b. Click the Format Painter button.
   c. Select the five bulleted paragraphs below the heading *Chapter 2 Questions*.
5. Save, print, and then close **3-Questions**.

Check Your Work

Activity 3 Sort Text in a Document on Online Shopping   1 Part

You will open a document on online shopping and then sort several different
paragraphs of text.

 Tutorial

Sorting Text in
Paragraphs

Sorting Text in Paragraphs

Paragraphs can be sorted alphabetically, numerically, or by date, based on the
first character or characters in each paragraph. If the first character is a letter,
Word will sort alphabetically from A to Z or from Z to A. This can be useful for
such things as a list of names or a glossary of terms. Paragraphs that begin with a
number, such as a dollar amount or measurement, can be arranged numerically in
ascending or descending order.

Sort

To sort text, select the specific paragraphs to be sorted. (If text is not selected,
Word sorts the entire document.) Click the Sort button in the Paragraph group on
the Home tab and the Sort Text dialog box displays. At this dialog box, click OK.

Quick Steps

**Sort Paragraphs
of Text**
1. Click Sort button.
2. Make changes as
   needed at Sort Text
   dialog box.
3. Click OK.

The *Type* option at the Sort Text dialog box provides the options *Text*, *Number*,
or *Date* depending on the text selected. Word attempts to determine the data type
and chooses one of the three options. For example, if numbers with mathematical
values are selected, Word assigns them the *Number* type. However, if a numbered
list is selected, Word assigns them the *Text* type since the numbers do not
represent mathematical values. Occasionally this will result in Word reorganizing a
numbered list incorrectly (as 1., 10., 11., 12., 2., for example). If this occurs,
change the *Type* option to *Number* to sort in correct numerical order.

Activity 3 Sorting Paragraphs Alphabetically and Numerically   Part 1 of 1

1. Open **OnlineShop** and then save it with the name **3-OnlineShop**.
2. Sort the bulleted paragraphs alphabetically by
   completing the following steps:
   a. Select the four bulleted paragraphs
      in the section *Advantages of Online
      Shopping*.
   b. Click the Sort button in the
      Paragraph group on the Home tab.
   c. At the Sort Text dialog box, make
      sure that *Paragraphs* displays in
      the *Sort by* option box and that
      the *Ascending* option is selected.
   d. Click OK.
3. Sort the numbered paragraphs by
   completing the following steps:
   a. Select the six numbered
      paragraphs in the section *Online
      Shopping Safety Tips*.
   b. Click the Sort button in the Paragraph group.
   c. Click OK at the Sort Text dialog box.

4. Sort alphabetically the three paragraphs below the title *REFERENCES* by completing the following steps:
  a. Select the paragraphs below the title *REFERENCES*.
  b. Click the Sort button in the Paragraph group.
  c. Click the *Type* option box arrow and then click *Text* at the drop-down list.
  d. Click OK.
5. Save, print, and then close **3-OnlineShop**.

4c

Sort Text   ?   ×

Sort by

Paragraphs   ▾   Type: Date ▾   ⦿ Ascending
                                            ○ Descending
                                    Text
Then by   Number
                                    Date
                          ▾   Type: ◉ Ascending
                                            ○ Descending

> Check Your Work

Activity 4 Prepare a Document on Workshops and Training Dates   4 Parts

You will set and move tabs on the horizontal ruler and at the Tabs dialog box and type tabbed text about workshops, training dates, and a table of contents.

Setting and Modifying Tabs

Tabs allow text to be aligned at different points in the document. The default setting for tabs in Word is a left tab set every 0.5 inch. When the Tab key is pressed, the insertion point moves to the right 0.5 inch. In some situations, these default tabs are appropriate; in others, custom tabs may be needed. Two methods are available for setting tabs: set tabs on the horizontal ruler or at the Tabs dialog box.

Setting and Modifying Tabs on the Horizontal Ruler

> Tutorial

Setting and Modifying Tabs on the Horizontal Ruler

Quick Steps

Set Tabs on Horizontal Ruler
1. Click Alignment button above vertical ruler.
2. Click tab locations on horizontal ruler.

💡 *Hint* When setting tabs on the horizontal ruler, a dotted guideline displays to help align them.

💡 *Hint* Position the insertion point in any paragraph of text, and tabs for the paragraph appear on the horizontal ruler.

Use the horizontal ruler to set, move, and delete tabs. If the ruler is not visible, click the View tab and then click the *Ruler* check box in the Show group to insert a check mark. By default, tabs are set every 0.5 inch on the horizontal ruler. To set a new tab, first click the Alignment button to the left of the ruler to specify how text will be aligned on the tab. The types of tabs that can be set on the ruler are left, center, right, decimal, and bar. These tab types are represented on the ruler with the symbols shown in Table 3.1. Text is aligned at the left edge of a left tab, in the middle of a center tab, at the right edge of a right tab, and at the decimal point with a decimal tab. Setting a bar tab causes a vertical bar (line) to be inserted in the document at the point where the tab is set. Refer to Figure 3.7 on page 76 to see an example of a document with a bar tab.

When the Alignment button displays the correct tab symbol, position the mouse pointer on the ruler where the tab should be set, and then click the left mouse button to set the tab. When a new tab is set, any default tabs to the left of it are automatically deleted by Word.

If the tab symbol on the Alignment button is changed, the symbol remains in place until it is changed again or Word is closed. If Word is closed and then reopened, the Alignment button displays with the left tab symbol.

To set a tab at a specific measurement on the horizontal ruler, press and hold down the Alt key, position the mouse pointer at the desired position, and then

---

Table 3.1 Alignment Button Tab Symbols

Alignment Button Symbol	Type of Tab
L	left
⊥	center
⌟	right
⊥.	decimal
I	bar

click and hold down the left mouse button. This displays two measurements in the white portion of the horizontal ruler. The first measurement is the location of the mouse pointer on the ruler in relation to the left margin. The second measurement is the distance from the mouse pointer to the right margin. With the left mouse button held down, position the tab symbol at the desired location and then release the mouse button followed by the Alt key.

Tabs can be used to type text in columns. Type text and then click the Tab key to create a new column. At the end of a line, press the Enter key or press Shift + Enter. If the Enter key is used to end each line, all lines of text in columns will need to be selected to make paragraph formatting changes. To make changes to columns of text with line breaks inserted using Shift + Enter, the insertion point needs to be positioned in only one location in the columns of text.

Activity 4a **Setting Left, Center, and Right Tabs on the Horizontal Ruler**   Part 1 of 4

1. Press Ctrl + N to open a new blank document.
2. Type WORKSHOPS and apply bold formatting and center alignment, as shown in Figure 3.5.
3. Press the Enter key and then change the paragraph alignment back to left and turn off bold formatting.
4. Set a left tab at the 0.5-inch mark, a center tab at the 3.25-inch mark, and a right tab at the 6-inch mark by completing the following steps:
   a. Click the Show/Hide ¶ button in the Paragraph group on the Home tab to turn on the display of nonprinting characters.
   b. Make sure the horizontal ruler is visible. (If it is not, click the View tab and then click the *Ruler* check box in the Show group to insert a check mark.)
   c. Make sure the left tab symbol displays in the Alignment button above the vertical ruler.
   d. Position the mouse pointer on the 0.5-inch mark on the horizontal ruler and then click the left mouse button.

e. Position the mouse pointer on the Alignment button and then click the left mouse button until the center tab symbol displays (see Table 3.1).

f. Position the mouse pointer on the 3.25-inch mark on the horizontal ruler. Press and hold down the Alt key and then click and hold down the left mouse button. Make sure the first measurement on the horizontal ruler displays as approximately *3.25"* and then release the mouse button followed by the Alt key. (If 3.25" does not display, consider increasing the zoom.)

g. Position the mouse pointer on the Alignment button and then click the left mouse button until the right tab symbol displays (see Table 3.1).

h. Position the mouse pointer below the 6-inch mark on the horizontal ruler. Press and hold down the Alt key and then click and hold down the left mouse button. Make sure the first measurement on the horizontal ruler displays as approximately *6"* and then release the mouse button followed the Alt key.

5. Type the text in columns, as shown in Figure 3.5. Press the Tab key before typing each column entry and press Shift + Enter after typing each entry in the third column. Apply bold formatting to column headings, as shown in the figure.

6. After typing the final entry in the last column entry, press the Enter key two times.

7. Press Ctrl + Q to remove paragraph formatting (tab settings) below the columns from the current paragraph.

8. Click the Show/Hide ¶ button to turn off the display of nonprinting characters.

9. Save the document and name it **3-Tabs**.

Check Your Work

Figure 3.5 Activity 4a

	WORKSHOPS	
Title	**Price**	**Date**
Quality Management	$240	Friday, February 5
Staff Development	229	Friday, February 19
Streamlining Production	175	Monday, March 1
Managing Records	150	Tuesday, March 16
Customer Service Training	150	Thursday, March 18
Sales Techniques	125	Tuesday, April 13

After a tab has been set on the horizontal ruler, it can be moved to a new location. To move a tab, position the mouse pointer on the tab symbol on the ruler, click and hold down the left mouse button, drag the symbol to the new location on the ruler, and then release the mouse button. To delete a tab from the ruler, position the mouse pointer on the tab symbol to be deleted, click and hold down the left mouse button, drag down into the document, and then release the mouse button.

Activity 4b Moving Tabs   Part 2 of 4

1. With **3-Tabs** open, position the insertion point anywhere in the first entry in the tabbed text.
2. Position the mouse pointer on the left tab symbol at the 0.5-inch mark on the horizontal ruler, click and hold down the left mouse button, drag the left tab symbol to the 1-inch mark on the ruler, and then release the mouse button. *Hint: Use the Alt key to help you position the tab symbol precisely*.

3. Position the mouse pointer on the right tab symbol at the 6-inch mark on the horizontal ruler, click and hold down the left mouse button, drag the right tab symbol to the 5.5-inch mark on the ruler, and then release the mouse button. *Hint: Use the Alt key to help you position the tab symbol precisely*.
4. Save **3-Tabs**.

Check Your Work

 Tutorial

Setting and
Clearing Tabs at
the Tabs Dialog Box

Quick Steps

Set Tabs at Tabs Dialog Box
1. Click Paragraph group dialog box launcher.
2. Click Tabs button.
3. Specify tab positions, alignments, and leader options.
4. Click OK.

Setting and Modifying Tabs at the Tabs Dialog Box

Use the Tabs dialog box, shown in Figure 3.6, to set tabs at specific measurements and clear one tab or all tabs. To display the Tabs dialog box, click the Paragraph group dialog box launcher. At the Paragraph dialog box, click the Tabs button in the lower left corner of the dialog box.

A left, right, center, decimal, or bar tab can be set at the Tabs dialog box. (For an example of a bar tab, refer to Figure 3.7 on page 76.) To set a tab, click the type of tab in the *Alignment* section of the dialog box, type the tab measurement in the *Tab stop position* text box, and then click the Set button. To clear an individual tab at the Tabs dialog box, select or enter the tab position and then click the Clear button. To clear all tabs, click the Clear All button.

Figure 3.6 Tabs Dialog Box

Type a tab measurement in this text box.

Choose a tab alignment with options in this section.

Choose a leader symbol with options in this section.

Activity 4c Setting Left Tabs and a Bar Tab at the Tabs Dialog Box

1. With **3-Tabs** open, press Ctrl + End to move the insertion point to the end of the document.
2. Type the title TRAINING DATES and apply bold formatting and center alignment, as shown in Figure 3.7. Press the Enter key, return the paragraph alignment to left, and then turn off bold formatting.
3. Display the Tabs dialog box and then set left tabs and a bar tab by completing the following steps:
   a. Click the Paragraph group dialog box launcher.
   b. At the Paragraph dialog box, click the Tabs button in the lower left corner of the dialog box.
   c. Make sure *Left* is selected in the *Alignment* section of the dialog box.
   d. Type 1.75 in the *Tab stop position* text box.
   e. Click the Set button.
   f. Type 4 in the *Tab stop position* text box and then click the Set button.
   g. Type 3.25 in the *Tab stop position* text box, click *Bar* in the *Alignment* section, and then click the Set button.
   h. Click OK to close the Tabs dialog box.

4. Type the text in columns, as shown in Figure 3.7. Press the Tab key before typing each column entry and press Shift + Enter to end each line. After typing *February 23*, press the Enter key.
5. Clear tabs below the columns from the current paragraph by completing the following steps:
   a. Click the Paragraph group dialog box launcher.
   b. At the Paragraph dialog box, click the Tabs button.
   c. At the Tabs dialog box, click the Clear All button.
   d. Click OK.
6. Press the Enter key.
7. Remove the 8 points of spacing after the last entry in the text by completing the following steps:
   a. Position the insertion point anywhere in the *January 26* entry.
   b. Click the Line and Paragraph Spacing button in the Paragraph group on the Home tab.
   c. Click the *Remove Space After Paragraph* option.
8. Save **3-Tabs**.

Check Your Work

Figure 3.7 Activity 4c

TRAINING DATES

January 8	February 5
January 14	February 11
January 20	February 17
January 26	February 23

Four types of tabs (left, right, center, and decimal) can be set with leaders at the Tabs dialog box. Leaders are useful in a table of contents or other material where the reader's eyes should be directed across the page. Figure 3.8 shows an example of leaders. Leaders can be periods (.), hyphens (-), or underlines (_). To add leaders to a tab, click the type of leader in the *Leader* section of the Tabs dialog box.

Activity 4d Setting a Left Tab and a Right Tab with Period Leaders

Part 4 of 4

1. With **3-Tabs** open, press Ctrl + End to move the insertion point to the end of the document.
2. Type the title TABLE OF CONTENTS and apply bold formatting and center alignment, as shown in Figure 3.8.
3. Press the Enter key and then return the paragraph alignment to left and turn off bold formatting.
4. Set a left tab and then a right tab with period leaders by completing the following steps:
   a. Click the Paragraph group dialog box launcher.
   b. Click the Tabs button.
   c. At the Tabs dialog box, make sure *Left* is selected in the *Alignment* section of the dialog box.
   d. With the insertion point positioned in the *Tab stop position* text box, type 1 and then click the Set button.
   e. Type 5.5 in the *Tab stop position* text box.
   f. Click *Right* in the *Alignment* section.
   g. Click *2 ......* in the *Leader* section and then click the Set button.
   h. Click OK to close the dialog box.
5. Type the text in columns, as shown in Figure 3.8. Press the Tab key before typing each column entry and press Shift + Enter to end each line.
6. Save, print, and then close **3-Tabs**.

Check Your Work

Figure 3.8 Activity 4d

```
TABLE OF CONTENTS
```

Activity 5 **Move and Copy Text in a Document on Online Shopping Tips**   **2 Parts**

You will open a document containing information on online shopping safety tips and then cut, copy, and paste text in the document.

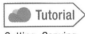

Tutorial

Cutting, Copying, and Pasting Text

Cutting, Copying, and Pasting Text

When editing a document, specific text may need to be deleted, moved to a different location in the document, or copied to various locations in the document. These activities can be completed using buttons in the Clipboard group on the Home tab.

Deleting and Cutting Text

 Cut

Cutting and deleting text are two ways to remove text from a document. Delete text by selecting it and then using the Delete key on the keyboard, or delete one character at a time with the Delete key or the Backspace key. To cut text, select it and then click the Cut button in the Clipboard group on the Home tab, or select it and then use the keyboard shortcut Ctrl + X. (Note: If text is accidentally cut or deleted, restore it by clicking the Undo button on the Quick Access Toolbar or with the keyboard shortcut Ctrl + Z before saving or closing the file. After a document has been saved and closed, the text cannot be restored.)

Hint The Clipboard content is deleted when the computer is turned off. Text you want to save permanently should be saved as a separate document.

When text is deleted, it is simply removed from the document. When text is cut, it is removed and stored temporarily in the Clipboard. The Clipboard holds text while it is being moved or copied to a new location in the document or to a different document.

Cutting and Pasting Text

 Paste

To move text to a different location in the document, select the text, click the Cut button, position the insertion point at the location the text is to be inserted, and then click the Paste button in the Clipboard group.

Quick Steps

Move Selected Text
1. Select text.
2. Click Cut button or use Ctrl + X.
3. Position insertion point.
4. Click Paste button or use Ctrl + V.

Selected text can also be moved using the shortcut menu. To do this, select the text and then position the insertion point inside the selected text until it turns into an arrow pointer. Click the right mouse button and then click *Cut* at the shortcut menu. Position the insertion point where the text is to be inserted, click the right mouse button, and then click *Paste* at the shortcut menu. Keyboard shortcuts are also available for cutting and pasting text. Use Ctrl + X to cut text and Ctrl + V to paste text.

Quick Steps

Move Text with Mouse
1. Select text.
2. Position mouse pointer in selected text.
3. Click and hold down left mouse button and drag to new location.
4. Release left mouse button.

When text is cut from a document, it will remain in the Clipboard while Word is open and can be pasted multiple times. The Clipboard holds only one item at a time. If another portion of text is cut to the Clipboard, the first selection will be removed.

Moving Text by Dragging with the Mouse

The mouse can be used to move text. To do this, select text to be moved and then click and drag the selection with the mouse pointer. As the text is being dragged, the mouse pointer will display as an arrow with a small gray box attached. Move to the location the selected text is to be inserted, and then release the button. If the selected text is inserted in the wrong location, click the Undo button immediately.

Activity 5a Cutting and Dragging Selected Text   Part 1 of 2

1. Open **ShoppingTips** and then save it with the name **3-ShoppingTips**.
2. Move a paragraph by completing the following steps:
   a. Select the paragraph that begins with *Only buy at secure sites,* including the blank line below the paragraph.
   b. Click the Cut button in the Clipboard group on the Home tab.
   c. Position the insertion point at the beginning of the paragraph that begins with *Watch for phony shopping apps.*
   d. Click the Paste button (make sure you click the Paste button and not the Paste button arrow) in the Clipboard group on the Home tab. (If the fourth and fifth paragraphs are not separated by a blank line, press the Enter key.)

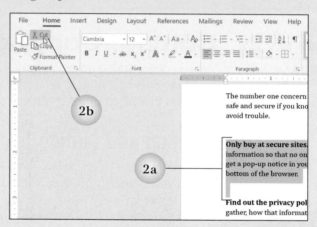

3. Following steps similar to those in Step 2, move the paragraph that begins with *Never provide your social* before the paragraph that begins *Watch for phony shopping apps* and after the paragraph that begins *Only buy at secure sites.*
4. Use the mouse to select the paragraph that begins with *Do not shop online using,* including one blank line below the paragraph.
5. Move the I-beam pointer inside the selected text until it displays as an arrow pointer.
6. Click and hold down the left mouse button, drag the arrow pointer (which displays with a small gray box attached) so that the insertion point (which displays as a black vertical bar) is positioned at the beginning of the paragraph that begins *Never provide your social* and then release the mouse button.
7. Deselect the text.
8. Save **3-ShoppingTips**.

Check Your Work

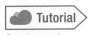

Tutorial

Copying and
Pasting Text and
Formatting

 Paste
Options

Using the Paste Options Button

When text is pasted in a document, the Paste Options button displays in the lower right corner of the text. Click this button (or press the Ctrl key on the keyboard) and the Paste Options gallery displays, as shown in Figure 3.9. The gallery can also be displayed by clicking the Paste button arrow in the Clipboard group.

The Paste Options gallery contains four buttons for specifying the formatting of pasted text. The first button, Keep Source Formatting, is the default and pastes the text with the original formatting. Click the second button, Merge Formatting, and pasted text will take on the formatting of the text where it is pasted. The third button, Picture, will paste selected text as an image. Click the last button, Keep Text Only, to paste only the text and not the text formatting. Hover the mouse pointer over a button in the gallery and the live preview displays the text in the document as it will appear when pasted.

Figure 3.9 Paste Options Button Drop-Down Gallery

Click the button that specifies the formatting for the pasted text.

Activity 5b Using the Paste Options Button   Part 2 of 2

1. With **3-ShoppingTips** open, open **Tip**.
2. In the **Tip** document, select the paragraph of text, including the blank line below the paragraph, and then click the Cut button in the Clipboard group on the Home tab.
3. Close **Tip**.
4. Press Ctrl + End to move the insertion point to the end of **3-ShoppingTips**.
5. Click the Paste button.
6. Click the Paste Options button at the end of the paragraph and then click the Merge Formatting button in the Paste Options gallery. (This changes the font so it matches the font of the other paragraphs in the document.)
7. Save, print, and then close **3-ShoppingTips**.

Check Your Work

Activity 6 Copy Text in a Staff Meeting Announcement   1 Part

You will copy and paste text in a document announcing a staff meeting for the Technical Support Team.

Copying and Pasting Text

Copy

Use copy and paste to copy text from one document and paste it into another. Or, paste copied text into one document multiple times to insert duplicate portions of text without needing to retype it. Copy selected text and then paste it in a different location using the Copy and Paste buttons in the Clipboard group on the Home tab or the keyboard shortcuts Ctrl + C and Ctrl + V.

Quick Steps

Copy Selected Text
1. Select text.
2. Click Copy button or use Ctrl + C.
3. Position insertion point.
4. Click Paste button or use Ctrl + V.

Text can also be copied and pasted using the mouse. To do this, select the text and then click inside the selected text. Hold down the left mouse button and also press and hold down the Ctrl key while dragging the selected text with the mouse. While text is being dragged, the pointer displays with a small gray box and a box containing a plus [+] symbol and a black vertical bar moves with the pointer. Position the black bar in the desired location, release the mouse button, and then release the Ctrl key to paste in the text.

Activity 6 Copying Text   Part 1 of 1

1. Open **StaffMtg** and then save it with the name **3-StaffMtg**.
2. Copy the text in the document to the end of the document by completing the following steps:
   a. Select all the text in the document and include one blank line below the text. ***Hint: Click the Show/Hide ¶ button to turn on the display of nonprinting characters. When you select the text, select one of the paragraph markers below the text***.
   b. Click the Copy button in the Clipboard group on the Home tab.
   c. Press Ctrl + End to move the insertion point to the end of the document.
   d. Click the Paste button.
3. Paste the text again at the end of the document. To do this, click the Paste button. (This inserts a copy of the text from the Clipboard.)
4. Select all the text in the document using the mouse and include one blank line below the text.
5. Move the I-beam pointer inside the selected text until it becomes an arrow pointer.
6. Click and hold down the Ctrl key and then the left mouse button. Drag the arrow pointer (which displays with a box containing a plus symbol) so the vertical black bar is positioned at the end of the document, release the mouse button, and then release the Ctrl key.
7. Deselect the text.
8. Make sure all the text fits on one page. If not, consider deleting any extra blank lines.
9. Save, print, and then close **3-StaffMtg**.

> 3:00 to 4:30 p.m., Room 20
>
> **TECHNICAL SUPPORT TEAM**
> **Staff Meeting**
> **Wednesday, March 10, 2021**
> **3:00 to 4:30 p.m., Room 20**
>
> **TECHNICAL SUPPORT TEAM**
> **Staff Meeting**
> **Wednesday, March 10, 2021**
> **3:00 to 4:30 p.m., Room 20**
>
> (6)
>
> (Ctrl) ▼

Check Your Work

Activity 7 Create a Contract Negotiations Document 1 Part

You will use the Clipboard task pane to copy and paste paragraphs to and from separate documents to create a contract negotiations document.

Quick Steps

Use the Clipboard
1. Click Clipboard group task pane launcher.
2. Select and copy or cut text.
3. Position insertion point.
4. Click option in Clipboard task pane.

Hint You can copy or cut items to the Clipboard from various Microsoft Office applications and then paste them into any Office file.

Using the Clipboard Task Pane

Use the Clipboard task pane to collect and paste multiple items. Up to 24 different items can be collected and then pasted in various locations. To display the Clipboard task pane, click the Clipboard group task pane launcher in the lower right corner of the Clipboard group on the Home tab. The Clipboard task pane displays at the left side of the screen in a manner similar to what is shown in Figure 3.10.

Select the text or object to be copied and then click the Copy button or Cut button in the Clipboard group. Continue selecting text or items and clicking the Copy or Cut button. To insert an item from the Clipboard task pane into the document, position the insertion point in the desired location and then click the option in the Clipboard task pane representing the item. Click the Paste All button to paste all the items in the Clipboard task pane into the document. If the copied or cut item is text, the first 50 characters display in the list box on the Clipboard task pane. When all the items are inserted, click the Clear All button to clear all items from the task pane.

Figure 3.10 Clipboard Task Pane

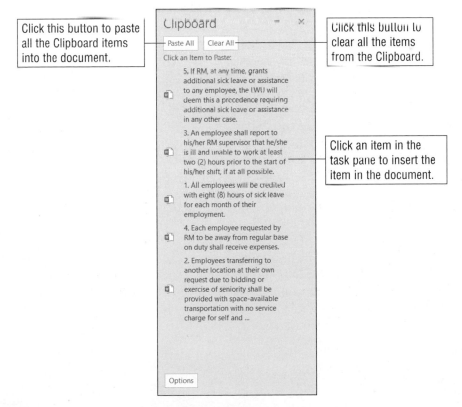

Click this button to paste all the Clipboard items into the document.

Click this button to clear all the items from the Clipboard.

Click an item in the task pane to insert the item in the document.

1. Open **ContractItems**.
2. Display the Clipboard task pane by clicking the Clipboard group task pane launcher in the bottom right corner of the Clipboard group on the Home tab. (If the Clipboard task pane list box contains any items, click the Clear All button at the top of the Clipboard task pane.)
3. Select paragraph 1 in the document (the *1.* is not selected) and then click the Copy button.
4. Select paragraph 3 in the document (the *3.* is not selected) and then click the Copy button.
5. Close **ContractItems**.
6. Paste the paragraphs by completing the following steps:
   a. Press Ctrl + N to open a new blank document. (If the Clipboard task pane does not display, click the Clipboard group task pane launcher.)
   b. Type CONTRACT NEGOTIATION ITEMS and apply bold formatting and center alignment.
   c. Press the Enter key, turn off bold formatting, and return the paragraph alignment to left.
   d. Click the Paste All button in the Clipboard task pane to paste both paragraphs in the document.
   e. Click the Clear All button in the Clipboard task pane.
7. Open **UnionContract**.
8. Select and then copy each of the following paragraphs:
   a. Paragraph 2 in the *Transfers and Moving Expenses* section.
   b. Paragraph 4 in the *Transfers and Moving Expenses* section.
   c. Paragraph 1 in the *Sick Leave* section.
   d. Paragraph 3 in the *Sick Leave* section.
   e. Paragraph 5 in the *Sick Leave* section.
9. Close **UnionContract**.
10. Make sure the insertion point is positioned at the end of the document on a new line and then paste the paragraphs by completing the following steps:
    a. Click the button in the Clipboard task pane representing paragraph 2. (When the paragraph is inserted in the document, the paragraph number changes to *3.*)
    b. Click the button in the Clipboard task pane representing paragraph 4.
    c. Click the button in the Clipboard task pane representing paragraph 3.
    d. Click the button in the Clipboard task pane representing paragraph 5.
11. Click the Clear All button.
12. Close the Clipboard task pane.
13. Save the document and name it **3-NegotiateItems**.
14. Print and then close **3-NegotiateItems**.

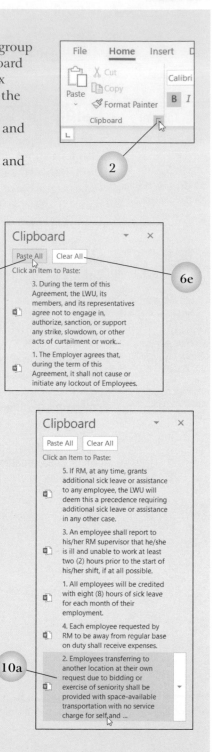

Check Your Work

Chapter Summary

- Number paragraphs using the Numbering button in the Paragraph group on the Home tab and insert bullets before paragraphs using the Bullets button in the Paragraph group on the Home tab.

- Remove all paragraph formatting from a paragraph by using the keyboard shortcut Ctrl + Q. Remove all character and paragraph formatting by clicking the Clear All Formatting button in the Font group.

- The AutoCorrect Options button displays when the AutoFormat feature inserts numbers or bullets. Click this button to display options for undoing and/or stopping automatic numbering or bulleting.

- A bulleted list with a hanging indent is automatically created when a paragraph begins with *, >, or -. The type of bullet inserted depends on the type of character entered.

- Automatic numbering and bulleting can be turned off at the AutoCorrect dialog box with the AutoFormat As You Type tab selected.

- A paragraph created in Word contains an invisible frame and a border can be added to this frame. Click the Borders button arrow in the Paragraph group on the Home tab to display a drop-down gallery of border options.

- Use options at the Borders and Shading dialog box with the Borders tab selected to add a customized border to a paragraph or selected paragraphs.

- Apply shading to selected text or paragraphs by clicking the Shading button arrow in the Paragraph group on the Home tab and then clicking a color at the drop-down gallery. Use options at the Borders and Shading dialog box with the Shading tab selected to add shading and/or a pattern to a paragraph or selected paragraphs.

- Use the Sort button in the Paragraph group on the Home tab to sort text in paragraphs alphabetically by the first character of each paragraph, which can be a number, symbol, or letter.

- By default, tabs are set every 0.5 inch. Tab settings can be changed on the horizontal ruler or at the Tabs dialog box.

- Use the Alignment button above the vertical ruler to select a left, right, center, decimal, or bar tab.

- When a tab is set on the horizontal ruler, any default tabs to the left are automatically deleted.

- After a tab has been set on the horizontal ruler, it can be moved or deleted using the mouse pointer.

- At the Tabs dialog box, any of the five types of tabs can be set at a specific measurement. Four types of tabs (left, right, center, and decimal) can be set with preceding leaders, which can be periods, hyphens, or underlines. Individual tabs or all tabs can be cleared at the Tabs dialog box.

- Cut, copy, and paste text using buttons in the Clipboard group on the Home tab, with options at the shortcut menu, or with keyboard shortcuts.

- When selected text is pasted, the Paste Options button displays in the lower right corner of the text. Click the button and the Paste Options gallery displays with buttons for specifying how text and formatting is pasted in the document.

- With the Clipboard task pane, up to 24 items can be copied and then pasted in various locations in a document or other document.

- Display the Clipboard task pane by clicking the Clipboard group task pane launcher in the Clipboard group on the Home tab.

Commands Review

FEATURE	RIBBON TAB, GROUP	BUTTON, OPTION	KEYBOARD SHORTCUT
borders	Home, Paragraph		
Borders and Shading dialog box	Home, Paragraph	, Borders and Shading	
bullets	Home, Paragraph		
clear all formatting	Home, Font		
clear paragraph formatting			Ctrl + Q
Clipboard task pane	Home, Clipboard		
copy text	Home, Clipboard		Ctrl + C
cut text	Home, Clipboard		Ctrl + X
numbering	Home, Paragraph		
Paragraph dialog box	Home, Paragraph		
paste text	Home, Clipboard		Ctrl + V
shading	Home, Paragraph		
Sort Text dialog box	Home, Paragraph		
Tabs dialog box	Home, Paragraph	, Tabs	

Word

Formatting Pages and Documents

Performance Objectives

Upon successful completion of Chapter 4, you will be able to:

1 Change margins, page orientation, and paper size

2 Format pages at the Page Setup dialog box

3 Insert a page break, blank page, and cover page

4 Insert and remove page numbers

5 Insert and edit predesigned headers and footers

6 Insert a watermark, page background color, and page border

7 Insert section breaks

8 Create and format text in columns

9 Hyphenate words automatically and manually

10 Create a drop cap

11 Use the Click and Type feature

12 Vertically align text

13 Find and replace text

Word provides a number of options for changing the layout of a document, such as adjusting page margins, orientation, and paper size. Word also includes features that can be inserted in a document such as a page break, blank page, cover page, and watermark, as well as page numbers, headers, footers, page color, and page borders. You will learn about these features in this chapter along with other page and document formatting options such as inserting section breaks, formatting text into columns, hyphenating words, creating a drop cap, and vertically aligning text. You will also learn how to find and replace text in a document.

Data Files

Before beginning chapter work, copy the WL1C4 folder to your storage medium and then make WL1C4 the active folder.

The online course includes additional training and assessment resources.

You will open a document containing information on guidelines for online etiquette and then change the margins, page orientation, and paper size.

Changing Page Setup

The Page Setup group on the Layout tab contains a number of options for changing the layout of pages in a document. Use options in the Page Setup group to perform such actions as changing margins, orientation, and paper size and inserting page breaks. The Pages group on the Insert tab contains three buttons for inserting a cover page, blank page, or page break.

Changing Margins

Margins

Changing Margins

Change page margins with options at the Margins button drop-down list, as shown in Figure 4.1. To display this drop-down list, click the Layout tab and then click the Margins button in the Page Setup group. To change the margins, click one of the preset margins in the drop-down list. Be aware that most printers require a minimum margin (between ¼ and ⅜ inch) because they cannot print to the edge of the page.

Changing Page Orientation

Orientation

Changing Page Orientation

Click the Orientation button in the Page Setup group on the Layout tab and two options display: *Portrait* and *Landscape*. At the portrait orientation, which is the default, the page is 8.5 inches wide and 11 inches tall. At the landscape orientation, the page is 11 inches wide and 8.5 inches tall. Change the page orientation and the page margins automatically shift: The left and right margin measurements become the top and bottom margin measurements.

Q̃uick Steps

Change Margins
1. Click Layout tab.
2. Click Margins button.
3. Click margin setting.

Change Page Orientation
1. Click Layout tab.
2. Click Orientation button.
3. Click *Portrait* or *Landscape*.

Change Paper Size
1. Click Layout tab.
2. Click Size button.
3. Click paper size.

Figure 4.1 Margins Button Drop-Down List

Tutorial

Changing Paper
Size

Size

Changing Paper Size

By default, Word formats documents for printing on standard letter-sized paper that is 8.5 inches wide and 11 inches tall. Change this default setting with options at the Size button drop-down list. Display this drop-down list by clicking the Size button in the Page Setup group on the Layout tab.

Activity 1a Changing Margins, Page Orientation, and Paper Size

Part 1 of 2

1. Open **Netiquette** and then save it with the name **4-Netiquette**.
2. Click the Layout tab.
3. Click the Margins button in the Page Setup group and then click the *Narrow* option.

4. Click the Orientation button in the Page Setup group and then click *Landscape* at the drop-down list.

5. Scroll through the document and notice how the text displays on the page in landscape orientation.
6. Click the Orientation button in the Page Setup group and then click *Portrait* at the drop-down list. (This changes the orientation back to the default.)

7. Click the Size button in the Page Setup group and then click the *Executive* option (*7.25" × 10.5"*). Paper size options may vary. If this option is not available, choose an option with a similar paper size.

8. Scroll through the document and notice how the text displays on the page.
9. Click the Size button and then click *Legal (8.5" × 14")*.
10. Scroll through the document and notice how the text displays on the page.
11. Click the Size button and then click *Letter (8.5" × 11")*. (This returns the size back to the default.)
12. Save **4-Netiquette**.

Check Your Work ⟩

Changing Margins at the Page Setup Dialog Box

Quick Steps

Change Margins at Page Setup Dialog Box
1. Click Layout tab.
2. Click Page Setup group dialog box launcher.
OR
2. Click Margins button, *Custom Margins*.
3. Specify margins.
4. Click OK.

Change Paper Size at Page Setup Dialog Box
1. Click Layout tab.
2. Click Size button.
3. Click *More Paper Sizes* at drop-down list.
4. Specify size.
5. Click OK.

The Margins button in the Page Setup group provides a number of preset margins. If these margins do not provide the desired margins, set specific margins at the Page Setup dialog box with the Margins tab selected, as shown in Figure 4.2. Display this dialog box by clicking the Page Setup group dialog box launcher on the Layout tab or by clicking the Margins button and then clicking *Custom Margins* at the bottom of the drop-down list.

To change one of the margins, select the current measurement in the *Top*, *Bottom*, *Left*, or *Right* measurement box and then type the new measurement, or click the measurement box up arrow to increase the measurement or the measurement box down arrow to decrease the measurement. As the margin measurements change at the Page Setup dialog box, the sample page in the *Preview* section shows the effects of the changes.

Changing Paper Size at the Page Setup Dialog Box

The Size button drop-down list contains a number of preset paper sizes. If these sizes do not provide the desired paper size, specify a size at the Page Setup dialog box with the Paper tab selected. Display this dialog box by clicking the Size button in the Page Setup group and then clicking *More Paper Sizes* at the bottom of the drop-down list.

Figure 4.2 Page Setup Dialog Box with the Margins Tab Selected

Notice the default settings for the top, bottom, left, and right margins.

Changes made to margins are reflected in this preview page.

Activity 1b Changing Margins and Paper Size at the Page Setup Dialog Box

Part 2 of 2

1. With **4-Netiquette** open, make sure the Layout tab is selected.
2. Click the Page Setup group dialog box launcher.
3. At the Page Setup dialog box with the Margins tab selected, click the *Top* measurement box up arrow until *0.7"* displays.
4. Click the *Bottom* measurement box up arrow until *0.7"* displays.
5. Select the current measurement in the *Left* measurement box and then type 0.75.
6. Select the current measurement in the *Right* measurement box and then type 0.75.
7. Click OK to close the dialog box.
8. Click the Size button in the Page Setup group and then click *More Paper Sizes* at the drop-down list.
9. At the Page Setup dialog box with the Paper tab selected, click the *Paper size* option box arrow and then click *Legal* at the drop-down list.
10. Click OK to close the dialog box.
11. Scroll through the document and notice how the text displays on the page.
12. Click the Size button in the Page Setup group and then click *Letter* at the drop-down list.
13. Save, print, and then close **4-Netiquette**.

Check Your Work

Activity 2 Customize a Report on Computer Input and Output Devices

3 Parts

You will open a document containing information on computer input and output devices and then insert page breaks, a blank page, a cover page, and page numbers.

Tutorial

Inserting and Removing a Page Break

Page Break

Inserting and Removing a Page Break

With the default top and bottom margins set at 1 inch, approximately 9 inches of text prints on the page. At approximately the 10-inch mark, Word automatically inserts a page break. Insert a page break manually in a document with the keyboard shortcut Ctrl + Enter or with the Page Break button in the Pages group on the Insert tab.

A page break inserted by Word is considered a *soft page break* and a page break inserted manually is considered a *hard page break*. Soft page breaks automatically adjust if text is added to or deleted from a document. Hard page breaks do not adjust and are therefore less flexible than soft page breaks.

Quick Steps

Insert Page Break
1. Click Insert tab.
2. Click Page Break button.
OR
Press Ctrl + Enter.

¶ Show/Hide ¶

If text is added to or deleted from a document containing a hard page break, check the break to determine whether it is still in a desirable location. Display a hard page break, along with other nonprinting characters, by clicking the Show/Hide ¶ button in the Paragraph group on the Home tab. A hard page break displays as a row of dots with the words *Page Break* in the center. To delete a hard page break, position the insertion point at the beginning of the page break and then press the Delete key or double-click the words *Page Break* and then press the Delete key. If the display of nonprinting characters is turned off, delete a hard page break by positioning the insertion point immediately below the page break and then pressing the Backspace key.

Activity 2a Inserting and Deleting Page Breaks

Part 1 of 3

1. Open **CompDevices** and then save it with the name **4-CompDevices**.
2. Change the top margin by completing the following steps:
   a. Click the Layout tab.
   b. Click the Page Setup group dialog box launcher.
   c. At the Page Setup dialog box with the Margins tab selected, type 1.5 in the *Top* measurement box.

   d. Click OK to close the dialog box.

3. Insert a page break at the beginning of the heading *Mouse* by completing the following steps:

   a. Position the insertion point at the beginning of the heading *Mouse* (at the bottom of page 1).

   b. Click the Insert tab and then click the Page Break button in the Pages group.

4. Move the insertion point to the beginning of the title *COMPUTER OUTPUT DEVICES* (on the second page) and then insert a page break by pressing Ctrl + Enter.

5. Move the insertion point to the beginning of the heading *Printer* and then press Ctrl + Enter to insert a page break.

6. Delete a page break by completing the following steps:

   a. Click the Home tab.

   b. Turn on the display of nonprinting characters by clicking the Show/Hide ¶ button in the Paragraph group.

   c. Scroll up to see the bottom of the third page and then double-click the words *Page Break*.

   d. Press the Delete key.

   e. Click the Show/Hide ¶ button to turn off the display of nonprinting characters.

7. Save **4-CompDevices**.

> **Check Your Work**

Inserting and Removing a Blank Page

Blank Page

Inserting and Removing a Blank Page

Click the Blank Page button in the Pages group on the Insert tab to insert a blank page at the position of the insertion point. This might be useful in a document where a blank page is needed for an illustration, graphic, or figure. When a blank page is inserted, Word inserts a page break and then inserts another page break to create the blank page. To remove a blank page, turn on the display of nonprinting characters and then delete the page breaks.

Inserting and Removing a Cover Page

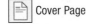

Cover Page

Inserting and Removing a Cover Page

Consider inserting a cover page to improve the visual appeal of a document or to prepare it for distribution to others. Use the Cover Page button in the Pages group on the Insert tab to insert a predesigned cover page and then type personalized text in the placeholders on the page. Click the Cover Page button and a drop-down list displays with visual representations of the cover pages. Scroll through the list and then click a predesigned cover page option.

Quick Steps

Insert Blank Page
1. Click Insert tab.
2. Click Blank Page button.

Insert Cover Page
1. Click Insert tab.
2. Click Cover Page button.
3. Click cover page option.

💡 **Hint** Adding a cover page gives a document a polished and professional look.

A predesigned cover page contains location placeholders, in which specific text is entered. For example, a cover page might contain the placeholder *[Document title]*. Click the placeholder to select it and then type the title of the document. Delete a placeholder by clicking to select it, clicking the placeholder tab, and then pressing the Delete key. Remove a cover page by clicking the Cover Page button and then clicking *Remove Current Cover Page* at the drop-down list.

Activity 2b Inserting and Removing a Blank Page and Inserting a Cover Page   Part 2 of 3

1. With **4-CompDevices** open, create a blank page by completing the following steps:
   a. Move the insertion point to the beginning of the heading *Touchpad and Touchscreen* on the second page.
   b. Click the Insert tab.
   c. Click the Blank Page button in the Pages group.
2. Insert a cover page by completing the following steps:
   a. Press Ctrl + Home to move the insertion point to the beginning of the document.
   b. Click the Cover Page button in the Pages group.
   c. Scroll down the drop-down list and then click the *Motion* option.
   d. Click the *[Document title]* placeholder and then type Computer Devices.

e. Click the *[Year]* placeholder, click the placeholder option box arrow, and then click the Today button at the bottom of the drop-down calendar.

f. Click the *[Company name]* placeholder and then type Drake Computing. (If a name appears in the placeholder, select the name and then type Drake Computing.)

g. Select the name above the company name and then type your first and last names. If instead of a name, the *[Author name]* placeholder displays above the company name, click the placeholder and then type your first and last names.

3. Remove the blank page you inserted in Step 1 by completing the following steps:

a. Move the insertion point immediately right of the period that ends the last sentence in the paragraph of text in the *Trackball* section (the last sentence on page 3).

b. Press the Delete key on the keyboard approximately six times until the heading *Touchpad and Touchscreen* displays on page 3.

4. Save **4-CompDevices**.

> **Trackball**
>
> A trackball is like an upside-down mouse. A mouse is move[d]
> and the user moves the ball with his or her fingers or palm.
> are incorporated into the design of the trackball.|
>
> **Touchpad and Touchscreen**
>
> A touchpad feels less mechanical than a mouse or trackball

3a-3b

 Check Your Work

Tutorial

Inserting and Removing Page Numbers

Inserting and Removing Page Numbers

Word by default does not include page numbers on pages. To insert page numbers in a document, click the Page Number button in the Header & Footer group on the Insert tab. A drop-down list displays with options for placing page numbers in the top margin of the page (in the Header pane) in the bottom margin of the page (in the Footer pane), in a page margin (either in a Header or Footer pane), or at the location of the insertion point. Click or point to an option and a drop-down list will appear showing several predesigned page number formats. Scroll through the list and then click an option.

Quick Steps

Insert Page Numbers
1. Click Insert tab.
2. Click Page Number button.
3. Click number option.

Choose a page number option other than *Current Position*, and the Header and Footer panes open. Changes can be made to the page numbering format in the Header pane or Footer pane. To do this, select the page number and then apply formatting such as a different font size, style, or color. A page number inserted in a document with the *Current Position* option is positioned in the document, not in the Header or Footer pane. Format the page number like any other text in the document.

After formatting page numbers inserted in the Header or Footer pane, click the Close Header and Footer button, or simply double-click anywhere in the document outside the header or footer. Remove page numbers from the document by clicking the Page Number button in the Header & Footer group and then clicking *Remove Page Numbers* at the drop-down list.

Activity 2c Inserting and Removing Predesigned Page Numbers

Part 3 of 3

1. With **4-CompDevices** open, insert page numbers by completing the following steps:
   a. Move the insertion point so it is positioned anywhere in the title *COMPUTER INPUT DEVICES*.
   b. If necessary, click the Insert tab.
   c. Click the Page Number button in the Header & Footer group and then point to *Top of Page*.
   d. Scroll through the drop-down list and then click the *Brackets 2* option.
2. Click the Close Header and Footer button in the Close group on the Header & Footer Tools Design tab.
3. Scroll through the document and notice the page numbers at the top of each page except the cover page. (The cover page and text are divided by a page break. Word does not include the cover page when numbering pages.)
4. Remove the page numbering by clicking the Insert tab, clicking the Page Number button, and then clicking *Remove Page Numbers* at the drop-down list.
5. Click the Page Number button, point to *Bottom of Page*, scroll down the drop-down list, and then click the *Accent Bar 2* option.

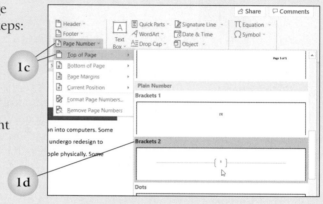

6. Click the Close Header and Footer button.
7. Save, print, and then close **4-CompDevices**.

Check Your Work

Activity 3 Add Elements to a Report on the Writing Process   3 Parts

You will open a document containing information on the process of writing
effectively, insert a predesigned header and footer, remove a header, and format
and delete header and footer elements.

Tutorial

Inserting and
Removing a
Predesigned
Header and Footer

Inserting Predesigned Headers and Footers

As mentioned in the last section, text that appears in the top margin of a page is
called a *header* and text that appears in the bottom margin of a page is referred
to as a *footer*. Headers and footers are common in manuscripts, textbooks,
reports, and other publications. They typically include page numbers and other
information such as the author's name, the title of the publication, and/or the
chapter title.

Header

Insert a predesigned header in a document by clicking the Insert tab and then
clicking the Header button in the Header & Footer group. This displays the
Header button drop-down list. At this drop-down list, click a predesigned header
option and the header is inserted in the document.

A predesigned header or footer may contain location placeholders such as
[Document title] or [Type here]. Click in the placeholder text to select it and
type the title of the document or other personalized text. Delete a placeholder by
clicking to select it and then pressing the Delete key. If the placeholder contains a
tab, delete the placeholder by clicking the tab and then pressing the Delete key.

To return to the document after inserting a header or footer, double-click in
the document outside the header or footer pane or click the Close Header and
Footer button.

Quick Steps

Insert Predesigned Header or Footer
1. Click Insert tab.
2. Click Header button or Footer button.
3. Click header or footer option.
4. Type text in specific placeholders in header or footer.
5. Click Close Header and Footer button.

Activity 3a Inserting a Predesigned Header   Part 1 of 3

1. Open **WritingProcess** and then save it with the name **4-WritingProcess**.
2. Press Ctrl + End to move the insertion point to the end of the document.
3. Move the insertion point to the beginning of the heading *REFERENCES* and then insert
   a page break by clicking the Insert tab and then clicking the Page Break button in the
   Pages group.

4. Press Ctrl + Home to move the insertion point to the beginning of the document and then insert a header by completing the following steps:

a. If necessary, click the Insert tab.

b. Click the Header button in the Header & Footer group.

c. Scroll to the bottom of the drop-down list and then click the *Sideline* option.

d. Click the *[Document title]* placeholder and then type The Writing Process.

e. Double-click in the document text. (This makes the document text active and dims the header.)

5. Scroll through the document to see how the header will print.

6. Save and then print **4-WritingProcess**.

Check Your Work

Footer

Insert a predesigned footer in the same manner as a header. Click the Footer button in the Header & Footer group on the Insert tab and a drop-down list displays that is similar to the Header button drop-down list. Click a footer and the predesigned footer is inserted in the document.

Removing a Header or Footer

Remove a header from a document by clicking the Insert tab and then clicking the Header button in the Header & Footer group. At the drop-down list, click the *Remove Header* option. Complete similar steps to remove a footer.

1. With **4-WritingProcess** open, press Ctrl + Home to move the insertion point to the beginning of the document.
2. Remove the header by clicking the Insert tab, clicking the Header button in the Header & Footer group, and then clicking the *Remove Header* option at the drop-down list.
3. Insert a footer in the document by completing the following steps:
   a. Click the Footer button in the Header & Footer group.
   b. Scroll down the drop-down list and then click *Ion (Light)*.

   c. Notice that Word inserted the document title at the left side of the footer. (Word remembered the document title you entered in the header.) Word also inserted your name at the right side of the footer. If the document title does not appear, click the *[DOCUMENT TITLE]* placeholder and then type THE WRITING PROCESS. If your name does not appear, click the *[AUTHOR NAME]* placeholder and then type your first and last names.
   d. Click the Close Header and Footer button to close the Footer pane and return to the document.
4. Scroll through the document to see how the footer will print.
5. Save and then print **4-WritingProcess**.

> Check Your Work

Editing a Predesigned Header or Footer

Predesigned headers and footers contain elements such as page numbers, a title, and an author's name. The formatting of an element can be changed by clicking the element and then applying formatting. Delete an element from a header or footer by selecting the element and then pressing the Delete key.

1. With **4-WritingProcess** open, remove the footer by clicking the Insert tab, clicking the Footer button, and then clicking *Remove Footer* at the drop-down list.
2. Insert and then format a header by completing the following steps:
   a. Click the Header button in the Header & Footer group on the Insert tab, scroll down the drop-down list, and then click *Grid*. (This header inserts the document title and a date placeholder.)
   b. Delete the date placeholder by clicking the *[Date]* placeholder, clicking the placeholder tab, and then pressing the Delete key.
   c. Double-click in the document text.
3. Insert and then format a footer by completing the following steps:
   a. Click the Insert tab.
   b. Click the Footer button, scroll down the drop-down list, and then click *Retrospect*.
   c. Select the name in the author placeholder at the left side of the footer and then type your first and last names.
   d. Select your name and the page number, apply bold formatting, and then change the font size to 10 points.
   e. Click the Close Header and Footer button.
4. Scroll through the document to see how the header and footer will print.
5. Save, print, and then close **4-WritingProcess**.

> **Check Your Work**

Activity 4 **Format a Report on Desirable Employee Qualities**   **2 Parts**

You will open a document containing information on desirable employee qualities and then insert a watermark, change the page background color, and insert a page border.

Formatting the Page Background

Quick Steps

Insert Watermark
1. Click Design tab.
2. Click Watermark button.
3. Click watermark option.

Apply Page Background Color
1. Click Design tab.
2. Click Page Color button.
3. Click color option.

The Page Background group on the Design tab contains three buttons for customizing the page background. Click the Watermark button and choose a predesigned watermark from options at the drop-down list. If a document will be shared electronically or published online, consider adding a page background color with the Page Color button. Use the Page Borders button to apply a border to the background of a page. Customize the style of the page border by using options in the Borders and Shading dialog box.

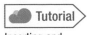

Tutorial

Inserting and
Removing a
Watermark

 Watermark

Inserting a Watermark

A watermark is a lightened image that displays behind the text in a document. Use a watermark to add visual appeal or to identify a document as a draft, sample, or confidential document. Word provides a number of predesigned watermarks. View watermark designs by clicking the Watermark button in the Page Background group on the Design tab. Scroll through the list and then click an option.

Tutorial

Applying Page
Background Color

 Page Color

Applying Page Background Color

Use the Page Color button in the Page Background group on the Design tab to apply a background color to a document. This background color is intended for documents that will be viewed on-screen or online, as color is visible on the screen but does not print. Insert a page color by clicking the Page Color button and then clicking a color at the drop-down color palette.

Activity 4a Inserting and Removing a Watermark and Applying a Page Background Color Part 1 of 2

1. Open **EmpQualities** and then save it with the name **4-EmpQualities**.
2. Insert a watermark by completing the following steps:
   a. With the insertion point positioned at the beginning of the document, click the Design tab.
   b. Click the Watermark button in the Page Background group.
   c. At the drop-down list, click the *CONFIDENTIAL 1* option.
3. Scroll through the document and notice how the watermark displays behind the text.
4. Remove the watermark and insert a different one by completing the following steps:
   a. Click the Watermark button and then click *Remove Watermark* at the drop-down list.
   b. Click the Watermark button and then click the *DO NOT COPY 1* option at the drop-down list.
5. Scroll through the document and notice how the watermark displays.
6. Move the insertion point to the beginning of the document.
7. Click the Page Color button in the Page Background group and then click the *Gray, Accent 3, Lighter 80%* option (seventh column, second row in the *Theme Colors* section).
8. Save **4-EmpQualities**.

 Check Your Work

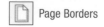 Page Borders

Inserting a Page Border

To improve the visual interest of a document, consider inserting a page border. When a page border is inserted in a multiple-page document, it prints on each page. To insert a page border, click the Page Borders button in the Page Background group on the Design tab. This displays the Borders and Shading dialog box with the Page Border tab selected, as shown in Figure 4.3. At this dialog box, specify the border style, color, and width.

The dialog box contains an option for inserting a page border containing an art image. To display the images available, click the *Art* option box arrow and then scroll through the drop-down list. Click an image to insert the art image page border in the document.

Changing Page Border Options

By default, a page border appears and prints 24 points from the top, left, right, and bottom edges of the page. Some printers, particularly inkjet printers, have a nonprinting area around the outside edges of the page that can interfere with the printing of a border. Before printing a document with a page border, click the File tab and then click the *Print* option. Look at the preview of the page at the right side of the Print backstage area and determine whether the entire border is visible. If a portion of the border is not visible in the preview page (generally at the bottom and right sides of the page), consider changing measurements at the Border and Shading Options dialog box, shown in Figure 4.4.

Display the Border and Shading Options dialog box by clicking the Design tab and then clicking the Page Borders button. At the Borders and Shading dialog box with the Page Border tab selected, click the Options button in the lower right corner of the dialog box. The options at the Border and Shading Options dialog box change depending on whether the Borders tab or the Page Border tab is selected when the Options button is clicked.

Figure 4.3 Borders and Shading Dialog Box with the Page Border Tab Selected

Figure 4.4 Border and Shading Options Dialog Box

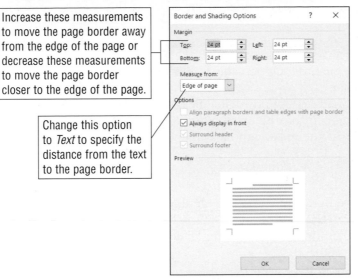

Increase these measurements to move the page border away from the edge of the page or decrease these measurements to move the page border closer to the edge of the page.

Change this option to *Text* to specify the distance from the text to the page border.

If a printer contains a nonprinting area and the entire page border will not print, consider increasing the spacing from the page border to the edge of the page. Do this with the *Top, Left, Bottom*, and/or *Right* measurement boxes. The *Measure from* option box has a default setting of *Edge of page*. To fit the border more closely around the text of the document, choose the *Text* option in the option box. This option sets the top and bottom margins at *1 pt* and the side margins at *4 pt*. These measurements can be increased or decreased by clicking the arrows in the measurement boxes.

Change the *Measure from* option to *Text* and the *Surround header* and *Surround footer* options become available and the check boxes contain check marks. With check marks in the check boxes, header and footer text is positioned inside the page border. To specify that header and footer text should be positioned outside the page border, remove the check marks from the check boxes.

Activity 4b Inserting a Page Border   Part 2 of 2

1. With **4-EmpQualities** open, remove the page color by clicking the Page Color button in the Page Background group on the Design tab and then clicking the *No Color* option.
2. Insert a page border by completing the following steps:
   a. Click the Page Borders button in the Page Background group on the Design tab.
   b. At the Borders and Shading dialog box with the Page Border tab selected, click the *Box* option in the *Setting* section.
   c. Scroll down the list of line styles in the *Style* list box to the last line style and then click the third line from the end.
   d. Click the *Color* option box arrow and then click the *Orange, Accent 2* option (sixth column, first row in the *Theme Colors* section).
   e. Click OK to close the dialog box.

3. Increase the spacing from the page border to the edges of the page by completing the following steps:
   a. Click the Page Borders button.
   b. At the Borders and Shading dialog box with the Page Border tab selected, click the Options button in the lower right corner.
   c. At the Border and Shading Options dialog box, click the *Top* measurement box up arrow until *31 pt* displays. (This is the maximum measurement allowed.)
   d. Increase the measurements in the *Left, Bottom,* and *Right* measurement boxes to *31 pt*.
   e. Click OK to close the Border and Shading Options dialog box.
   f. Click OK to close the Borders and Shading dialog box.
4. Save **4-EmpQualities** and then print page 1.
5. Insert an art image page border and change the page border spacing options by completing the following steps:
   a. Click the Page Borders button.
   b. Click the *Art* option box arrow and then click the border image shown at the right (approximately one-third of the way down the drop-down list).
   c. Click the Options button in the lower right corner of the Borders and Shading dialog box.
   d. At the Border and Shading Options dialog box, click the *Measure from* option box arrow and then click *Text* at the drop-down list.
   e. Click the *Top* measurement box up arrow until *10 pt* displays.
   f. Increase the measurement in the *Bottom* measurement box to *10 pt* and the measurements in the *Left* and *Right* measurement boxes to *14 pt*.
   g. Click the *Surround header* check box to remove the check mark.
   h. Click the *Surround footer* check box to remove the check mark.
   i. Click OK to close the Border and Shading Options dialog box.
   j. Click OK to close the Borders and Shading dialog box.
6. Save, print, and then close **4-EmpQualities**.

Chapter 4 | Formatting Pages and Documents

Check Your Work

In a document on computer input devices, you will format text into columns, improve the readability by hyphenating long words, and improve the visual interest by inserting a drop cap.

Tutorial

Inserting and
Deleting a Section
Break

Breaks

Quick Steps

Insert Section Break
1. Click Layout tab.
2. Click Breaks button.
3. Click section break
   option.

Hint When you
delete a section break,
the text that follows
takes on the formatting
of the text preceding
the break.

Inserting a Section Break

Some documents may have several sections of text that need to be formatted in different ways. To help make formatting easier, insert section breaks. Formatting changes that are made to one section—such as narrower margins, a paragraph border, colored text, and so on—will only apply to that section and not to the rest of the document.

Insert a section break in a document by clicking the Breaks button in the Page Setup group on the Layout tab. Choose from four types of section breaks in the drop-down list: Next Page, Continuous, Even Page, and Odd Page. Click *New Page* to insert a section break and start a new section on the next page. Click *Continuous* to insert a section break and start a new section on the same page. Click *Even Page* or *Odd Page* to insert a section break and then start a new section on either the next even or the next odd page.

To see the locations of section breaks in a document, click the Show/Hide ¶ button on the Home tab to turn on the display of nonprinting characters. A section break is shown in the document as a double row of dots with the words *Section Break* in the middle. Word will identify the type of section break. For example, if a continuous section break is inserted, the words *Section Break (Continuous)* display in the middle of the row of dots. To delete a section break, click the Show/Hide ¶ button to turn on the display of nonprinting characters, click on the section break, and then press the Delete key.

Activity 5a **Inserting a Continuous Section Break**   Part 1 of 6

1. Open **InputDevices** and then save it with the name **4-InputDevices**.
2. Insert a continuous section break by completing the following steps:
   a. Move the insertion point to the beginning of the heading *Keyboard*.
   b. Click the Layout tab.
   c. Click the Breaks button in the Page Setup group and then click *Continuous* in the *Section Breaks* section of the drop-down list.
3. Click the Home tab, click the Show/Hide ¶ button in the Paragraph group, and then notice the section break at the end of the first paragraph of text.
4. Click the Show/Hide ¶ button to turn off the display of nonprinting characters.

5. With the insertion point positioned at the beginning of the heading *Keyboard*, change the left and right margins to 1.5 inches. (The margin changes affect only the text after the continuous section break.)

6. Save and then print **4-InputDevices**.

> Check Your Work

Tutorial

Formatting Text into Columns

Formatting Text into Columns

When preparing a document containing text, an important point to consider is its readability. *Readability* refers to the ease with which a person can read and understand groups of words. The line length of text in a document can enhance or detract from its readability. If the line length is too long, the reader may lose his or her place and have a difficult time moving to the next line below.

To improve the readability of a document, consider formatting the text in columns. One common type is the newspaper column, which is typically used for text in newspapers, newsletters, and magazines.

Columns

Format text in one, two, or three columns with the Columns button in the Page Setup group on the Layout tab. To customize the column width and spacing, click the *More Columns* option to open the Columns dialog box. Adjust the measurement to create columns of varying widths. A document can include as many columns as will fit on the page. Word determines how many columns can be included based on the page width, the margin widths, and the size and spacing of the columns. Columns should be at least 0.5 inch in width.

Quick Steps

Create Columns
1. Click Layout tab.
2. Click Columns button.
3. Click number of columns.

Activity 5b Formatting Text into Columns

Part 2 of 6

1. With **4-InputDevices** open, make sure the insertion point is positioned below the section break and then change the left and right margins back to 1 inch.
2. Delete the section break by completing the following steps:
   a. Click the Show/Hide ¶ button in the Paragraph group on the Home tab to turn on the display of nonprinting characters.
   b. Click on *Section Break (Continuous)* at the end of the first paragraph below the title in the document. (This moves the insertion point to the beginning of the section break.)

COMPUTER·INPUT·DEVICES¶

Engineers·have·been·especially·creative·in·designing·new·ways·to·get·information·into·computers.·Some· input·methods·are·highly·specialized·and·unusual,·while·common·devices·often·undergo·redesign·to· improve·their·capabilities·or·their·ergonomics,·the·ways·in·which·they·affect·people·physically.·Some· common·input·devices·include·keyboards,·mice,·trackballs,·and·touchpads.¶══Section Break (Continuous)══

Keyboard¶

A·keyboard·can·be·an·external·device·that·is·attached·by·means·of·a·cable,·or·it·can·be·attached·to·the·

2b

   c. Press the Delete key.
   d. Click the Show/Hide ¶ button to turn off the display of nonprinting characters.

3. Move the insertion point to the beginning of the first paragraph of text below the title and then insert a continuous section break.
4. Format the text into columns by completing the following steps:
   a. Make sure the insertion point is positioned below the section break.
   b. If necessary, click the Layout tab.
   c. Click the Columns button in the Page Setup group.
   d. Click *Two* at the drop-down list.
5. Save **4-InputDevices**.

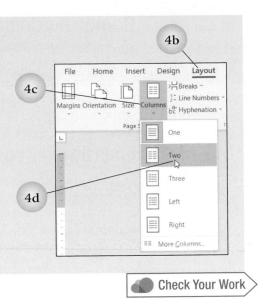

Check Your Work

Creating Columns with the Columns Dialog Box

Quick Steps

Create Columns at Columns Dialog Box
1. Click Layout tab
2. Click Columns button.
3. Click *More Columns*.
4. Specify column options.
5. Click OK.

Use the Columns dialog box to create newspaper columns that are equal or unequal in width. To display the Columns dialog box, shown in Figure 4.5, click the Columns button in the Page Setup group on the Layout tab and then click *More Columns* at the drop-down list.

With options at the Columns dialog box, specify the style and number of columns, enter specific column measurements, create unequal columns, and insert a line between columns. By default, column formatting is applied to the whole document. This can be changed to *This point forward* at the *Apply to* option box at the bottom of the Columns dialog box. With the *This point forward* option, a section break is inserted and the column formatting is applied to text from the location of the insertion point to the end of the document or until another column format is encountered. The *Preview* section of the dialog box shows an example of how the columns will appear in the document.

Figure 4.5 Columns Dialog Box

Choose the number of columns in this section or with this measurement box.

Specify column width and spacing with options in this section.

Use this option box to apply column formatting to the whole document, from the insertion point to the end of the document, or to a specific section.

Click this check box to insert a line between columns.

Preview the effects of column settings in this section.

Removing Column Formatting

To remove column formatting using the Columns button, position the insertion point in the section containing columns, click the Layout tab, click the Columns button, and then click *One* at the drop-down list. Column formatting can also be removed at the Columns dialog box by selecting the *One* option in the *Presets* section.

Inserting a Column Break

Hint You can also insert a column break with the keyboard shortcut Ctrl + Shift + Enter.

When formatting text into columns, Word automatically breaks the columns to fit the page. At times, automatic column breaks may appear in undesirable locations. Insert a manual column break by positioning the insertion point where the column is to end, clicking the Layout tab, clicking the Breaks button in the Page Setup group, and then clicking *Column* at the drop-down list.

Activity 5c Formatting Text into Columns at the Columns Dialog Box

Part 3 of 6

1. With **4-InputDevices** open, delete the section break by completing the following steps:
   a. If necessary, click the Home tab.
   b. Click the Show/Hide ¶ button in the Paragraph group to turn on the display of nonprinting characters.
   c. Click on *Section Break (Continuous)* and then press the Delete key.
   d. Click the Show/Hide ¶ button to turn off the display of nonprinting characters.
2. Remove column formatting by clicking the Layout tab, clicking the Columns button, and then clicking *One* at the drop-down list.
3. Format the text into columns by completing the following steps:
   a. If necessary, position the insertion point at the beginning of the first paragraph of text below the title.
   b. Click the Columns button and then click *More Columns* at the drop-down list.
   c. At the Columns dialog box, click *Two* in the *Presets* section.
   d. Click the *Spacing* measurement box down arrow until *0.3"* displays.
   e. Click the *Line between* check box to insert a check mark.
   f. Click the *Apply to* option box arrow and then click *This point forward* at the drop-down list.
   g. Click OK to close the dialog box.

4. Insert a column break by completing the following steps:
   a. Position the insertion point at the beginning of the heading *Mouse*.
   b. Click the Breaks button in the Page Setup group and then click *Column* at the drop-down list.
5. Save and then print **4-InputDevices**.

Check Your Work

Balancing Columns on a Page

In a document containing text formatted into columns, Word automatically lines up (balances) the last lines of text at the bottoms of the columns, except on the last page. Text in the last column of the last page may end far short of the bottom of the page, and the page will look unbalanced. Balance columns by inserting a continuous section break at the end of the text.

Activity 5d **Formatting and Balancing Columns of Text**   Part 4 of 6

1. With **4-InputDevices** open, delete the column break by positioning the insertion point at the beginning of the heading *Mouse*, if necessary, and then pressing the Backspace key.
2. Select the entire document and then change the font to 12-point Constantia.
3. Move the insertion point to the end of the document and then balance the columns by clicking the Layout tab, clicking the Breaks button in the Page Setup group, and then clicking *Continuous* at the drop-down list.

> A touchscreen allows the user to choose options by pressing the appropriate part of the screen. Touchscreens are widely used
>
> in bank ATMs and in kiosks at retail outlets and in tourist areas.
>
> 3

4. Apply the Green, Accent 6, Lighter 60% paragraph shading (last column, third row) to the title *COMPUTER INPUT DEVICES*.
5. Apply the Green, Accent 6, Lighter 80% paragraph shading (last column, second row) to each heading in the document.
6. Insert page numbers that print at the bottom center of each page using the *Plain Number 2* option.
7. Double-click in the document to make it active.
8. Save **4-InputDevices**.

Check Your Work

Hyphenating Words

In some Word documents, especially those with left and right margins wider than 1 inch or those with text set in columns, the right margin may appear quite ragged. To make the margin neater and more uniform, use hyphens to break longer words that fall at the end of the line. Use the hyphenation feature to hyphenate words automatically or manually.

Automatically Hyphenating Words

 Hyphenation

To automatically hyphenate words in a document, click the Layout tab, click the Hyphenation button in the Page Setup group, and then click *Automatic* at the drop-down list. Scroll through the document and check to see whether hyphens were added in appropriate locations within the words. To undo hyphenation, immediately click the Undo button on the Quick Access Toolbar.

Hint Avoid dividing words at the ends of more than two consecutive lines.

Manually Hyphenating Words

To control where hyphens appear in words during hyphenation, choose manual hyphenation. To do this, click the Layout tab, click the Hyphenation button in the Page Setup group, and then click *Manual* at the drop-down list. This displays the Manual Hyphenation dialog box, as shown in Figure 4.6. (The word in the *Hyphenate at* text box will vary.)

At this dialog box, click Yes to hyphenate the word as indicated in the *Hyphenate at* text box, click No if the word should not be hyphenated, or click Cancel to cancel hyphenation. The hyphen can be repositioned in the word in the *Hyphenate at* text box. Word shows the word with syllable breaks indicated by hyphens. Each place the word will be hyphenated displays as a blinking black bar. To hyphenate a word at a different place, click and drag the blinking black bar to the position desired and then click Yes. Continue clicking Yes or No at the Manual Hyphenation dialog box.

Quick Steps

Automatically Hyphenate Document
1. Click Layout tab.
2. Click Hyphenation button.
3. Click *Automatic*.

Manually Hyphenate Document
1. Click Layout tab.
2. Click Hyphenation button.
3. Click *Manual*.
4. Click Yes or No to hyphenate indicated words.
5. When complete, click OK.

Figure 4.6 Manual Hyphenation Dialog Box

Click Yes to hyphenate the word at this location, or move to a different syllable break and then click Yes.

1. With **4-InputDevices** open, hyphenate words automatically by completing the following steps:
   a. Press Ctrl + Home.
   b. Click the Layout tab.
   c. Click the Hyphenation button in the Page Setup group and then click *Automatic* at the drop-down list.

2. Scroll through the document and notice the hyphenation.
3. Click the Undo button to remove the hyphens.
4. Manually hyphenate words by completing the following steps:
   a. Click the Hyphenation button in the Page Setup group and then click *Manual* at the drop-down list.
   b. At the Manual Hyphenation dialog box, make one of the following choices:
      - Click Yes to hyphenate the word as indicated in the *Hyphenate at* text box.
      - Click and drag the hyphen in the word to break the word on a different syllable and then click Yes.
      - Click No if the word should not be hyphenated.
   c. Continue clicking Yes or No at the Manual Hyphenation dialog box.
   d. At the message indicating that hyphenation is complete, click OK.
5. Save **4-InputDevices**.

Check Your Work

Creating a Drop Cap

Tutorial

Creating and Removing a Drop Cap

 Drop Cap

Quick Steps

Create Drop Cap
1. Click Insert tab.
2. Click Drop Cap button.
3. Click drop cap option.

Use a drop cap to enhance the appearance of text. A drop cap is the first letter of the first word of a paragraph that is set into the paragraph with formatting that differentiates it from the rest of the paragraph. Drop caps can be used to identify the beginnings of major sections or parts of a document.

Create a drop cap with the Drop Cap button in the Text group on the Insert tab. The drop cap can be set in the paragraph or in the margin. At the Drop Cap dialog box, specify a font, the number of lines the letter should drop, and the distance the letter should be positioned from the text of the paragraph. Add a drop cap to the entire first word of a paragraph by selecting the word and then clicking the Drop Cap button.

1. With **4-InputDevices** open, create a drop cap by completing the following steps:
   a. Position the insertion point in the first word of the first paragraph below the title (the word *Engineers*).
   b. Click the Insert tab.
   c. Click the Drop Cap button in the Text group.
   d. Click *In margin* at the drop-down gallery.

2. Looking at the drop cap, you decide that you do not like it positioned in the margin and want it to be a little smaller. To change the drop cap, complete the following steps:
   a. With the *E* in the word *Engineers* selected, click the Drop Cap button and then click *None* at the drop-down gallery.
   b. Click the Drop Cap button and then click *Drop Cap Options* at the drop-down gallery.
   c. At the Drop Cap dialog box, click *Dropped* in the *Position* section.
   d. Click the *Font* option box arrow, scroll up the drop-down list, and then click *Cambria*.
   e. Click the *Lines to drop* measurement box down arrow to change the number to *2*.
   f. Click OK to close the dialog box.
   g. Click outside the drop cap to deselect it.
3. Save, print, and then close **4-InputDevices**.

Check Your Work

Activity 6 Create an Announcement about Supervisory Training   2 Parts

You will create an announcement about upcoming supervisor training and use the Click and Type feature to center and right-align text. You also will vertically center the text on the page.

Tutorial

Using Click and Type

Using the Click and Type Feature

Word contains a Click and Type feature that allows text to be aligned left, right, or center beginning at a specific point in the document. This feature can be used to position text as it is being typed rather than typing the text and then selecting and formatting the text, which requires multiple steps.

Quick Steps
Use Click and Type
1. Hover mouse at left margin, between left and right margins, or at right margin.
2. When horizontal lines display next to mouse pointer, double-click left mouse button.

To use the Click and Type feature, open a new blank document and move the mouse pointer slowly over the page, going from left to right. The pointer will appear as an I-beam with horizontal lines representing the text alignment. Near the left margin, the horizontal lines are left-aligned. In the center of the page, the lines are centered. At the right margin, the horizontal lines are right-aligned. Double-click in the document and begin typing. Text should automatically align to match the horizontal lines indicated on the I-beam pointer. (Note: Make sure the horizontal lines display near the mouse pointer before double-clicking the mouse button. Double-clicking when the alignment lines are not shown will insert a tab instead of changing the text alignment.)

Activity 6a   Using Click and Type   Part 1 of 2

1. At a blank document, create the centered text shown in Figure 4.7 by completing the following steps:
   a. Position the I-beam pointer between the left and right margins at about the 3.25-inch mark on the horizontal ruler and at the top of the vertical ruler.
   b. When the center-alignment lines display below the I-beam pointer, double-click the left mouse button.

   c. Type the centered text shown in Figure 4.7. Press Shift + Enter to end each line except the last line.
2. Change to right alignment by completing the following steps:
   a. Position the I-beam pointer near the right margin at approximately the 1-inch mark on the vertical ruler until the right-alignment lines display at the left of the I-beam pointer.

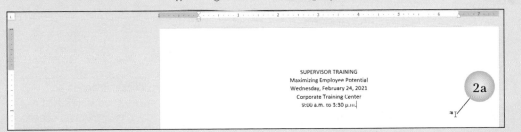

   b. Double-click the left mouse button.
   c. Type the right-aligned text shown in Figure 4.7. Press Shift + Enter to end the first line.
3. Select the centered text and then change the font to 14-point Candara bold and the line spacing to double spacing.
4. Select the right-aligned text, change the font to 10-point Candara bold, and then deselect the text.
5. Save the document and name it **4-Training**.

Check Your Work

Figure 4.7 Activity 6a

SUPERVISOR TRAINING
Maximizing Employee Potential
Wednesday, February 24, 2021
Corporate Training Center
9:00 a.m. to 3:30 p.m.

Sponsored by
Cell Systems

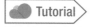
Tutorial

Changing Vertical
Alignment

Changing Vertical Alignment

Text or items in a Word document are aligned at the top of the page by default. Change this alignment with the *Vertical alignment* option box at the Page Setup dialog box with the Layout tab selected, as shown in Figure 4.8. Display this dialog box by clicking the Layout tab, clicking the Page Setup group dialog box launcher, and then clicking the Layout tab at the Page Setup dialog box.

The *Vertical alignment* option box in the *Page* section of the Page Setup dialog box contains four choices: *Top*, *Center*, *Justified*, and *Bottom*. The default setting is *Top*, which aligns text and items such as images at the top of the page. Choose *Center* to position the text in the middle of the page vertically. The *Justified* option aligns text between the top and bottom margins. The *Center* option positions text in the middle of the page vertically, while the *Justified* option adds space between paragraphs of text (not within) to fill the page from the top to the bottom margins. Choose the *Bottom* option to align text at the bottom of the page.

Quick Steps

Vertically Align Text

1. Click Layout tab.
2. Click Page Setup group dialog box launcher.
3. Click Layout tab.
4. Click *Vertical alignment* option box.
5. Click alignment.
6. Click OK.

Figure 4.8 Page Setup Dialog Box with the Layout Tab Selected

Page Setup dialog box — Layout tab selected. Section start: New page. Suppress endnotes. Headers and footers: Different odd and even; Different first page. From edge: Header 0.5"; Footer 0.5". Page — Vertical alignment: Top.

Click this option box arrow to display a list of vertical alignment options.

Preview. Apply to: Whole document. Line Numbers... Borders... Set As Default. OK. Cancel.

1. With **4-Training** open, click the Layout tab and then click the Page Setup group dialog box launcher.
2. At the Page Setup dialog box, click the Layout tab.
3. Click the *Vertical alignment* option box arrow in the *Page* section and then click *Center* at the drop-down list.

Page Setup

| Margins | Paper | Layout |

Section

Section start: New page

2

☐ Suppress endnotes

Headers and footers

☐ Different odd and even

☐ Different first page

From edge: Header: 0.5" Footer: 0.5"

Page

Vertical alignment: Top

Top
Center
Justified
Bottom

3

Preview

4. Click OK to close the dialog box.
5. Save, print, and then close **4-Training**.

Check Your Work

Activity 7 Format a Lease Agreement
3 Parts

You will open a lease agreement, search for specific text, and then search for specific text and replace it with other text.

Editing Text with Find and Replace

 Find

 Replace

The Editing group on the Home tab contains the Find button and the Replace button. Use the Find button to search for specific text in a document and use the Replace button to search for and then replace specific text.

Tutorial

Finding Text

Finding Text

Quick Steps
Find Text
1. Click Find button.
2. Type search text.
3. Click Next button.

Click the Find button in the Editing group on the Home tab (or press the keyboard shortcut Ctrl + F) and the Navigation pane displays at the left side of the screen with the Results tab selected. With this tab selected, type search text in the search text box and any occurrence of the text in the document is highlighted. A fragment of the text surrounding the search text is shown in a thumbnail in the Navigation pane. For example, when searching for *Lessee* in **4-LeaseAgrmnt** in Activity 7a (on page 115), the screen displays as shown in Figure 4.9. Any occurrence of *Lessee* displays highlighted in yellow in the document and the Navigation pane shows thumbnails of the text surrounding the occurrences of *Lessee*.

Click a text thumbnail in the Navigation pane and the occurrence of the search text is selected in the document. Hover the mouse pointer over a text thumbnail in the Navigation pane and the page number location displays in a small box near the mouse pointer. Move to the next occurrence of the search text by clicking the Next button (contains a down arrow) below and to the right of the search text box. Click the Previous button (contains an up arrow) to move to the previous occurrence of the search text.

Click the down arrow at the right side of the search text box and a drop-down list displays. It shows options for displaying dialog boxes, such as the Find Options dialog box and the Find and Replace dialog box. It also shows options for specifying what should be found in the document, such as figures, tables, and equations.

The search text in a document can be highlighted with options at the Find and Replace dialog box with the Find tab selected. Display this dialog box by clicking the Find button arrow in the Editing group on the Home tab and then clicking *Advanced Find* at the drop-down list. Another method for displaying the Find and Replace dialog box is to click the down arrow at the right side of the search text box in the Navigation pane and then click the *Advanced Find* option at the drop-down list. To highlight found text, type the search text in the *Find what* text box, click the Reading Highlight button, and then click *Highlight All* at the drop-down list. All occurrences of the text in the document are highlighted. To remove highlighting, click the Reading Highlight button and then click *Clear Highlighting* at the drop-down list.

Figure 4.9 Navigation Pane Showing Search Results

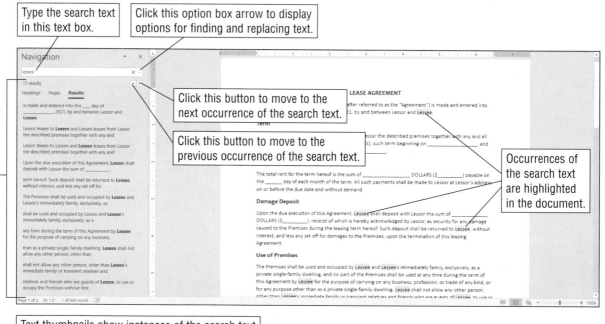

Type the search text in this text box.

Click this option box arrow to display options for finding and replacing text.

Click this button to move to the next occurrence of the search text.

Click this button to move to the previous occurrence of the search text.

Occurrences of the search text are highlighted in the document.

Text thumbnails show instances of the search text along with the sentence or phrase it is found in.

1. Open **LeaseAgrmnt** and then save it with the name **4-LeaseAgrmnt**.
2. Find all occurrences of *lessee* by completing the following steps:
   a. Click the Find button in the Editing group on the Home tab.
   b. If necessary, click the Results tab in the Navigation pane.
   c. Type lessee in the search text box in the Navigation pane.
   d. After a moment, all occurrences of *lessee* in the document are highlighted and text thumbnails display in the Navigation pane. Click a couple of the text thumbnails in the Navigation pane to select the text in the document.
   e. Click the Previous button (contains an up arrow) to select the previous occurrence of *lessee* in the document.

3. Use the Find and Replace dialog box with the Find tab selected to highlight all occurrences of *Premises* in the document by completing the following steps:
   a. Click in the document and press Ctrl + Home to move the insertion point to the beginning of the document.
   b. Click the search option box arrow in the Navigation pane and then click *Advanced Find* at the drop-down list.
   c. At the Find and Replace dialog box with the Find tab selected (and *lessee* selected in the *Find what* text box), type Premises.
   d. Click the Reading Highlight button and then click *Highlight All* at the drop-down list.
   e. Click in the document to make it active and then scroll through the document and notice the occurrences of highlighted text.
   f. Click in the dialog box to make it active.
   g. Click the Reading Highlight button and then click *Clear Highlighting* at the drop-down list.
   h. Click the Close button to close the Find and Replace dialog box.
4. Close the Navigation pane by clicking the Close button in the upper right corner of the pane.

 Tutorial

Finding and
Replacing Text

Quick Steps

Find and Replace Text
1. Click Replace button.
2. Type search text.
3. Press Tab key.
4. Type replacement text.
5. Click Replace or Replace All button.

Finding and Replacing Text

To find and replace text, click the Replace button in the Editing group on the Home tab or use the keyboard shortcut Ctrl + H. This displays the Find and Replace dialog box with the Replace tab selected, as shown in Figure 4.10. Type the search text in the *Find what* text box, press the Tab key, and then type the replacement text in the *Replace with* text box.

The Find and Replace dialog box contains several command buttons. Click the Find Next button to tell Word to find the next occurrence of the text. Click the Replace button to replace the text and find the next occurrence. If all occurrences of the text in the *Find what* text box are to be replaced with the text in the *Replace with* text box, click the Replace All button.

Figure 4.10 Find and Replace Dialog Box with the Replace Tab Selected

Type the search text in the *Find what* text box.

Type the replacement text in the *Replace with* text box.

Click to display additional options for completing a search.

Activity 7b Finding and Replacing Text

1. With **4-LeaseAgrmnt** open, make sure the insertion point is positioned at the beginning of the document.
2. Find all occurrences of *Lessor* and replace them with *Tracy Hartford* by completing the following steps:
   a. Click the Replace button in the Editing group on the Home tab.
   b. At the Find and Replace dialog box with the Replace tab selected and *Premises* selected in the *Find what* text box, type Lessor.
   c. Press the Tab key to move the insertion point to the *Replace with* text box.
   d. Type Tracy Hartford.
   e. Click the Replace All button.
   f. At the message stating that 11 replacements were made, click OK. (Do not close the Find and Replace dialog box.)
3. With the Find and Replace dialog box still open, complete steps similar to those in Step 2 to find all occurrences of *Lessee* and replace them with *Michael Iwami*.
4. Click the Close button to close the Find and Replace dialog box.
5. Save **4-LeaseAgrmnt**.

Check Your Work

Specifying Search Options

The Find and Replace dialog box provides more options for completing a search. To display these options, click the More button in the lower left corner of the dialog box. This causes the Find and Replace dialog box to expand, as shown in Figure 4.11. Search Options in the dialog box are described in Table 4.1. Click check boxes to select options for customizing the search, and then click the Less button (previously the More button) to hide the options and shrink the dialog box again. If a mistake was made when replacing text, close the Find and Replace dialog box and then click the Undo button on the Quick Access Toolbar.

Figure 4.11 Expanded Find and Replace Dialog Box

Click this button to remove the display of search options.

Specify search options using the check boxes in this section.

Table 4.1 Options at the Expanded Find and Replace Dialog Box

Choose this option	To
Match case	Exactly match the case of the search text. For example, search for *Book* and select the *Match case* option and Word will stop at *Book* but not *book* or *BOOK*.
Find whole words only	Find a whole word, not a part of a word. For example, search for *her* without selecting *Find whole words only* and Word will stop at *there*, *here*, *hers*, and so on.
Use wildcards	Use special characters as wildcards to search for specific text.
Sounds like (English)	Match words that sound alike but are spelled differently, such as *know* and *no*.
Find all word forms (English)	Find all forms of the word entered in the *Find what* text box. For example, enter *hold* and Word will stop at *held* and *holding*.
Match prefix	Find only those words that begin with the letters in the *Find what* text box. For example, enter *per* and Word will stop at words such as *perform* and *perfect* but skip words such as *super* and *hyperlink*.
Match suffix	Find only those words that end with the letters in the *Find what* text box. For example, enter *ly* and Word will stop at words such as *accurately* and *quietly* but skip words such as *catalyst* and *lyre*.
Ignore punctuation characters	Ignore punctuation within characters. For example, enter *US* in the *Find what* text box and Word will stop at *U.S.*
Ignore white-space characters	Ignore spaces between letters. For example, enter *F B I* in the *Find what* text box and Word will stop at *FBI*.

1. With **4-LeaseAgrmnt** open, make sure the insertion point is positioned at the beginning of the document.
2. Find all word forms of the word *lease* and replace them with *rent* by completing the following steps:
   a. Click the Replace button in the Editing group on the Home tab.
   b. At the Find and Replace dialog box with the Replace tab selected, type lease in the *Find what* text box.
   c. Press the Tab key and then type rent in the *Replace with* text box.
   d. Click the More button.
   e. Click the *Find all word forms (English)* check box. (This inserts a check mark in the check box.)
   f. Click the Replace All button.
   g. At the message stating that Replace All is not recommended with Find All Word Forms, click OK.
   h. At the message stating that six replacements were made, click OK.
   i. Click the *Find all word forms* check box to remove the check mark.

3. Find the word *less* and replace it with the word *minus* and specify that you want Word to find only those words that end in *less* by completing the following steps:
   a. At the expanded Find and Replace dialog box, select the text in the *Find what* text box and then type less.
   b. Select the text in the *Replace with* text box and then type minus.
   c. Click the *Match suffix* check box to insert a check mark (telling Word to find only words that end in *less*).
   d. Click the Replace All button.
   e. Click OK at the message stating that two replacements were made.
   f. Click the *Match suffix* check box to remove the check mark.
   g. Click the Less button.
   h. Close the Find and Replace dialog box.
4. Save, print, and then close **4-LeaseAgrmnt**.

Check Your Work

Chapter Summary

- By default, a Word document contains 1-inch top, bottom, left, and right margins. Change margins with preset margin settings at the Margins button drop-down list or with options at the Page Setup dialog box with the Margins tab selected.

- The default page layout is portrait orientation. It can be changed to landscape orientation with the Orientation button in the Page Setup group on the Layout tab.

- The default paper size is 8.5 inches wide by 11 inches tall. It can be changed with options at the Size button drop-down list or options at the Page Setup dialog box with the Paper tab selected.

- A page break that Word inserts automatically is a *soft page break*. A page break inserted manually is a *hard page break*. Insert a hard page break using the Page Break button in the Pages group on the Insert tab or by pressing Ctrl + Enter.

- Insert a predesigned and formatted cover page by clicking the Cover Page button in the Pages group on the Insert tab and then clicking an option at the drop-down list.

- Insert predesigned and formatted page numbers by clicking the Page Number button in the Header & Footer group on the Insert tab, specifying the location of the page number, and then clicking a page numbering option.

- Insert predesigned headers and footers in a document with the Header button and the Footer button in the Header & Footer group on the Insert tab.

- A watermark is a lightened image that displays behind the text in a document. Use the Watermark button in the Page Background group on the Design tab to insert a watermark.

- Insert a page background color in a document with the Page Color button in the Page Background group on the Design tab. The page background color is designed for viewing a document on-screen and does not print.

- Click the Page Borders button in the Page Background group on the Design tab and the Borders and Shading dialog box with the Page Border tab selected displays. Use options at this dialog box to insert a page border or an art image page border in a document.

- Apply formatting to a portion of a document by inserting a continuous section break or a section break that begins a new page. Turn on the display of nonprinting characters to display section breaks.

- Set text in columns to improve the readability of documents such as newsletters and reports. Format text in columns using the Columns button in the Page Setup group on the Layout tab or with options at the Columns dialog box.

- Remove column formatting with the Columns button in the Page Setup group on the Layout tab or at the Columns dialog box. Balance column text on the last page of a document by inserting a continuous section break at the end of the text.

- Improve the appearance of text by hyphenating long words that fall at the ends of lines. Use the hyphenation feature to hyphenate words automatically or manually.

- To enhance the appearance of text, use drop caps to identify the beginnings of major sections or paragraphs. Create drop caps with the Drop Cap button in the Text group on the Insert tab.

- Use the Click and Type feature to center, right-align, and left-align text.

- Vertically align text in a document with the *Vertical alignment* option box at the Page Setup dialog box with the Layout tab selected.
- Use the Find button in the Editing group on the Home tab to search for specific text. Use the Replace button to search for specific text and replace it with other text.
- At the Find and Replace dialog box, click the Find Next button to find the next occurrence of the text. Click the Replace button to replace the text and find the next occurrence or click the Replace All button to replace all occurrences of the text.
- Click the More button at the Find and Replace dialog box to display additional search options.

Commands Review

FEATURE	RIBBON TAB, GROUP	BUTTON, OPTION	KEYBOARD SHORTCUT
blank page	Insert, Pages		
Border and Shading Options dialog box	Design, Page Background	, Options	
Borders and Shading dialog box with Page Border tab selected	Design, Page Background		
column break	Layout, Page Setup	, *Column*	Ctrl + Shift + Enter
columns	Layout, Page Setup		
Columns dialog box	Layout, Page Setup	, *More Column*	
continuous section break	Layout, Page Setup	, *Continuous*	
cover page	Insert, Pages		
drop cap	Insert, Text		
Find and Replace dialog box with Find tab selected	Home, Editing	, *Advanced Find*	
Find and Replace dialog box with Replace tab selected	Home, Editing		Ctrl + H
footer	Insert, Header & Footer		
header	Insert, Header & Footer		
hyphenate words automatically	Layout, Page Setup	, *Automatic*	
Manual Hyphenation dialog box	Layout, Page Setup	, *Manual*	
margins	Layout, Page Setup		
Navigation pane	Home, Editing		Ctrl + F

FEATURE	RIBBON TAB, GROUP	BUTTON, OPTION	KEYBOARD SHORTCUT
orientation	Layout, Page Setup		
page background color	Design, Page Background		
page break	Insert, Pages		Ctrl + Enter
page numbers	Insert, Header & Footer		
Page Setup dialog box with Margins tab selected	Layout, Page Setup	, *Custom Margins* OR	
Page Sctup dialog box with Paper tab selected	Layout, Page Setup	, *More Paper Sizes*	
paper size	Layout, Page Setup		
watermark	Design, Page Background		

Microsoft®

Word Level 1

Unit 2

Enhancing and Customizing Documents

Microsoft®

Word

Inserting and Formatting Objects

Performance Objectives

Upon successful completion of Chapter 5, you will be able to:

1 Insert symbols, special characters, and the date and time

2 Insert, format, and customize images, text boxes, shapes, and WordArt

3 Insert and customize a screenshot

4 Insert, format, and modify a SmartArt graphic

Documents in Word may include special characters and symbols as well as the current date and time. The visual interest of a document can be enhanced by graphics such as images, text boxes, shapes, WordArt, and screenshots. Word's SmartArt feature can be used to insert a graphic such as a diagram or organizational chart. This chapter covers how to insert and customize these elements using buttons in the Illustrations group, the Text group, and the Symbols group on the Insert tab.

◖ Data Files 〉

Before beginning chapter work, copy the WL1C5 folder to your storage medium and then make WL1C5 the active folder.

The online course includes additional training and assessment resources.

Activity 1 Format a Document on Computer Input Devices 2 Parts

In a document on computer input devices, you will insert a special character, symbols, and the date and time.

Inserting Symbols and Special Characters

Tutorial
Inserting Symbols

Tutorial
Inserting Special Characters

Symbol

Quick Steps

Insert Symbol
1. Click Insert tab.
2. Click Symbol button.
3. Click symbol.
OR
1. Click Insert tab.
2. Click Symbol button.
3. Click *More Symbols*.
4. Double-click symbol.
5. Click Close.

Quick Steps

Insert Special Character
1. Click Insert tab.
2. Click Symbol button.
3. Click *More Symbols*.
4. Click Special Characters tab.
5. Double-click special character.
6. Click Close.

Use the Symbol button on the Insert tab to insert special symbols in a document. Click the button and a drop-down list displays the most recently inserted symbols. Click one of the symbols in the list to insert it in the document or click the *More Symbols* option to display the Symbol dialog box, as shown in Figure 5.1. Double-click a symbol to insert it, or click it once and then click the Insert button. Click Close to exit the dialog box. Another method for selecting a symbol at the Symbol dialog box is to type the symbol code in the *Character code* text box. Click a symbol in the dialog box and the character code displays in the *Character code* text box. If a symbol is used on a regular basis, remembering the character code can be useful for inserting the symbol in a document.

At the Symbol dialog box with the Symbols tab selected, the font can be changed with the *Font* option box. When the font is changed, different symbols display in the dialog box. Click the Special Characters tab at the Symbol dialog box and a list of special characters displays along with keyboard shortcuts for creating them.

Figure 5.1 Symbol Dialog Box with the Symbols Tab Selected

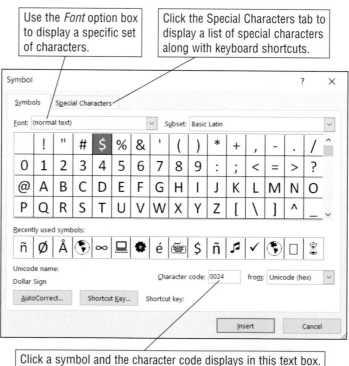

1. Open **InputDevices** and then save it with the name **5-InputDevices**.
2. Press Ctrl + End to move the insertion point to the end of the document.
3. Type Prepared by: and then press the spacebar.
4. Type the first name Matthew and then press the spacebar.
5. Insert the last name *Viña* by completing the following steps:
   a. Type Vi.
   b. Click the Insert tab.
   c. Click the Symbol button in the Symbols group.
   d. Click *More Symbols* at the drop-down list.
   e. At the Symbol dialog box, make sure *(normal text)* appears in the *Font* option box and then double-click the *ñ* symbol (located in approximately the twelfth row).
   f. Click the Close button.
   g. Type a.
6. Press Shift + Enter.
7. Insert the keyboard symbol (⌨) by completing the following steps:
   a. Click the Symbol button and then click *More Symbols*.
   b. At the Symbol dialog box, click the *Font* option box arrow and then click *Wingdings* at the drop-down list. (You will need to scroll down the list to see this option.)
   c. Select the current number in the *Character code* text box and then type 55.
   d. Click the Insert button and then click the Close button.
8. Type SoftCell Technologies.
9. Insert the registered trademark symbol (®) by completing the following steps:
   a. Click the Symbol button and then click *More Symbols*.
   b. At the Symbol dialog box, click the Special Characters tab.
   c. Double-click the ® symbol (tenth option from the top).
   d. Click the Close button.
   e. Press Shift + Enter.
10. Select the keyboard symbol (⌨) and then change the font size to 18 points.
11. Save **5-InputDevices**.

Check Your Work

Inserting the Date and Time

Use the Date & Time button in the Text group on the Insert tab to insert the current date and time in a document. Click this button and the Date and Time dialog box displays, as shown in Figure 5.2. (Your date will vary from what you see in the figure.) At the Date and Time dialog box, click the desired date and/or time format in the *Available formats* list box.

If the *Update automatically* check box does not contain a check mark, the date and/or time are inserted in the document as text that can be edited in the normal manner. The date and/or time can also be inserted as a field. The advantage to using a field is that the date and time are updated when a document is reopened. Insert a check mark in the *Update automatically* check box to insert the date and/or time as a field. The date can also be inserted as a field using the keyboard shortcut Alt + Shift + D, and the time can be inserted as a field with the keyboard shortcut Alt + Shift + T.

A date or time field will automatically update when a document is reopened. The date and time can also be updated in the document by clicking the date or time field and then clicking the Update tab that appears above the field, by right-clicking the date or time field and then clicking *Update Field* at the shortcut menu, or by pressing the F9 function key.

Figure 5.2 Date and Time Dialog Box

Click the desired option in this list box.

Insert a check mark in this check box if you want the date and/or time inserted as a field and updated each time you reopen the document.

Activity 1b Inserting the Date and Time

Part 2 of 2

1. With **5-InputDevices** open, press Ctrl + End and make sure the insertion point is positioned below the company name.
2. Insert the current date by completing the following steps:
   a. Click the Insert tab.
   b. Click the Date & Time button in the Text group.
   c. At the Date and Time dialog box, click the third option from the top in the *Available formats* list box. (Your date and time will vary from what you see in the image at the right.)
   d. Click in the *Update automatically* check box to insert a check mark.
   e. Click OK to close the dialog box.

3. Press Shift + Enter.
4. Insert the current time by pressing Alt + Shift + T.
5. Save **5-InputDevices**.
6. Update the time by clicking the time and then pressing the F9 function key.
7. Save, print, and then close **5-InputDevices**.

Check Your Work

Activity 2 Insert Images in a Travel Document   2 Parts

You will open a document with information on an Australian tour and add visual interest to the document by inserting and formatting images.

Tutorial

Inserting, Sizing, and Positioning an Image

Pictures

Online Pictures

Inserting and Formatting Images

Insert an image, such as a photo or clip art, in a Word document with buttons in the Illustrations group on the Insert tab. Use the Pictures button in the Illustrations group to insert an image from a folder on the computer's hard drive or removable drive or use the Online Pictures button to locate an online image.

Inserting an Image

Click the Pictures button in the Illustrations group on the Insert tab to display the Insert Pictures dialog box. At this dialog box, navigate to the drive and folder where images are saved, and then double-click an image to insert it in the document.

Click the Online Pictures button and the Online Pictures window displays. At this window, type the search term or topic in the search text box and then press the Enter key. Images that match the search term or topic are shown in the window. Click an image and then click the Insert button and the image is inserted in the document. Be aware that many of the images available online are copyrighted. Before using an image in a document that will be shared publicly, make sure the image is either in the public domain (and thus not copyrighted) or determine how to get permission to use the image.

Sizing and Cropping an Image

When an image is inserted in a document, the Picture Tools Format tab is active. The Size group on the Picture Tools Format tab contains buttons for changing the size of an image and cropping an image. Change the size of an image by typing a measurement in the *Shape Height* and/or *Shape Width* measurement boxes or by clicking the up or down arrows in the measurement box.

Images in Word can also be sized using the mouse. Click an image to select it and circular sizing handles display around the image. Position the mouse pointer on a sizing handle until the pointer turns into a double-headed arrow and then click and hold down the left mouse button. Drag the sizing handle in or out to decrease or increase the size of the image and then release the mouse button. Use the middle sizing handles at the left and right sides of the image to make the image wider or thinner. Use the middle sizing handles at the top and bottom of the image to make the image taller or shorter. Use the sizing handles at the corners of the image to change both the width and height at the same time.

Crop

Use the Crop button in the Size group to remove any unnecessary parts of an image. Click the Crop button and crop handles display around the image. Position the mouse pointer on a crop handle and the mouse pointer displays as a crop tool. Drag a crop handle to remove parts of the image.

Arranging an Image

The Arrange group on the Picture Tools Format tab contains buttons for positioning, aligning, and rotating images. The group also contains buttons for wrapping text around an image and specifying if an image should appear in front of or behind text or other items.

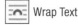 Wrap Text

Use the Wrap Text button in the Arrange group to specify how text or other objects in the document should wrap around a selected image. The Wrap Text button drop-down list contains options for specifying square or tight wrapping, wrapping text above or below the image, and positioning the image behind or in front of text. The Layout Options button can also be used to specify text wrapping. When an image is selected, the Layout Options button displays outside the upper right corner of the image. Click the Layout Options button and then click a wrapping option at the drop-down list. Another method for specifying text wrapping is to right-click an image, point to *Wrap Text* at the shortcut menu, and click a text wrapping option at the side menu.

 Layout Options

Move an image to a specific location on the page with options at the Position button drop-down gallery in the Arrange group. Choose an option from this gallery and the image is moved to the specified location and square text wrapping is applied to it.

 Position

Rotate an image by positioning the mouse pointer on the rotation handle, a circular arrow that appears above a selected image. The pointer will display with a black circular arrow attached. Click and hold down the left mouse button, drag in the desired direction, and then release the mouse button. An image can also be rotated or flipped with options at the Rotate button drop-down gallery in the Arrange group. For example, the image can be rotated left or right or flipped horizontally or vertically.

 Rotate

Moving an Image

In addition to the Position button in the Arrange group on the Picture Tools Format tab, an image can be moved using the mouse. Before moving an image with the mouse, specify how text should wrap around the image. After specifying text wrapping, position the mouse pointer on the image until the mouse pointer displays with a four-headed arrow attached. Click and hold down the left mouse button, drag the image to the new location, and then release the mouse button.

As an image is moved to the top, left, right, or bottom margin or to the center of the document, green alignment guides display. Use these guides to help position the image on the page. If alignment guides do not display, turn them on by clicking the Align button in the Arrange group and then clicking *Use Alignment Guides* at the drop-down list. In addition to alignment guides, gridlines can be turned on to help position an image precisely. Turn on the display of gridlines by clicking the Align button and then clicking *View Gridlines*.

 Align

1. Open **Tour** and then save it with the name **5-Tour**.
2. Insert an image by completing the following steps:
   a. Click the Insert tab and then click the Pictures button in the Illustrations group.
   b. At the Insert Picture dialog box, navigate to your WL1C5 folder.
   c. Double-click the *Uluru* image file in the Content pane.

3. Crop the image by completing the following steps:
   a. Click the Crop button in the Size group on the Picture Tools Format tab.
   b. Position the mouse pointer on the bottom middle crop handle (which appears as a short black line) until the pointer turns into the crop tool (which appears as a small black T).
   c. Click and hold down the left mouse button, drag up to just below the rock (as shown at the right), and then release the mouse button.
   d. Click the Crop button in the Size group to turn the feature off.

TRAVEL ADVANTAGE

4. Change the size of the image by clicking in the *Shape Height* measurement box in the Size group, typing 3, and then pressing the Enter key.
5. Specify text wrapping by clicking the Wrap Text button in the Arrange group and then clicking *Tight* at the drop-down list.
6. Change to a different text wrapping by completing the following steps:
   a. Click the Layout Options button outside the upper right corner of the image.
   b. Click the *Behind Text* option at the side menu (second column, second row in the *With Text Wrapping* section).
   c. Close the side menu by clicking the Close button in the upper right corner of the side menu.
7. Rotate the image by clicking the Rotate button in the Arrange group and then clicking *Flip Horizontal* at the drop-down gallery.

8. Position the mouse pointer on the border of the selected image until the pointer displays with a four-headed arrow attached. Click and hold down the left mouse button, drag the image

up and slightly to the left until you see green alignment guides at the top margin and the center of the page, and then release the mouse button. (If the green alignment guides do not display, turn on the guides by clicking the Align button in the Arrange group on the Picture Tools Format tab and then clicking the *Use Alignment Guides* option.)
9. Save **5-Tour**.

Check Your Work

Tutorial

Formatting an Image

Remove Background

Corrections

Color

Artistic Effects

Transparency

Compress Pictures

Change Picture

Reset Picture

Adjusting an Image

The Adjust group on the Picture Tools Format tab contains buttons for adjusting the background, color, brightness, and contrast of an image. Click the Remove Background button to display the Background Removal tab with buttons for removing unwanted portions of an image. Change the brightness and/or contrast of an image with options at the Corrections button drop-down gallery. This gallery also includes options for sharpening or softening an image. Use options at the Color button drop-down gallery to change the image color as well as the color saturation and color tone. The Color button drop-down gallery also includes the *Set Transparent Color* option. Click this option and the mouse pointer displays as a dropper tool. Click a color in the image and that color becomes transparent.

The Artistic Effects button drop-down gallery offers a variety of effects that can be applied to an image. Lighten an image with options at the Transparency button drop-down gallery. For example, make an image more transparent to display any text or other objects behind the image. Use the Compress Pictures button to compress the size of images in a document. Remove or replace an image with the Change Picture button and discard all formatting changes and reset an image with the Reset Picture button.

Applying a Picture Style

Word provides a number of predesigned picture styles that can be applied to an image. Click a picture style in the Picture Styles group or click the More Picture Styles button to display a drop-down gallery of picture styles.

Creating Alternative Text for an Image

When an image is inserted in a document, consider adding *alternative text*. Alternative text, also known as alt text, is a brief description of an image or object that can be read by a screen reader and helps a person with a visual impairment understand what the image or object represents. Create alternative text at the

Alt Text

Alt Text task pane. Display this task pane by clicking the Alt Text button in the Accessibility group on the Picture Tools Format tab or by right-clicking the image and then clicking *Edit Alt Text* at the shortcut menu. At the Alt Text task pane, type a description of the image. If the image is only decorative and not important for understanding the content of the document, insert a check mark in the *Mark as decorative* check box. An image marked as decorative will not include any description for screen readers.

1. With **5-Tour** open and the image selected, apply an artistic effect by clicking the Artistic Effects button in the Adjust group and then clicking the *Watercolor Sponge* option (second column, third row).
2. Lighten the image by clicking the Transparency button in the Adjust group and then clicking the *Transparency: 30%* option (third option in the drop-down gallery).
3. After looking at the new color, artistic effect, and transparency, return to the original color and remove the artistic effect and transparency by clicking the Reset Picture button in the Adjust group.
4. Sharpen the image by clicking the Corrections button in the Adjust group and then clicking the *Sharpen: 25%* option (fourth option in the *Sharpen/Soften* section).
5. Change the contrast of the image by clicking the Corrections button in the Adjust group and then clicking the *Brightness: 0% (Normal) Contrast: +40%* option (third column, bottom row in the *Brightness/Contrast* section).
6. Compress the image by completing the following steps:
    a. Click the Compress Pictures button in the Adjust group.

    b. At the Compress Pictures dialog box, make sure check marks appear in the check boxes for both options in the *Compression options* section and then click OK.
7. Apply a picture style by clicking the More Pictures Styles button in the Picture Styles group and then clicking the *Simple Frame, Black* option (second column, second row at the drop-down gallery).
8. Add alternative text to the image by completing the following steps:
    a. Click the Alt Text button in the Accessibility group.
    b. Click in the text box in the Alt Text task pane and then type the description Uluru (also known as Ayers Rock).
    c. Click the Close button to close the task pane.

9. Click outside the image to deselect it.
10. Insert an image of Australia (with the Northern Territory highlighted) by completing the following steps:
    a. Click the Insert tab.
    b. Click the Pictures button in the Illustrations group.
    c. At the Insert Picture dialog box, with your WL1C5 folder active, double-click the *NT-Australia* image file in the Content pane.
11. Position and size the image by completing the following steps:
    a. Click the Position button in the Arrange group.
    b. Click the *Position in Top Right with Square Text Wrapping* option (third column, first row in the *With Text Wrapping* section).
    c. Click the Wrap Text button.
    d. Click the *Behind Text* option at the drop-down gallery.
    e. Click in the *Shape Height* measurement box in the Size group, type 1, and then press the Enter key.
12. Make the white background of the image transparent by completing the following steps:
    a. Click the Color button in the Adjust group.
    b. Click the *Set Transparent Color* option at the bottom of the drop-down list. (The mouse pointer turns into a dropper tool.)
    c. Position the dropper tool on the white background of the image and then click the left mouse button.
13. Click the Color button and then click the *Orange, Accent color 2 Dark* option (third column, second row in the *Recolor* section).
14. Insert an airplane image by clicking the Insert tab, clicking the Pictures button, and then double-clicking the *Airplane* image file in your WL1C5 folder.
15. With the airplane image selected, remove the background by completing the following steps:
    a. Click the Remove Background button in the Adjust group on the Picture Tools Format tab.
    b. Click the Mark Areas to Remove button. (The mouse pointer changes to a pen.)
    c. Position the mouse pointer (pen) in the blue background at the left of the tail of the airplane, press and hold down the left mouse button, drag in the blue background (left of the airplane tail), and then release the mouse button. Do not drag through any portion of the airplane. (The blue background the mouse pointer passes through should be removed.)
    d. If necessary, use the mouse pointer to drag in the blue background at the right of the tail of the airplane. (Do not drag through any portion of the airplane.
    e. If you are not satisfied with the background removal, click the Discard All Changes button and start again. If you are satisfied with the background removal, click the Keep Changes button.

16. Position the airplane by clicking the Position button and then clicking the *Position in Top Left with Square Text Wrapping* option (first column, top row in the *With Text Wrapping* section).
17. Specify text wrapping by clicking the Wrap Text button and then clicking the *Behind Text* option.
18. Change the image width by clicking in the *Shape Width* measurement box, typing 2.1, and then pressing the Enter key.
19. Save, print, and then close **5-Tour**.

Check Your Work

Activity 3 Customize a Report on Robots   2 Parts

You will open a report on robots and then add a pull quote using a predesigned text box and draw a text box and type information about an upcoming conference.

Tutorial

Inserting a Text Box

A Text Box

Inserting a Text Box

Add interest or create a location in a document for text by inserting or drawing a text box. Click the Insert tab and then click the Text Box button in the Text group and a drop-down list displays with predesigned text boxes and the *Draw Text Box* option. Choose one of the predesigned text boxes, which already contain formatting, or draw a text box and then customize or apply formatting to it with options and buttons on the Drawing Tools Format tab.

Inserting a Predesigned Text Box

Quick Steps
Insert Predesigned Text Box
1. Click Insert tab.
2. Click Text Box button.
3. Click option at drop-down list.

One use for a text box in a document is to insert a pull quote. A pull quote is a quote from the text that is "pulled out" and enlarged and positioned in an attractive location on the page. Some advantages of using pull quotes are that they reinforce important concepts, summarize the message, and break up text blocks to make them easier to read. If a document contains multiple pull quotes, keep them in the order in which they appear in the text to ensure clear comprehension by readers.

A text box for a pull quote can be drawn in a document or a predesigned text box can be inserted in the document. To insert a predesigned text box, click the Insert tab, click the Text Box button, and then click the predesigned text box at the drop-down list.

Tutorial

Formatting a Text Box

Formatting a Text Box

When a text box is selected, the Drawing Tools Format tab is active. This tab contains buttons for formatting and customizing the text box. Use options in the Insert Shapes group on the Drawing Tools Format tab to insert a shape in the text box or in another location in the document. Apply predesigned styles to a text box and change the shape fill, outline, and effects with options in the Shape Styles group. Change the formatting of the text in the text box with options in

Text Fill

Text Outline

Text Effects

the WordArt Styles group. Click the More WordArt Styles button in the WordArt Styles group and then click a style at the drop-down gallery. Further customize the formatting of text in the text box with the Text Fill, Text Outline, and Text Effects buttons in the Text group. Use options in the Arrange group to position the text box on the page, specify text wrapping in relation to the text box, align the text box with other objects in the document, and rotate the text box. Specify the text box size with the *Shape Height* and *Shape Width* measurement boxes in the Size group.

Activity 3a   Inserting a Predesigned Text Box

Part 1 of 2

1. Open **Robots** and then save it with the name **5-Robots**.
2. Insert a predesigned text box by completing the following steps:
   a. Click the Insert tab.
   b. Click the Text Box button in the Text group.
   c. Scroll down the drop-down list and then click the *Ion Quote (Dark)* option.

3. Type the following text in the text box: "The task of creating a humanlike body has proven incredibly difficult."
4. Delete the line and the source placeholder in the text box by pressing the F8 function key (which turns on the Selection mode), pressing Ctrl + End (which selects text from the location of the insertion point to the end of the text box), and then pressing the Delete key.
5. With the Drawing Tools Format tab active, click the More Shape Styles button in the Shape Styles group and then click the *Subtle Effect - Blue, Accent 5* option (sixth column, fourth row in the *Theme Styles* section).
6. Click the Shape Effects button in the Shape Styles group, point to *Shadow*, and then click the *Offset: Bottom Right* option (first column, first row in the *Outer* section).

7. Position the mouse pointer on the border of the selected text box until the pointer turns into a four-headed arrow and then drag the text box so it is positioned as shown below.

Visual Perception

Visual perception is an area of great complexity. A large percentage of the human brain is dedicated to processing data coming from the eyes. As our most powerful sense, sight is the primary means through which we understand the world around us.

A single camera is not good enough to simulate the eye. Two cameras are needed to give stereoscopic vision, which allows depth and movement perception. Even with two cameras, visual perception is incomplete because the cameras cannot

"The task of creating a humanlike body has proven incredibly difficult."

understand or translate what they see. Processing the image is the difficult part. In order for a robot to move through a room full of furniture it must build a mental map of that room, complete with obstacles. The robot must judge the distance and size of objects before it can figure out how to move around them.

Audio Perception

⑦

8. Click outside the text box to deselect it.
9. Save **5-Robots**.

☁ Check Your Work ⟩

Drawing a Text Box

Quick Steps

Draw Text Box
1. Click Insert tab.
2. Click Text Box button.
3. Click *Draw Text Box*.
4. Click or drag in document to create box.

To draw a text box rather than inserting a predesigned one, click the Insert tab, click the Text Box button in the Text group, and then click *Draw Text Box* at the drop-down list. With the mouse pointer displaying as crosshairs (a plus [+] symbol), click in the document to insert the text box or position the crosshairs in the document and then drag to create the text box with the desired size and dimensions. When a text box is selected, the Drawing Tools Format tab is active. Use buttons on this tab to format a drawn text box in the same manner as a built-in text box.

Activity 3b Inserting and Formatting a Text Box   Part 2 of 2

1. With **5-Robots** open, press Ctrl + End to move the insertion point to the end of the document.
2. Insert a text box by completing the following steps:
   a. Click the Insert tab.
   b. Click the Text Box button and then click the *Draw Text Box* option.
   c. Position the mouse pointer (displays as crosshairs) on the insertion point and then click the left mouse button. (This inserts the text box in the document.)
3. Change the text box height and width by completing the following steps:
   a. Click in the *Shape Height* measurement box in the Size group, type 1.2, and then press the Tab key.
   b. Type 4.5 in the *Shape Width* measurement box and then press the Enter key.
4. Center the text box by clicking the Align button in the Arrange group and then clicking *Align Center* at the drop-down list.

5. Apply a shape style by clicking the More Shape Styles button in the Shape Styles group and then clicking the *Subtle Effect - Blue, Accent 1* option (second column, fourth row in the *Theme Styles* section).

6. Apply a bevel shape effect by clicking the Shape Effects button, pointing to the *Bevel* option, and then clicking the *Soft Round* option at the side menu (second column, second row in the *Bevel* section).

7. Apply a 3-D shape effect by clicking the Shape Effects button, pointing to *3-D Rotation*, and then clicking the *Perspective: Above* option (first column, second row in the *Perspective* section).

8. Insert and format text in the text box by completing the following steps:
   a. Press the Enter key two times. (The insertion point should be positioned in the text box.)
   b. Click the Home tab.
   c. Change the font size to 14 points, apply bold formatting, and change the font color to *Dark Blue* (ninth option in the *Standard Colors* section).
   d. Click the Center button in the Paragraph group.
   e. Type International Conference on Artificial Intelligence Summer 2022.
   f. Click outside the text box to deselect it. (Your text box should appear as shown at the right.)

9. Save, print, and then close **5-Robots**.

8f

International Conference on Artificial Intelligence Summer 2022

Check Your Work

<table>
<tr><td>

Activity 4 Prepare a Company Flyer   **2 Parts**

You will create a company flyer document and increase the visual interest in the document by inserting and customizing shapes and WordArt.

</td></tr>
</table>

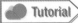

Inserting, Sizing, and Positioning a Shape and Line

Formatting a Shape and Line

 Shapes

Quick Steps

Draw Shape
1. Click Insert tab.
2. Click Shapes button.
3. Click shape.
4. Click or drag in document to create shape.

💡 **Hint** To draw a square, choose the Rectangle shape and then press and hold down the Shift key while drawing.

Drawing Shapes

Use the Shapes button in the Illustrations group on the Insert tab to draw shapes in a document, including lines, basic shapes, block arrows, flow chart shapes, stars and banners, and callouts. Click a shape and the mouse pointer displays as crosshairs. Position the crosshairs in the document where the shape is to be inserted and then click the left mouse button or click and hold down the left mouse button, drag to create the shape, and then release the mouse button. The shape is inserted in the document and the Drawing Tools Format tab is active.

A shape selected from the *Lines* section of the drop-down list and then drawn in the document is considered a *line drawing*. A shape selected from another section of the drop-down list and then drawn in the document is considered an *enclosed object*. When drawing an enclosed object, maintain the proportions of the shape by pressing and holding down the Shift key while dragging with the mouse to create the shape.

Copying Shapes

To copy a shape, select the shape and then click the Copy button in the Clipboard group on the Home tab. Position the insertion point at the location the copied shape is to be inserted and then click the Paste button. A selected shape can also be copied by right-clicking the shape and then clicking *Copy* at the shortcut menu. Position the insertion point where the shape is to be copied, right-click and then click *Paste* at the shortcut menu. Another method for copying shapes is to press and hold down the Ctrl key while dragging a copy of the shape to the new location.

Activity 4a Drawing and Copying Arrow Shapes   **Part 1 of 2**

1. At a blank document, press the Enter key two times and then draw an arrow shape by completing the following steps:
   a. Click the Insert tab.
   b. Click the Shapes button in the Illustrations group and then click the *Arrow: Striped Right* shape (fifth column, second row in the *Block Arrows* section).
   c. Position the mouse pointer (which displays as crosshairs) on the insertion point and then click the left mouse button. (This inserts the arrow shape in the document.)
2. Format the arrow by completing the following steps:
   a. Click in the *Shape Height* measurement box in the Size group, type 2.4, and then press the Tab key.
   b. Type 4.5 in the *Shape Width* measurement box and then press the Enter key.

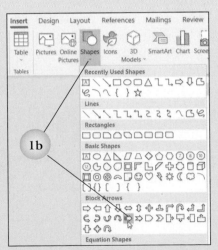

c. Horizontally align the arrow by clicking the Align button in the Arrange group and then clicking *Distribute Horizontally* at the drop-down list.

d. Click the More Shape Styles button in the Shape Styles group and then click the *Intense Effect - Green, Accent 6* option (last option in the *Theme Styles* section at the drop-down gallery).

e. Click the Shape Effects button in the Shape Styles group, point to *Bevel*, and then click the *Angle* option (first column, second row in the *Bevel* section).

f. Click the Shape Outline button arrow in the Shape Styles group and then click the *Dark Blue* option (ninth option in the *Standard Colors* section).

3. Copy the arrow by completing the following steps:

a. With the mouse pointer positioned in the arrow (mouse pointer displays with a four-headed arrow attached), press and hold down the Ctrl key and click and hold down the left mouse button. Drag down until the copied arrow appears just below the top arrow, release the mouse button, and then release the Ctrl key.

b. Copy the selected arrow by pressing and holding down the Ctrl key and clicking and holding down the left mouse button and then dragging the copied arrow just below the second arrow.

4. Flip the middle arrow by completing the following steps:

a. Click the middle arrow to select it.

b. Click the Rotate button in the Arrange group on the Drawing Tools Format tab and then click the *Flip Horizontal* option at the drop-down gallery.

5. Insert the text *Financial* in the top arrow by completing the following steps:

a. Click the top arrow to select it.

b. Type Financial.

c. Select *Financial*.

d. Click the Home tab.

e. Change the font size to 16 points, apply bold formatting, and change the font color to Dark Blue (ninth option in the *Standard Colors* section).

6. Complete steps similar to those in Step 5 to insert the word *Direction* in the middle arrow.

7. Complete steps similar to those in Step 5 to insert the word *Retirement* in the bottom arrow.

8. Save the document and name it **5-FinConsult**.

9. Print the document.

Check Your Work

Tutorial

Inserting, Sizing, and Positioning WordArt

Tutorial

Formatting WordArt

$\boxed{A}$ WordArt

Quick Steps

Create WordArt Text
1. Click Insert tab.
2. Click WordArt button.
3. Click option.
4. Type WordArt text.

Creating and Formatting WordArt

Use the WordArt feature to distort or modify text to conform to a variety of shapes. This is useful for creating company logos, letterheads, flyer titles, and headings.

To insert WordArt in a document, click the Insert tab and then click the WordArt button in the Text group. At the drop-down list, click an option and a WordArt text box is inserted in the document containing the words *Your text here* and the Drawing Tools Format tab is active. Type the WordArt text and then format the WordArt with options on the Drawing Tools Format tab. Existing text can also be formatted as WordArt. To do this, select the text, click the WordArt button on the Insert tab, and then click the WordArt option at the drop-down list.

Activity 4b **Inserting and Modifying WordArt**   Part 2 of 2

1. With **5-FinConsult** open, press Ctrl + Home to move the insertion point to the beginning of the document.
2. Insert WordArt text by completing the following steps:
   a. Type Miller Financial Services and then select *Miller Financial Services*.
   b. Click the Insert tab.
   c. Click the WordArt button in the Text group and then click the option in the third column, first row (orange fill and outline).

2c

3. Format the WordArt text by completing the following steps:
   a. Make sure the WordArt text border displays as a solid line.
   b. Click the Text Fill button arrow in the WordArt Styles group on the Drawing Tools Format tab and then click the *Light Green* option (fifth option in the *Standard Colors* section).
   c. Click the Text Outline button arrow in the WordArt Styles group and then click the *Green, Accent 6, Darker 50%* option (last option in the *Theme Colors* section).

3b

d. Click the Text Effects button in the WordArt Styles group, point to *Glow*, and then click the *Glow: 5 point; Blue, Accent color 1* option (first column, first row in the *Glow Variations* section).

e. Click in the *Shape Height* measurement box in the Size group, type 1, and then press the Tab key.

f. Type 6 in the *Shape Width* measurement box in the Size group and then press the Enter key.

g. Click the Text Effects button in the WordArt Styles group, point to *Transform*, and then click the *Warp Up* option (third column, fourth row in the *Warp* section).

h. Click the Position button in the Arrange group and then click the *Position in Top Center with Square Text Wrapping* option (second column, first row in the *With Text Wrapping* section).

4. Click outside the WordArt to deselect it.

5. Move the arrows as needed to ensure they do not overlap the WordArt or each other and that they all fit on one page.

6. Save, print, and then close **5-FinConsult**.

Check Your Work

Activity 5 Insert and Format Screenshots

2 Parts

You will create a document with screenshots of the Print and Export backstage areas and create another document with screen clippings of sample cover pages.

Inserting a Screenshot

The Illustrations group on the Insert tab contains a Screenshot button, which captures a screen or part of a screen as an image. To capture the entire screen, open a new document, click the Insert tab, click the Screenshot button in the Illustrations group, and then click the screen thumbnail at the drop-down list. (The currently active document does not appear as a thumbnail at the drop-down list—only other documents or files that are open.) Click the specific thumbnail at the drop-down list and a screenshot is inserted as an image in the open document. Once the screenshot is inserted in the document, the Picture Tools Format tab is active. Use buttons on this tab to customize the screenshot image.

Activity 5a Inserting and Formatting Screenshots

Part 1 of 2

1. Make sure that Word is the only program open and then press Ctrl + N to open a blank document.
2. Press Ctrl + N to open a second blank document, type Print Backstage Area at the left margin, and then press the Enter key.
3. Save the document and name it **5-BackstageAreas**.
4. Point to the Word button on the taskbar and then click the thumbnail representing the blank document.
5. Display the Print backstage area by clicking the File tab and then clicking the *Print* option.
6. Point to the Word button on the taskbar and then click the thumbnail representing **5-BackstageAreas**.
7. Insert and format a screenshot of the Print backstage area by completing the following steps:
   a. Click the Insert tab.
   b. Click the Screenshot button in the Illustrations group and then click the thumbnail in the drop-down list. (This inserts a screenshot of the Print backstage area in the document.)
   c. With the screenshot image selected, click the *Drop Shadow Rectangle* picture style option (fourth option in the Picture Styles gallery).
   d. Select the measurement in the *Shape Width* measurement box, type 5.5, and then press the Enter key.
8. Press Ctrl + End and then press the Enter key. (The insertion point should be positioned below the screenshot image and at the left margin. You may need to press the Enter key again so the insertion point is positioned at the left margin.)
9. Type Info Backstage Area at the left margin and then press the Enter key.
10. Point to the Word button on the taskbar and then click the thumbnail representing the blank document (with the Print backstage area displayed).
11. At the backstage area, click the *Info* option. (This displays the Info backstage area.)
12. Point to the Word button on the taskbar and then click the thumbnail representing **5-BackstageAreas**.
13. Insert and format a screenshot of the Info backstage area by completing steps similar to those in Step 7.
14. Press Ctrl + Home to move the insertion point to the beginning of the document.
15. Save, print, and then close **5-BackstageAreas**.
16. At the Info backstage area, press the Esc key to redisplay the blank document.
17. Close the blank document.

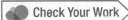

To create a screenshot of only part of the image on the screen, use the *Screen Clipping* option at the Screenshot button drop-down list. Click this option and the other open document, file, or Windows Start screen or desktop displays in a dimmed manner and the mouse pointer displays as crosshairs. Using the mouse, draw a border around the specific area of the screen to be captured. The area identified is inserted in the other document as an image, the image is selected, and the Picture Tools Format tab is active.

Activity 5b Inserting and Formatting a Screen Clipping

Part 2 of 2

1. Open **NSSLtrhd** and then save it with the name **5-NSSCoverPages**.
2. Type the text Sample Cover Pages and then press the Enter key two times.
3. Select the text you just typed, change the font to 18-point Copperplate Gothic Bold, and then center the text.
4. Press Ctrl + End to move the insertion point below the text.
5. Open **NSSCoverPg01** and then change the zoom to 50% by clicking approximately five times on the Zoom Out button at the left of the Zoom slider bar on the Status bar.
6. Point to the Word button on the taskbar and then click the thumbnail representing **5-NSSCoverPages**.
7. Insert and format a screen clipping image by completing the following steps:
   a. Click the Insert tab.
   b. Click the Screenshot button and then click the *Screen Clipping* option.

   c. When **NSSCoverPg01** displays in a dimmed manner, position the mouse crosshairs in the upper left corner of the cover page, click and hold down the left mouse button, drag down to the lower right corner of the cover page, and then release the mouse button. (See the image below and to the right.)
   d. With the cover page screen clipping image inserted in **5-NSSCoverPages**, make sure the image is selected. (The sizing handles should appear around the cover page image.)
   e. Click the Wrap Text button in the Arrange group on the Picture Tools Format tab and then click *Square* at the drop-down gallery.
   f. Select the current measurement in the *Shape Width* measurement box, type 3, and then press the Enter key.
   g. Click the Picture Border button arrow and then click the *Black, Text 1* option (second column, first row in the *Theme Colors* section).
8. Point to the Word button on the Taskbar and then click the thumbnail representing **NSSCoverPg01**.

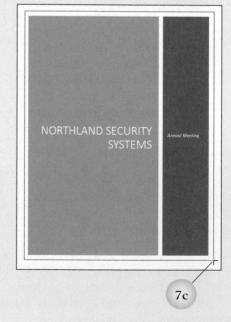

9. Close **NSSCoverPg01**.
10. Open **NSSCoverPg02** and then, if necessary, change the zoom to 50%.
11. Point to the Word button on the Taskbar and then click the thumbnail representing **5-NSSCoverPages**.
12. Insert and format a screen clipping image of the cover page by completing steps similar to those in Step 7.
13. Using the mouse, position the two cover page screenshot images side by side in the document.
14. Save, print, and then close **5-NSSCoverPages**.
15. With **NSSCoverPg02** the active document, change the zoom to 100% and then close the document.

> Check Your Work

Activity 6 Prepare and Format a SmartArt Graphic   2 Parts

You will prepare SmartArt process graphics that identify steps in the production process and then apply formatting to enhance the graphics.

Creating SmartArt

💡 **Hint** Use SmartArt to communicate your message and ideas in a visual manner.

Use Word's SmartArt feature to insert graphics such as diagrams and organizational charts in a document. SmartArt offers a variety of predesigned graphics that are available at the Choose a SmartArt Graphic dialog box, as shown in Figure 5.3. At this dialog box, *All* is selected by default in the left panel and all the available predesigned SmartArt graphics are shown in the middle panel.

Figure 5.3 Choose a SmartArt Graphic Dialog Box

Double-click a SmartArt graphic in this panel.

Choose a SmartArt graphic category from options in this panel.

Click a SmartArt graphic in the middle panel and then read a description of it here.

Tutorial

Inserting, Sizing,
and Positioning
SmartArt

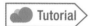 SmartArt

Quick Steps

**Insert SmartArt
Graphic**
1. Click Insert tab.
2. Click SmartArt
   button.
3. Double-click graphic.

Inserting a SmartArt Graphic

To insert a SmartArt graphic, click the Insert tab and then click the SmartArt button in the Illustrations group to open the Choose a SmartArt Graphic dialog box (see Figure 5.3). Predesigned SmartArt graphics are shown in the middle panel of the dialog box. Use the scroll bar at the right side of the middle panel to scroll down the list of choices. Click a graphic in the middle panel and its name displays in the right panel along with a description. SmartArt includes graphics for presenting a list of data; showing processes, cycles, and relationships; and presenting data in a matrix or pyramid. Double-click a graphic in the middle panel of the dialog box (or click the graphic and then click OK) and the graphic is inserted in the document.

When a SmartArt graphic is inserted in a document, a text pane may appear at the left of the graphic. Type text in the text pane or type directly in the graphic.

Tutorial

Formatting a
SmartArt Graphic

💡 **Hint** Limit the
number of shapes and
amount of text in your
SmartArt graphic.

Formatting a SmartArt Graphic

Apply formatting to a SmartArt graphic with options at the SmartArt Tools Design tab. This tab becomes active when the graphic is inserted in the document. Use options and buttons on this tab to add objects, change the graphic layout, apply a style to the graphic, and reset the graphic to the original formatting.

Formatting can also be applied to a SmartArt graphic with options on the SmartArt Tools Format tab. Use options and buttons on this tab to change the sizes and shapes of objects in the graphic; apply shape styles and WordArt styles; change the shape fill, outline, and effects; and arrange and size the graphic.

Activity 6a Inserting and Formatting SmartArt Graphics

Part 1 of 2

1. At a blank document, insert the SmartArt graphic shown in Figure 5.4 by completing the following steps:
   a. Click the Insert tab.
   b. Click the SmartArt button in the Illustrations group.
   c. At the Choose a SmartArt Graphic dialog box, click *Process* in the left panel and then double-click the *Alternating Flow* graphic (second column, second row).
   d. If a *Type your text here* text pane does not appear at the left of the graphic, click the Text Pane button in the Create Graphic group on the SmartArt Tools Design tab to display it.
   e. With the insertion point positioned after the top bullet in the *Type your text here* text pane, type Design.
   f. Click the *[Text]* placeholder below *Design* and then type Mock-up.
   g. Continue clicking occurrences of the *[Text]* placeholder and typing text so the text pane displays as shown at the right.
   h. Close the text pane by clicking the Close button in the upper right corner of the pane. (You can also click the Text Pane button in the Create Graphic group.)

2. Change the graphic colors by clicking the Change Colors button in the SmartArt Styles group and then clicking the *Colorful Range - Accent Colors 5 to 6* option (last option in the *Colorful* section).

3. Apply a style by clicking the More SmartArt Styles button in the SmartArt Styles group and then clicking the *Inset* option (second option in the *3-D* section).

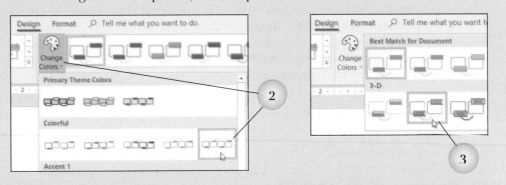

4. Copy the graphic and then change the layout by completing the following steps:
   a. Click inside the SmartArt graphic border but outside any shapes.
   b. Click the Home tab and then click the Copy button in the Clipboard group.
   c. Press Ctrl + End, press the Enter key, and then press Ctrl + Enter to insert a page break.
   d. Click the Paste button in the Clipboard group.
   e. Click inside the copied SmartArt graphic border but outside any shapes.
   f. Click the SmartArt Tools Design tab.
   g. Click the More Layouts button in the Layouts group and then click the *Continuous Block Process* layout (second column, second row).
   h. Click outside the graphic to deselect it.
5. Save the document and name it **5-SAGraphics**.

Check Your Work

Figure 5.4 Activity 6a

Arranging and Moving a SmartArt Graphic

 Position

Wrap Text

Position a SmartArt graphic by clicking the Position button in the Arrange group on the SmartArt Tools Format tab. Apply text wrapping to a SmartArt graphic using options in the Arrange group, with the Layout Options button, or by right-clicking the graphic and clicking *Wrap Text* at the shortcut menu.

Move a SmartArt graphic by positioning the mouse pointer on the graphic until the pointer displays with a four-headed arrow attached, clicking and holding down the left mouse button, and then dragging the graphic to the new location. The SmartArt graphic or shapes within it can also be moved using the up, down, left, and right arrow keys on the keyboard.

Activity 6b Formatting SmartArt Graphics   Part 2 of 2

1. With **5-SAGraphics** open, format shapes by completing the following steps:
   a. Click the SmartArt graphic on the first page to select it (a border surrounds the graphic).
   b. Click the SmartArt Tools Format tab.
   c. In the SmartArt graphic, click the rectangle shape containing the word *Design*.
   d. Press and hold down the Shift key and then click the shape containing the word *Development*.
   e. With the Shift key still held down, click the shape containing the word *Implementation* and then release the Shift key. (All three shapes should now be selected.)
   f. Click the Change Shape button in the Shapes group.
   g. Click the pentagon arrow shape (seventh column, second row in the *Block Arrows* section).
   h. With the shapes still selected, click the Larger button in the Shapes group.
   i. With the shapes still selected, click the Shape Outline button arrow in the Shape Styles group and then click the *Dark Blue* option (ninth option in the *Standard Colors* section).

   j. Click inside the SmartArt graphic border but outside any shapes. (This deselects the shapes but keeps the graphic selected.)
2. Click in the *Shape Height* measurement box in, type 4, and then press the Enter key.

3. Click the Position button and then click the *Position in Middle Center with Square Text Wrapping* option (second column, second row in the *With Text Wrapping* section).
4. Click outside the SmartArt graphic to deselect it.
5. Format the bottom SmartArt graphic by completing the following steps:

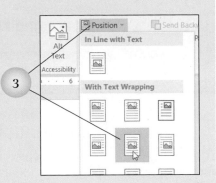

    a. Press Ctrl + End to move to the end of the document and then click in the bottom SmartArt graphic to select it.

    b. Press and hold down the Shift key and then click each of the three shapes.

    c. Click the More WordArt Styles button in the WordArt Styles group on the SmartArt Tools Format tab.

    d. Click the option in the first column, first row (black fill, shadow).

    e. Click the Text Outline button arrow in the WordArt Styles group and then click the *Dark Blue* option (ninth color in the *Standard Colors* section)

    f. Click the Text Effects button in the WordArt Styles group, point to *Glow* at the drop-down list, and then click the *Glow: 5 point; Orange, Accent color 2* option (second column, first row).

    g. Click inside the SmartArt graphic border but outside any shapes.
6. Click the Position button in the Arrange group and then click the *Position in Middle Center with Square Text Wrapping* option (second column, second row in the *With Text Wrapping* section).
7. Click outside the SmartArt graphic to deselect it.
8. Save, print, and then close **5-SAGraphics**.

Check Your Work

Activity 7 Prepare and Format a Company Organizational Chart
1 Part

You will prepare an organizational chart for a company and then apply formatting to enhance the appearance of the chart.

Creating an Organizational Chart with SmartArt

Quick Steps

Insert Organizational Chart
1. Click Insert tab.
2. Click SmartArt button.
3. Click *Hierarchy*.
4. Double-click organizational chart.

To visually illustrate hierarchical data, consider using a SmartArt option to create an organizational chart. To display organizational chart SmartArt options, click the Insert tab and then click the SmartArt button in the Illustrations group. At the Choose a SmartArt Graphic dialog box, click *Hierarchy* in the left panel. Organizational chart options are shown in the middle panel of the dialog box. Double-click an organizational chart and the chart is inserted in the document. Type text in a SmartArt graphic by selecting the shape and then typing text in it or type text in the *Type your text here* window at the left of the graphic. Format a SmartArt organizational chart with options and buttons on the SmartArt Tools Design tab and the SmartArt Tools Format tab, and with the Layout Options button.

Activity 7 Creating and Formatting a SmartArt Organizational Chart
Part 1 of 1

1. At a blank document, create the SmartArt organizational chart shown in Figure 5.5. To begin, click the Insert tab.
2. Click the SmartArt button in the Illustrations group.
3. At the Choose a SmartArt Graphic dialog box, click *Hierarchy* in the left panel of the dialog box and then double-click the *Organization Chart* option (first option in the middle panel).
4. If a *Type your text here* pane displays at the left of the organizational chart, close it by clicking the Text Pane button in the Create Graphic group.
5. Delete one of the boxes in the organizational chart by clicking the border of the box in the lower right corner to select it and then pressing the Delete key. (Make sure that the selection border surrounding the box is a solid line and not a dashed line. If a dashed line appears, click the box border again. This should change the border to a solid line.)
6. With the bottom right box selected, click the Add Shape button arrow in the Create Graphic group and then click the *Add Shape Below* option.
7. Click the *[Text]* placeholder in the top box, type Blaine Willis, press Shift + Enter, and then type President. Click in each of the remaining boxes and type the text as shown in Figure 5.5. (Press Shift + Enter after typing each name.)
8. Click the More SmartArt Styles button in the SmartArt Styles group and then click the *Inset* style (second option in the *3-D* section).
9. Click the Change Colors button and then click the *Colorful Range - Accent Colors 4 to 5* option (fourth option in the *Colorful* section).

10. Click the SmartArt Tools Format tab.
11. Click the text pane control (displays with a left-pointing arrow) at the left side of the graphic border. (This displays the *Type your text here* window.)
12. Using the mouse, select all the text in the *Type your text here* window.
13. Click the Change Shape button in the Shapes group and then click the *Rectangle: Top Corners Rounded* option (eighth option in the *Rectangles* section).

14. Click the Shape Outline button arrow in the Shape Styles group and then click the *Dark Blue* option (ninth option in the *Standard Colors* section).
15. Close the *Type your text here* window.
16. Click inside the organizational chart border but outside any shapes.
17. Click in the *Shape Height* measurement box, type 4, and then press the Enter key.
18. Click in the *Shape Width* measurement box, type 6.5, and then press the Enter key.
19. Click outside the organizational chart to deselect it.
20. Save the document and name it **5 OrgChart**.
21. Print and then close the document.

Check Your Work

Figure 5.5 Activity 7

Chapter Summary

- Insert symbols with options at the Symbol dialog box with the Symbols tab selected, and insert special characters with options at the Symbol dialog box with the Special Characters tab selected.

- Click the Date & Time button in the Text group on the Insert tab to display the Date and Time dialog box. Insert the date or time with options at this dialog box or with keyboard shortcuts. If the date or time is inserted as a field, update the field by clicking the Update tab or the F9 function key.

- Insert an image, such as a photo or clip art, with buttons in the Illustrations group on the Insert tab.

- To insert an image from a folder on the computer's hard drive or removable drive, click the Insert tab and then click the Pictures button in the Illustrations group. At the Insert Picture dialog box, navigate to the specific folder and then double-click the image file.

- To insert an online image, click the Insert tab and then click the Online Pictures button. At the Online Pictures window, type the search text or topic and then press the Enter key. Click an image to select it and then click the Insert button.

- Use the *Shape Height* and *Shape Width* measurement boxes in the Size group on the Picture Tools Format tab to change the size of an image. The size of an image can also be changed with the sizing handles around a selected image.

- Use the Crop button in the Size group to remove unnecessary parts of an image. To crop an image, click the Crop button and then use the crop handles to specify what part of the image should be cropped.

- The Arrange group on the Picture Tools Format tab contains buttons for positioning, aligning, and rotating text.

- Use the Wrap Text button in the Arrange group to specify how text or other objects should wrap around a selected image. The Layout Options button that displays outside the upper right corner of a selected image can also be used to specify text wrapping.

- Move an image using options at the Position button drop-down gallery on the Picture Tools Format tab or by choosing a text wrapping style and then moving the image by dragging it with the mouse.

- Rotate a selected image using the mouse pointer on the rotation handle (circular arrow) that appears above the image.

- The Adjust group on the Picture Tools Format tab contains buttons for adjusting the background, color, brightness, and contrast of an image. An artistic effect can be applied to a selected image using the Artistic Effects button in the Adjust group. Use the *Set Transparent Color* option at the Color button drop-down gallery to make a color transparent in the selected image. Adjust the transparency of an image with options at the Transparency button drop-down gallery.

- Apply a predesigned picture style to a selected image with styles in the Picture Styles group on the Picture Tools Format tab.

- Create alternative text to describe images in a document for readers with visual impairments. Type a description of an image at the Alt Text task pane. Display this task pane by clicking the Alt Text button on the Picture Tools Format tab or right-clicking an image and then clicking *Edit Alt Text* at the shortcut menu.

- Click the Text Box button in the Text group on the Insert tab to display a drop-down list of predesigned text boxes (text boxes that already contain formatting) that can be inserted in a document.

- Draw a text box by clicking the Text Box button in the Text group on the Insert tab, clicking the *Draw Text Box* option at the drop-down list, and then clicking or dragging in the document.

- Customize a text box with buttons on the Drawing Tools Format tab.

- Draw shapes in a document by clicking the Shapes button in the Illustrations group on the Insert tab, clicking a shape at the drop-down list, and then clicking or dragging in the document to draw the shape. Customize a shape with options on the Drawing Tools Format tab.

- Copy a selected shape by clicking the Copy button in the Clipboard group on the Home tab, positioning the insertion point in the new location, and then clicking the Paste button. Another method for copying a selected shape is to press and hold down the Ctrl key while dragging the selected shape.

- Use WordArt to distort or modify text to conform to a variety of shapes. Customize WordArt with options on the Drawing Tools Format tab.

- Use the Screenshot button in the Illustrations group on the Insert tab to capture part or all of a window visible on the screen. Use buttons on the Picture Tools Format tab to customize a screenshot image.

- Use the SmartArt feature to insert predesigned graphics and organizational charts in a document. Click the SmartArt button in the Illustrations group on the Insert tab to display the Choose a SmartArt Graphic dialog box containing a variety of graphics.

- Format a SmartArt graphic with options and buttons on the SmartArt Tools Design tab and the SmartArt Tools Format tab.

- Position a SmartArt graphic by clicking the Position button in the Arrange group on the SmartArt Tools Format tab and then clicking a position option at the drop-down gallery.

- Specify how text or other objects should wrap around a SmartArt graphic with options at the Wrap Text button drop-down gallery. The Layout Options button that appears outside the upper right corner of the selected SmartArt graphic can also be used to specify text wrapping.

- Move a selected SmartArt graphic by dragging it with the mouse or using the up, down, left, and right arrow keys on the keyboard. Before moving a SmartArt graphic, apply text wrapping.

- Use a SmartArt option to create an organizational chart, which is a visual illustration of hierarchical data.

Commands Review

FEATURE	RIBBON TAB, GROUP	BUTTON, OPTION	KEYBOARD SHORTCUT
Alt Text task pane	Picture Tools Format, Accessibility		
Choose a SmartArt Graphic dialog box	Insert, Illustrations		
Date and Time dialog box	Insert, Text		
insert date as field			Alt + Shift + D
Insert Picture dialog box	Insert, Illustrations		
insert time as field			Alt + Shift + T
predesigned text box	Insert, Text		
screenshot	Insert, Illustrations		
shapes	Insert, Illustrations		
Symbol dialog box	Insert, Symbols	Ω, *More Symbols*	
text box	Insert, Text		
update field			F9
WordArt	Insert, Text		

Microsoft®

Word

CHAPTER

6

Managing Documents

Performance Objectives

Upon successful completion of Chapter 6, you will be able to:

1 Change the view of a document

2 Use learning tools to aid reading fluency and comprehension

3 Change page movement, display percentage, and ribbon display options

4 Hide and show white space

5 Split a window, view documents side by side, and open a new window

6 Insert a file into an open document

7 Preview and print specific text and pages in a document

8 Prepare and print envelopes and labels

9 Create a document using a template

10 Save documents in different file formats

11 Save a template and open a template using File Explorer

Word provides a number of options for managing documents, including customizing the document view, using learning tools, changing the display and display percentage, and changing ribbon display options. Managing documents can also include working with windows and performing such actions as arranging windows, splitting windows, viewing documents side by side, and opening a new window. In this chapter, you will learn these techniques, as well as saving documents in different file formats and saving and opening a template. You will also learn how to create and print envelopes and labels.

 Data Files

Before beginning chapter work, copy the WL1C6 folder to your storage medium and then make WL1C6 the active folder.

The online course includes additional training and assessment resources.

You will open a document on navigating and searching the web, change the document view, use learning tools, change page movement to side to side, change display percentages, and hide and show white space at the tops and bottoms of pages.

Tutorial

Changing the
Document View

Changing the Document View

By default, a Word document displays in Print Layout view. This view displays the document on the screen as it will appear when printed. Other views are available, such as Draft and Read Mode. Change views with buttons in the view area on the Status bar (see Figure 6.1) or with options on the View tab.

Displaying a Document in Draft View

[≣] Draft

Change to Draft view and the document displays in a format for efficient editing and formatting. In this view, margins and other features such as headers and footers do not appear on the screen. Change to Draft view by clicking the View tab and then clicking the Draft button in the Views group.

Displaying a Document in Web Layout View

[▦] Web Layout

To see what a document would look like as a web page, click the Web Layout button on the View tab. In Web Layout view, the document margins are wider; this can be useful for viewing objects such as tables and graphics.

Displaying a Document in Read Mode View

[▤] Read Mode

[▤] Read Mode

Read Mode view displays a document in a format for easy viewing and reading. Change to Read Mode view by clicking the Read Mode button in the view area on the Status bar or by clicking the View tab and then clicking the Read Mode button in the Views group. Navigate in Read Mode view using the keys on the keyboard, as shown in Table 6.1. Another way to navigate in Read Mode is to click the Next and Previous arrow buttons at the right and left sides of the screen to page forward and backward through the document.

The File, Tools, and View tabs appear in the upper left corner of the screen in Read Mode view. Click the File tab to display the backstage area. Click the Tools tab and a drop-down list displays options for finding specific text in the document, searching for information on the internet using the Smart Lookup feature, and translating text in the document.

Figure 6.1 View Buttons and the Zoom Slider Bar

Table 6.1 Keyboard Commands in Read Mode View

Press this key	To complete this action
Page Down key, Right Arrow key, or spacebar	display next two pages
Page Up key, Left Arrow key, or Backspace key	display previous two pages
Home	display first page in document
End	display last page in document
Esc	return to previous view

Click the View tab to customize Read Mode view. Use View tab options to display the Navigation pane to navigate to specific locations in the document or to show comments inserted in the document. The View tab also includes options for making text more readable by changing column width, page color, and page layout; increasing spacing between characters, words, and lines; showing syllable breaks; and hearing text read aloud. These options are also available on the Immersive Learning Tools tab, described on the next page.

If a document contains an object such as a table, SmartArt graphic, image, or shape, zoom in on the object in Read Mode view by double-clicking it. The display size of the object increases and a button containing a magnifying glass with a plus symbol inside (⊕) appears just outside the upper right corner of the object. Click the magnifying glass to zoom in and out. Click outside the object to exit the zoom view. To close Read Mode view and return to the previous view, press the Esc key or click the View tab and then click *Edit Document* at the drop-down list.

Activity 1a Changing Views

Part 1 of 3

1. Open **WebReport** and then save it with the name **6-WebReport**.
2. Display the document in Draft view by clicking the View tab and then clicking the Draft button in the Views group.

3. Click the Web Layout button in the Views group to display the document as it would appear if published as a web page.
4. Display the document in Read Mode view by clicking the Read Mode button in the view area on the Status bar.

5. If a speaker is connected to your computer, have the text read out loud by clicking the View tab and then clicking the *Read Aloud* option at the drop-down list. After listening for a short period of time, turn off the reading by clicking the View tab and then clicking the *Read Aloud* option.

6. Increase the display size of the table at the right of the screen by double-clicking the table. (If the table is not visible, click the Next button at the right of the screen to view the next page.)

7. Click the button containing a magnifying glass with a plus symbol that displays outside the upper right corner of the table. (This increases the zoom.)

8. Click outside the table to return it to the original display size.

9. Practice navigating in Read Mode view using the actions shown in Table 6.1 (except the last action).

10. Press the Esc key to return to the Print Layout view.

Tutorial
Using Learning Tools

Using Learning Tools

Column Width

Page Color

Line Focus

Text Spacing

Syllables

Read Aloud

The same learning tools available in Read Mode view can also be found on the Immersive Learning Tools tab, along with several additional options. Click the View tab and then click the Learning Tools button in the Immersive group and the Immersive Learning Tools tab displays as shown in Figure 6.2.

Text in narrow columns is easier to read. Click the Column Width button on the Immersive Learning Tools tab and choose from *Very Narrow*, *Narrow*, *Moderate*, and *Wide*. Adding color to a page can also make text easier to read and reduce eye strain. Use the Page Color button to change the background color to *Sepia* (a light reddish-brown background color); or, select *Inverse* to see white text on a black background. Improve focus and comprehension by choosing the Line Focus button to read text one, three, or five lines at a time. Click the Text Spacing button to make text easier to read by increasing space between words, characters, and lines. Click the Syllables button to display syllable breaks in words, making words easier to recognize and pronounce.

If audio output is available, click the Read Aloud button to hear the text read aloud. Each word is highlighted as it is being read. A playback toolbar displays with buttons for controlling the narration, as shown in Figure 6.3. Turn off reading by clicking the Stop button on the playback toolbar or by clicking the Read Aloud button again.

Figure 6.2 Immersive Learning Tools Tab

Figure 6.3 Playback Toolbar

Begins reading at
the beginning of the
previous paragraph

Pauses reading

Displays a drop-down list with options
for specifying the reading speed and
changing the reading voice

Stops reading

Begins reading at the beginning
of the next paragraph

Activity 1b Using Learning Tools

1. With **6-WebReport** open, display learning tools by clicking the View tab, if necessary, and then clicking the Learning Tools button in the Immersive group.
2. Change column width by clicking the Column Width button on the Immersive Learning Tools tab and then clicking *Moderate* at the drop-down list.
3. Change page background color by clicking the Page Color button and then clicking the *Sepia* option.
4. Focus on only a few lines in the document by clicking the Line Focus button and then clicking *Five Lines* at the drop-down list.

5. Click the down arrow at the right side of the screen to scroll down five lines in the document.
6. Remove the focus by clicking the Line Focus button and then clicking *None* at the drop-down list.
7. Apply text spacing by clicking the Text Spacing button.
8. After viewing the document with extra spacing, click the Text Spacing button to turn off text spacing.
9. Click the Syllables button to display word syllable breaks.
10. After viewing the document with syllable breaks added to words, click the Syllables button to turn off syllable breaks.
11. If audio output is available, click the Read Aloud button.

12. Listen to the reading for a short time and then click the Pause button on the playback toolbar to pause the reading.
13. Click the Play button (previously the Pause button) to resume the reading.
14. Click the Next button on the playback toolbar to begin the reading with the next paragraph of text.
15. Change the reading voice by clicking the Settings button on the playback toolbar. At the drop-down list, click the *Voice Selection* option box arrow and then click *Microsoft Zira*.
16. After listening to the reading by Microsoft Zira, return to the default reading voice by clicking the Settings button, clicking the *Voice Selection* option box arrow, and then clicking *Microsoft David*.
17. Click the Stop button on the playback toolbar to turn off reading.
18. Remove the sepia page color by clicking the Page Color button and then clicking *None* at the drop-down list.
19. Close the Immersive Learning Tools tab by clicking the Close Learning Tools button.

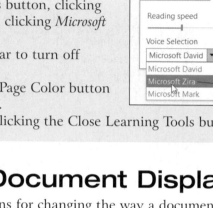

Changing the Document Display

Word includes a number of options for changing the way a document displays on the screen. Show pages in a document like pages in a book with the Side to Side button in the Page Movement group on the View tab. Use options on the Zoom slider bar or the Zoom dialog box to change the display percentage. Show more of the document by turning off the ribbon, including tabs and commands, or turning off the display of commands but keeping the tabs visible. Another method for showing more of a document is to hide the white space that appears at the top and bottom of each page.

 Tutorial

Changing Page Movement

 Side to Side

Changing Page Movement

Paging through a document occurs by default in a vertical (up and down) manner. To view a document more like a book, with two pages visible at one time and other pages cascaded behind them, change to side-to-side page movement by clicking the Side to Side button in the Page Movement group on the View tab. Figure 6.4 shows how pages appear in the 6-WebReport document with the Side to Side button active.

Scroll through pages on a touch screen using a finger to flip through pages. If the computer screen is not a touch screen, use the horizontal scroll bar or the mouse wheel to scroll through pages. To use the horizontal scroll bar, click the Next button (right-pointing triangle) at the right side of the scroll bar to display the next page or click the Previous button (left-pointing triangle) at the left side of the scroll bar to display the previous page; drag the scroll box on the scroll bar; or click to the left or right of the scroll box. The mouse wheel can also be used to scroll through pages.

Figure 6.4 Side-to-Side Page Movement

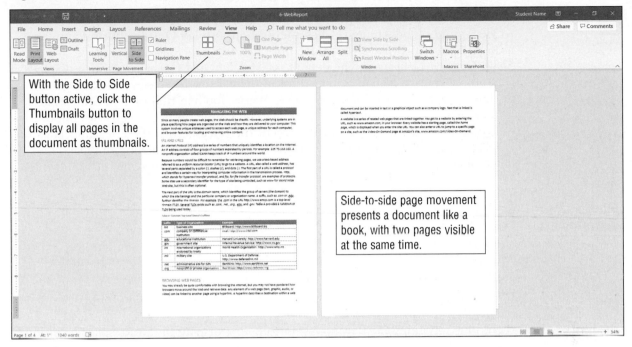

With the Side to Side button active, click the Thumbnails button to display all pages in the document as thumbnails.

Side-to-side page movement presents a document like a book, with two pages visible at the same time.

 Thumbnails

When the Side to Side button is active, the Thumbnails button appears in the Zoom group on the View tab and other options in the Zoom group are unavailable. Click the Thumbnails button and all pages in the document display as thumbnails. Click a thumbnail to move the insertion point to the beginning of the page represented by the thumbnail and that page along with the next or previous page displays side to side. Another method for displaying page thumbnails is to hold down the Ctrl key while moving the mouse wheel. Return to the default vertical page movement by clicking the Vertical button in the Page Movement group on the View tab.

 Vertical

 Tutorial

Changing the Display Percentage

Changing the Display Percentage

By default, a document displays at 100%. This display percentage can be changed with the Zoom slider bar at the right side of the Status bar (see Figure 6.1 on page 156) and with options in the Zoom group on the View tab. To change the display percentage with the Zoom slider bar, drag the button on the bar to increase or decrease the percentage. Click the Zoom Out button at the left of the slider bar to decrease the display percentage or click the Zoom In button to increase the display percentage.

 Zoom

100%

One Page

Multiple Pages

Page Width

Click the Zoom button in the Zoom group on the View tab to display the Zoom dialog box, which contains options for changing the display percentage. If the display percentage has been changed, return to the default by clicking the 100% button in the Zoom group on the View tab. Click the One Page button to display the entire page on the screen and click the Multiple Pages button to display multiple pages on the screen. Click the Page Width button and the document expands across the screen.

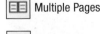 **Hint** Click 100% at the right of the Zoom slider bar to display the Zoom dialog box.

Changing Ribbon Display Options

Ribbon Display Options

Use the Ribbon Display Options button in the upper right corner of the screen to view more of a document. Click the Ribbon Display Options button and a drop-down list displays with three options: *Auto-hide Ribbon*, *Show Tabs*, and *Show Tabs and Commands*. The default is *Show Tabs and Commands*, which displays the Quick Access Toolbar, ribbon, and Status bar on the screen. Click the first option, *Auto-hide Ribbon*, and the Quick Access Toolbar, ribbon, and Status bar are hidden, allowing more of the document to be visible on the screen. To temporarily redisplay these features, click at the top of the screen. Turn these features back on by clicking the Ribbon Display Options button and then clicking the *Show Tabs and Commands* option. Click the *Show Tabs* option at the drop-down list and the tabs display on the ribbon while the buttons and commands remain hidden.

Hiding and Showing White Space

> **Tutorial**
>
> Hiding and Showing White Space
>
> **Hide White Space**
>
> **Show White Space**

In Print Layout view, a page appears as it will when printed, including the white spaces at the top and the bottom of the page representing the document's margins. To save space on the screen in Print Layout view, the white space can be removed from view by positioning the mouse pointer at the top edge or bottom edge of a page or between pages until the pointer displays as the Hide White Space icon and then double-clicking the left mouse button. To redisplay the white space, position the mouse pointer on the thin gray line separating pages until the pointer turns into the Show White Space icon and then double-click the left mouse button.

Activity 1c Changing Views, Changing Display, and Hiding/Showing White Space   Part 3 of 3

1. With **6-WebReport** open, press Ctrl + Home to move the insertion point to the beginning of the document.
2. Change to side-to-side page movement by clicking the View tab and then clicking the Side to Side button in the Page Movement group. (This displays pages 1 and 2 side by side.)
3. Click the Next button at the right side of the horizontal scroll bar to display pages 2 and 3.
4. Display page thumbnails by clicking the Thumbnails button in the Zoom group.
5. Click the page 4 thumbnail.

6. Return to the default page movement by clicking the Vertical button in the Page Movement group.

7. Click the Zoom button in the Zoom group on the View tab.
8. At the Zoom dialog box, click the *75%* option and then click OK.
9. Return the display percentage to the default by clicking the 100% button in the Zoom group.
10. Click the Ribbon Display Options button in the upper right corner of the screen and then click *Auto-hide Ribbon* at the drop-down list.
11. Press the Page Up key until the beginning of the document displays.
12. Click at the top of the screen to temporarily redisplay the Quick Access Toolbar, ribbon, and Status bar.
13. Click the Ribbon Display Options button and then click *Show Tabs* at the drop-down list.
14. Click the Ribbon Display Options button and then click *Show Tabs and Commands* at the drop-down list.
15. Hide the white spaces at the tops and bottoms of pages by positioning the mouse pointer at the top edge of the page until the pointer turns into the Hide White Space icon and then double-clicking the left mouse button.
16. Scroll through the document and notice the appearance of pages.
17. Redisplay the white spaces at the tops and bottoms of pages by positioning the mouse pointer on any thin gray line separating pages until the pointer turns into the Show White Space icon and then double-clicking the left mouse button.
18. Close **6-WebReport**.

Activity 2 Manage Multiple Documents   7 Parts

You will arrange, maximize, restore, and minimize windows; move selected text between split windows; compare formatting of documents side by side; and print specific text, pages, and multiple copies.

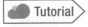
Tutorial

Working with Windows

Hint Press Ctrl + F6 to switch between open documents.

Working with Windows

Multiple documents can be opened in Word, the insertion point can be moved between documents, and information can be moved or copied from one document and pasted into another. When a new document is opened, it displays on top of any previously opened document. With multiple documents open, the window containing each document can be resized to see all or a portion of it on the screen.

A Word button appears on the taskbar when a document is open. If more than one document is open, another button will appear behind the first in a cascading manner. To see all documents that are currently open in Word, hover the mouse pointer over the Word button. A thumbnail of each document will appear. To make a change to a document, click the thumbnail that represents the document.

 Switch Windows

Another method for determining what documents are open is to click the View tab and then click the Switch Windows button in the Window group. The document name in the list with the check mark in front of it is the active document. The active document contains the insertion point. To make a different document active, click the document name. To switch to another document using the keyboard, type the number shown in front of the document.

Arranging Windows

Quick Steps

Arrange Windows
1. Open documents.
2. Click View tab.
3. Click Arrange All button.

If several documents are open, they can be arranged so a portion of each appears. The portion that appears includes the title (if present) and the opening paragraph of each document. To arrange a group of open documents, click the View tab and then click the Arrange All button in the Window group.

 Arrange All

Maximizing, Restoring, and Minimizing Documents

 Hint The keyboard shortcut to maximize a document is Ctrl + F10.

Use the Maximize and Minimize buttons in the upper right corner of the active document to change the size of a document window. The two buttons are at the left of the Close button. (The Close button is in the upper right corner of the screen and contains an X.)

 Maximize

 Minimize

If all the open documents are arranged on the screen, clicking the Maximize button in the active document causes that document to expand to fill the screen. Any other open windows will be hidden behind it. In addition, the Maximize button changes to the Restore button. To return the active document back to its original size, click the Restore button. Click the Minimize button in the active document and the document is reduced to a button on the taskbar. To maximize a document that has been minimized, hover the mouse pointer over the taskbar button and click the thumbnail of the document.

Restore

Activity 2a **Arranging, Maximizing, Restoring, and Minimizing Windows** **Part 1 of 7**

Note: If you are using Word on a network system that contains a virus checker, you may not be able to open multiple documents at once. Continue by opening each document individually.

1. Open the following documents: **AptLease**, **CompSoftware**, **IntelProp**, and **NSS**. (To open all of the documents at one time, display the Open dialog box, hold down the Ctrl key, click each document name, release the Ctrl key, and then click the Open button.)
2. Arrange the windows by clicking the View tab and then clicking the Arrange All button in the Window group.
3. Make **AptLease** the active document by clicking the Switch Windows button in the Window group on the View tab of the document at the top of your screen and then clicking *AptLease* at the drop-down list.
4. Close **AptLease**.
5. Make **IntelProp** active and then close it.

---

6. Make **CompSoftware** active and minimize it by clicking the Minimize button in the upper right corner of the active window.
7. Maximize **NSS** by clicking the Maximize button immediately left of the Close button.
8. Close **NSS**.
9. Restore **CompSoftware** by clicking the button on the taskbar that represents the document.
10. Maximize **CompSoftware**.

Splitting a Window

Quick Steps

Split Window
1. Open document.
2. Click View tab.
3. Click Split button.

 Split

Hint The keyboard shortcut to split a window is Alt + Ctrl + S.

Remove Split

A window can be split into two panes so that two different parts of a document can be seen at once. For example, show an outline for a report in one pane and the part of the report to be edited in the other pane. The original window is split into two panes that extend horizontally across the screen.

Split a window by clicking the View tab and then clicking the Split button in the Window group. This splits the window in two with a split bar and another horizontal ruler. The location of the split bar can be changed by positioning the mouse pointer on the split bar until the pointer displays as an up-and-down-pointing arrow with two small lines in the middle, holding down the left mouse button, dragging to the new location, and then releasing the mouse button.

When a window is split, the insertion point is positioned in the bottom pane. To move the insertion point to the other pane with the mouse, position the I-beam pointer in the other pane and then click the left mouse button. To remove the split bar from the document, click the View tab and then click the Remove Split button in the Window group. The split bar can also be double-clicked or dragged to the top or bottom of the screen.

Activity 2b Moving Selected Text between Split Windows   **Part 2 of 7**

1. With **CompSoftware** open, save the document and name it **6-CompSoftware**.
2. Click the View tab and then click the Split button in the Window group.
3. Move the first section below the second section by completing the following steps:
   a. Click in the top pane and then click the Home tab.
   b. Select the section *SECTION 1: PERSONAL-USE SOFTWARE* from the title to right above *SECTION 2: GRAPHICS AND MULTIMEDIA SOFTWARE*.
   c. Click the Cut button in the Clipboard group on the Home tab.
   d. Click in the bottom pane and then move the insertion point to the end of the document.
   e. Click the Paste button in the Clipboard group on the Home tab.
   f. Reverse the numbers in the two titles to *SECTION 1: GRAPHICS AND MULTIMEDIA SOFTWARE* and *SECTION 2: PERSONAL-USE SOFTWARE*.

4. Remove the split from the window by clicking the View tab and then clicking the Remove Split button in the Window group.
5. Press Ctrl + Home to move the insertion point to the beginning of the document.
6. Save **6-CompSoftware**.

 Check Your Work

Viewing Documents Side by Side

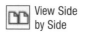 View Side by Side

Synchronous Scrolling

Quick Steps

View Documents Side by Side

1. Open two documents.
2. Click View tab.
3. Click View Side by Side button.

The contents of two documents can be compared on screen by opening both documents, clicking the View tab, and then clicking the View Side by Side button in the Window group. The documents are arranged on the screen side by side, as shown in Figure 6.5. By default, synchronous scrolling is active. With this feature active, scrolling in one document causes the same scrolling in the other document. This feature is useful for comparing the text, formatting, or other features between documents. To scroll in one document and not the other, click the Synchronous Scrolling button in the Window group to turn it off.

Figure 6.5 Viewing Documents Side by Side

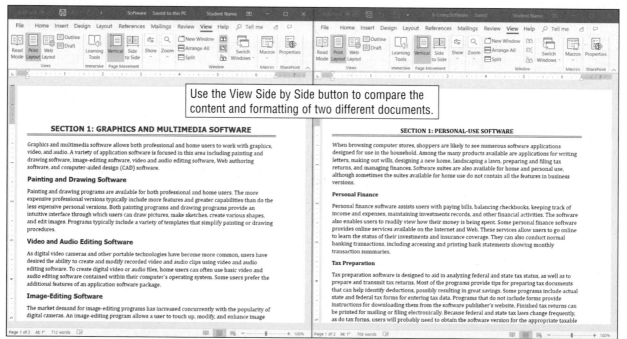

1. With **6-CompSoftware** open, open **Software**.
2. Click the View tab and then click the View Side by Side button in the Window group.
3. Scroll through both documents simultaneously. Notice the difference between the two documents. (The titles and headings are set in different fonts and colors.) Format the title and headings in **6-CompSoftware** so they match the formatting in **Software**. *Hint: Use the* *Format Painter button to copy the formatting.*
4. Turn off synchronous scrolling by clicking the Synchronous Scrolling button in the Window group on the View tab.
5. Scroll through the document and notice that no scrolling occurs in the other document.
6. Make **Software** the active document and then close it.
7. Save **6-CompSoftware**.

> **Check Your Work**

Opening a New Window

A second copy of a document can be opened in a new window so that two copies of the same document may be viewed side by side. To do this, first open a document and then click the New Window button in the Window group on the View tab. When a new window is opened, the document name in the Title bar is followed by - *2*. The document name in the original window is followed by - *1*. Any change made to the document in one window is reflected in the document in the other window, as both windows display the exact same file.

1. With **6-CompSoftware** open, open a second copy of the document in a new window by clicking the New Window button in the Window group on the View tab. (Notice that the document name in the Title bar displays followed by - *2*.)
2. Click the View tab and then click the View Side by Side button in the Window group.
3. Click the Window button on the View tab and then click the Synchronous Scrolling button to turn off synchronous scrolling.
4. Click in the **6-CompSoftware - 2** window to make the document active. Look at the first paragraph of text and notice the order in which the different types of software are listed in the last sentence of the paragraph (painting and drawing software, image-editing software, video and audio editing software, and computer-aided design [CAD] software).
5. Click in the **6-CompSoftware - 1** window and then cut and paste the headings and text so each type of software is described in the order it was listed in the first paragraph.
6. Click the Save button on the Quick Access Toolbar.
7. Close the second copy of the document by clicking the Word button on the taskbar and then clicking the Close button in the upper right corner of the **6-CompSoftware - 2** thumbnail (above the Word button on the taskbar).

> **Check Your Work**

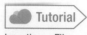

Object

Inserting a File into a Document

The contents of one document can be inserted into another using the Object button in the Text group on the Insert tab. Click the Object button arrow and then click *Text from File* and the Insert File dialog box displays. This dialog box contains similar features as the Open dialog box. Navigate to the specific folder and then double-click the document to be inserted in the open document.

Quick Steps

Insert File
1. Click Insert tab.
2. Click Object button arrow.
3. Click *Text from File*.
4. Navigate to folder.
5. Double-click document.

Activity 2e Inserting a File

Part 5 of 7

1. With **6-CompSoftware** open, move the insertion point to the end of the document.
2. Insert a file into the open document by completing the following steps:
   a. Click the Insert tab.
   b. Click the Object button arrow in the Text group and then click *Text from File* at the drop-down list.
   c. At the Insert File dialog box, navigate to your WL1C6 folder and then double-click *EduComp*.
3. Save **6-CompSoftware**.

2b

Check Your Work

Previewing and Printing

Use options at the Print backstage area, shown in Figure 6.6, to specify what is to be printed and to preview pages before printing them. To display the Print backstage area, click the File tab and then click the *Print* option. The Quick Access Toolbar can be customized to include the Print Preview and Print button that when clicked will display the Print backstage area. Insert the button on the Quick Access Toolbar by clicking the Customize Quick Access Toolbar button at the right side of the toolbar and then clicking *Print Preview and Print* at the drop-down list.

💡 **Hint** The Print backstage area can also be displayed with the keyboard shortcut Ctrl + P.

Previewing Pages

Zoom to Page

At the Print backstage area, a preview of the current page is shown (see Figure 6.6). Click the Next Page button to view the next page in the document preview, and click the Previous Page button to display the previous page. Use the Zoom slider bar to increase or decrease the size of the page and click the Zoom to Page button to fit the entire page in the viewing area.

Figure 6.6 Print Backstage Area

preview area

Print

Copies: 1

Print

Printer
HP LaserJet 1160
Ready

Printer Properties

Settings

Print All Pages
The whole thing

Pages:

Print One Sided
Only print on one side of the p...

Collated
1,2,3   1,2,3   1,2,3

Portrait Orientation

Letter
8.5" x 11"

Normal Margins
Left: 1"   Right: 1"

1 Page Per Sheet

Page Setup

SECTION 1: GRAPHICS AND MULTIMEDIA SOFTWARE

Graphics and multimedia software allows both professional and home users to work with graphics, video, and audio. A variety of application software is focused in this area including painting and drawing software, image-editing software, video and audio editing software, and computer-aided design (CAD) software.

Painting and Drawing Software

Painting and drawing programs are available for both professional and home users. The more expensive professional versions typically include more features and greater capabilities than do the less expensive personal versions. Both painting programs and drawing programs provide an intuitive interface through which users can draw pictures, make sketches, create various shapes, and edit images. Programs typically include a variety of templates that simplify painting or drawing procedures.

Image-Editing Software

The market demand for image-editing programs has increased concurrently with the popularity of digital cameras. An image-editing program allows a user to touch up, modify, and enhance image quality. Once edited, images can be stored in a variety of forms and inserted into other files, such as letters, advertisements, and electronic scrapbooks.

Video and Audio Editing Software

As digital video cameras and other portable technologies have become more common, users have desired the ability to create and modify recorded video and audio clips using video and audio editing software. To create digital video or audio files, home users can often use basic video and audio editing software contained within their computer's operating system. Some users prefer the additional features of an application software package.

Computer-aided Design Software

Computer-aided design software is a sophisticated kind of drawing software, providing tools that enable professionals to create architectural, engineering, product, and scientific designs. Engineers can use the software to design buildings or bridges, and scientists can create graphical designs of plant, animal, and chemical structures. Some software programs display designs in three-dimensional form so they can be viewed from various angles. Once a design has been created, changes can be easily made until it is finalized.

SECTION 2: PERSONAL-USE SOFTWARE

When browsing computer stores, shoppers are likely to see numerous software applications designed for use in the household. Among the many products available are applications for writing letters, making out wills, designing a new home, landscaping a lawn, preparing and filing tax returns, and managing finances. Software suites are also available for home and personal use, although sometimes the suites available for home use do not contain all the features in business versions.

Personal Finance

Personal finance software assists users with paying bills, balancing checkbooks, keeping track of income and expenses, maintaining investment records, and other financial activities. The software also enables users to readily view how their money is being spent. Some personal finance software provides online services available on the Internet and Web. These services allow users to go online to learn the status of their investments and insurance coverage. They can also conduct normal banking transactions, including accessing and printing bank statements showing monthly transaction summaries.

Tax Preparation

Tax preparation software is designed to aid in analyzing federal and state tax status, as well as to prepare and transmit tax returns. Most of the programs provide tips for preparing tax documents that can help identify deductions, possibly resulting in great savings. Some programs include actual state and federal tax forms for entering tax data. Programs that do not include forms provide instructions for downloading them from the software publisher's website. Finished tax returns can be printed for mailing or filing electronically. Because federal and state tax laws change frequently, as do tax forms, users will probably need to obtain the software version for the appropriate taxable years or period.

Legal Documents

Legal software is designed to help analyze, plan, and prepare a variety of legal documents, including wills and trusts. It can also be used to prepare other legal documents, such as the forms required for real estate purchases or sales, rental contracts, and estate planning. Included in most packages are standard templates for various legal documents, along with suggestions for preparing them.

Educational and Reference Software

The widespread use of home computers has brought about an increase in the availability of educational and reference software, making computers popular learning and reference tools. Examples of educational and reference software include encyclopedias, dictionaries, and tutorials.

Encyclopedias and Dictionaries

Almost everyone has used an encyclopedia or dictionary at one time or another. An encyclopedia is a comprehensive reference work containing detailed articles on a broad range of subjects. Before computers, encyclopedias were only available in print form. They are now available electronically and many new PCs include a CD-based encyclopedia.

A standard dictionary is a reference work containing an alphabetical listing of words, with definitions that provide the word's meaning, pronunciation, and usage. Examples include *Webster's Dictionary* and *Webster's New World Dictionary of Computer Terms*. Other specialized dictionaries, such as multi-language dictionaries, contain words along with their equivalent in another language for use in translation. Many dictionaries are available on CD.

Learning Tutorials

Many people learn skills by using CD- or Internet-based tutorials. A tutorial is a form of instruction in which students are guided step by step through the learning process. Tutorials are available for

Zoom Out button   Zoom In button

61%

Zoom slider bar   Zoom to Page button

Previous Page button   Next Page button

Activity 2f Previewing Pages

Part 6 of 7

1. With **6-CompSoftware** open, press Ctrl + Home to move the insertion point to the beginning of the document.
2. Insert the Print Preview and Print button on the Quick Access Toolbar by clicking the Customize Quick Access Toolbar button and then clicking *Print Preview and Print* at the drop-down list.
3. Preview the document by clicking the Print Preview and Print button on the Quick Access Toolbar.
4. Click the Zoom In button (plus [+] symbol) at the right of the Zoom slider bar two times. (This increases the size of the preview page.)
5. At the Print backstage area, click the Next Page button below and to the left of the preview page. (This displays page 2 in the preview area.)
6. Click the Zoom Out button (minus [–] symbol) at the left of the Zoom slider bar until two pages of the document display in the preview area.

Word Level 1 | Unit 2

Chapter 6 | Managing Documents   **169**

7. Change the zoom at the Zoom dialog box by completing the following steps:
   a. Click the percentage number at the left of the Zoom slider bar.
   b. At the Zoom dialog box, click the *Many pages* option in the *Zoom to* section.
   c. Click OK to close the dialog box. (Notice that all the pages in the document appear as thumbnails in the preview area.)
8. Click the Zoom to Page button at the right of the Zoom slider bar. (This returns the page to the default size.)
9. Click the Back button to return to the document.
10. Remove the Print Preview and Print button from the Quick Access Toolbar by clicking the Customize Quick Access Toolbar button and then clicking *Print Preview and Print* at the drop-down list.

Printing Specific Text and Pages

Hint Save a document before printing it.

Control what prints in a document with options at the Print backstage area. Click the first gallery in the *Settings* category and a drop-down list displays with options for printing. All the pages in the document may be printed; or, print only selected text, the current page, or a custom range of pages.

Print a portion of a document by selecting the text and then choosing the *Print Selection* option at the Print backstage area. With this option, only the selected text prints. (If no text is selected, this option is dimmed.) Click the *Print Current Page* option to print only the page on which the insertion point is located. Use the *Custom Print* option to identify a specific page, multiple pages, or a range of pages to print. To print specific pages, use a comma (,) to indicate *and* and use a hyphen (-) to indicate *through*. For example, to print pages 2 and 5, type 2,5 in the *Pages* text box and to print pages 6 through 10, type 6-10.

With the other galleries available in the *Settings* category of the Print backstage area, specify whether to print on one or both sides of the page, change the page orientation (portrait or landscape), specify how the pages are collated, choose a paper size, and specify document margins. The last gallery contains options for printing 1, 2, 4, 6, 8, or 16 pages of a multiple-page document on one sheet of paper. This gallery also contains the *Scale to Paper Size* option. Click this option and then use the side menu to choose the paper size to scale the document.

To print more than one copy of a document, use the *Copies* measurement box to the right of the Print button. If several copies of a multiple-page document are printed, Word collates the pages as they print so that pages appear in sequential order in each copy. For example, if two copies of a three-page document are printed, pages 1, 2, and 3 are grouped together as one copy, and then the pages print a second time. Collated copies take slightly longer to print. If copies do not need to be collated, reduce printing time by clicking the *Collated* gallery in the Print backstage area and then clicking the *Uncollated* option.

To send a document directly to the printer without displaying the Print backstage area, consider adding the Quick Print button to the Quick Access Toolbar. To do this, click the Customize Quick Access Toolbar button at the right side of the toolbar and then click *Quick Print* at the drop-down gallery. Click the Quick Print button and all the pages of the active document will print.

Activity 2g Printing Specific Text and Pages

1. With **6-CompSoftware** open, print selected text by completing the following steps:
   a. Select the heading *Painting and Drawing Software* and the paragraph of text that follows it.
   b. Click the File tab and then click the *Print* option.
   c. At the Print backstage area, click the first gallery in the *Settings* category (displays with *Print All Pages*) and then click *Print Selection* at the drop-down list.
   d. Click the Print button.
2. Change the margins and page orientation and then print only the first page by completing the following steps:
   a. Press Ctrl + Home to move the insertion point to the beginning of the document.
   b. Click the File tab and then click the *Print* option.
   c. At the Print backstage area, click the fourth gallery (displays with *Portrait Orientation)* in the *Settings* category and then click *Landscape Orientation* at the drop-down list.
   d. Click the sixth gallery (displays with *Normal Margins*) in the *Settings* category and then click *Narrow* at the drop-down list.
   c. Click the first gallery (displays with *Print All Pages*) in the *Settings* category and then click *Print Current Page* at the drop-down list.
   f. Click the Print button. (The first page of the document prints in landscape orientation with 0.5-inch margins.)

3. Print all the pages as thumbnails on one page by completing the following steps:
   a. Click the File tab and then click the *Print* option.
   b. At the Print backstage area, click the bottom gallery (displays with *1 Page Per Sheet*) in the *Settings* category and then click *4 Pages Per Sheet* at the drop-down list.
   c. Click the first gallery (displays with *Print Current Page*) in the *Settings* category and then click *Print All Pages* at the drop-down list.
   d. Click the Print button.
4. Select the entire document, change the line spacing to 1.5 lines, and then deselect the text.
5. Print two copies of specific pages by completing the following steps:
   a. Click the File tab and then click the *Print* option.
   b. Click the fourth gallery (displays with *Landscape Orientation*) at the *Settings* category and then click *Portrait Orientation* in the drop-down list.
   c. Click in the *Pages* text box below the first gallery in the *Settings* category and then type 1,3.
   d. Click the *Copies* measurement box up arrow (located to the right of the Print button) to display *2*.
   e. Click the third gallery (displays with *Collated*) in the *Settings* category and then click *Uncollated* at the drop-down list.
   f. Click the bottom gallery (displays with *4 Pages Per Sheet*) in the *Settings* category and then click *1 Page Per Sheet* at the drop-down list.
   g. Click the Print button. (The first page of the document will print two times and then the third page will print two times.)
6. Save and then close **6-CompSoftware**.

Check Your Work

You will create an envelope document and type the return address and delivery address using envelope addressing guidelines issued by the United States Postal Service. You will also open a letter document and then prepare an envelope using the inside address on the business letter.

☁ Tutorial

Preparing an
Envelope

✉ Envelopes

Preparing and Printing Envelopes

Word automates the creation of envelopes with options at the Envelopes and Labels dialog box with the Envelopes tab selected, as shown in Figure 6.7. Display this dialog box by clicking the Mailings tab and then clicking the Envelopes button in the Create group. At the dialog box, type the delivery address in the *Delivery address* text box and the return address in the *Return address* text box. Print the envelope immediately by clicking the Print button, or prepare the envelope to be printed along with a letter or other document by clicking the Add to document button.

When a return address is entered in the dialog box, Word will display the question *Do you want to save the new return address as the default return address?* At this question, click Yes to save the current return address for future envelopes or click No if the return address should not be used as the default. To omit a return address, insert a check mark in the *Omit* check box.

The Envelopes and Labels dialog box contains a *Preview* sample box and a *Feed* sample box. The *Preview* sample box shows how the envelope will appear when printed and the *Feed* sample box shows how the envelope should be fed into the printer.

Ȯuick Steps

Prepare Envelope
1. Click Mailings tab.
2. Click Envelopes button.
3. Type delivery address.
4. Click in *Return address* text box.
5. Type return address.
6. Click Add to Document button or Print button.

Figure 6.7 Envelopes and Labels Dialog Box with the Envelopes Tab Selected

When addressing envelopes, consider following general guidelines issued by the United States Postal Service (USPS). The USPS guidelines suggest using all capital letters with no commas or periods for return and delivery addresses. Figure 6.8 shows envelope addresses that follow the USPS guidelines. Use abbreviations for street suffixes (such as *ST* for *Street* and *AVE* for *Avenue*). For a complete list of address abbreviations, visit the USPS.com website and then search for *Official USPS Abbreviations*.

Activity 3a Printing an Envelope

1. At a blank document, create an envelope document with the delivery address and return address shown in Figure 6.8. Begin by clicking the Mailings tab.
2. Click the Envelopes button in the Create group.
3. At the Envelopes and Labels dialog box with the Envelopes tab selected, type the delivery address shown in Figure 6.8 (the one containing the name *GREGORY LINCOLN*). (Press the Enter key to end each line in the name and address.)
4. Click in the *Return address* text box. (If any text displays in the *Return address* text box, select and then delete it.)
5. Type the return address shown in Figure 6.8 (the one containing the name *WENDY STEINBERG*). (Press the Enter key to end each line in the name and address.)
6. Click the Add to Document button.
7. At the message *Do you want to save the new return address as the default return address?*, click No.
8. Save the document and name it **6-Env**.
9. Print and then close **6-Env**. *Note: Manual feed of the envelope may be required. Please check with your instructor.*

Check Your Work

Figure 6.8 Activity 3a

WENDY STEINBERG
4532 S 52 ST
BOSTON MA 21002-2334

GREGORY LINCOLN
4455 SIXTH AVE
BOSTON MA 21100-4409

After typing a letter in Word, prepare an envelope to mail the letter by clicking the Envelopes button. Word automatically inserts the first address in the document in the *Delivery address* text box. (Note: Each line of the address must end with a press of the Enter key, and not Shift + Enter, for Word to recognize it.)

Alternately, select the delivery address in the letter document and then click the Envelopes button. When using this method, the address will be formatted exactly as it appears in the letter and may not conform to the USPS guidelines; however, these guidelines are only suggestions, not requirements.

Activity 3b Creating an Envelope in an Existing Document

Part 2 of 2

1. Open **LAProgram**.
2. Click the Mailings tab.
3. Click the Envelopes button in the Create group.
4. At the Envelopes and Labels dialog box (with the Envelopes tab selected), make sure the delivery address appears properly in the *Delivery address* text box.
5. If any text appears in the *Return address* text box, insert a check mark in the *Omit* check box (located to the right of the *Return address* option). (This tells Word not to print the return address on the envelope.)
6. Click the Print button.
7. Close **LAProgram** without saving the changes.

Envelopes and Labels

Envelopes Labels

Delivery address:

Mr. and Mrs. Matthew Adair
12201 North 21st Street
Jennings, LA 70563

☐ Add electronic postage

Return address: ☐ Omit

Verify that an envelope is loaded before printing.

Print   Add to Document

> Check Your Work

Activity 4 Prepare and Print Labels

2 Parts

You will create mailing labels containing different names and addresses, labels with the same name and address, and labels with an image.

Preparing and Printing Labels

Use Word's Labels feature to print text on mailing labels, file folder labels, and other types of labels. Word formats text for a variety of brands and sizes of labels that can be purchased at most office supply stores. Use the Labels feature to create a sheet of mailing labels with a different name and address on each label or with the same name and address or image on each label.

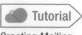 Tutorial

Creating Mailing
Labels with
Different Names
and Addresses

 Labels

Creating Mailing Labels with Different Names and Addresses

To create a sheet of mailing labels with a different name and address on each label, click the Labels button in the Create group on the Mailings tab. At the Envelopes and Labels dialog box with the Labels tab selected, as shown in Figure 6.9, leave the *Address* text box empty and then click the New Document button to insert the labels in a new document. The insertion point is positioned in the first label. Type the name and address in the label and then press the Tab key one or two times (depending on the label) to move the insertion point to the next label. Pressing Shift + Tab will move the insertion point to the preceding label.

Changing Label Options

Click the Options button at the Envelopes and Labels dialog box with the Labels tab selected and the Label Options dialog box displays, as shown in Figure 6.10. At the Label Options dialog box, choose the type of printer, the type and brand of label, and the product number. This dialog box also provides information about the selected label, such as type, height, width, and paper size. When a label is selected, Word automatically determines the label margins. To customize these default settings, click the Details button at the Label Options dialog box.

Figure 6.9 Envelopes and Labels Dialog Box with the Labels Tab Selected

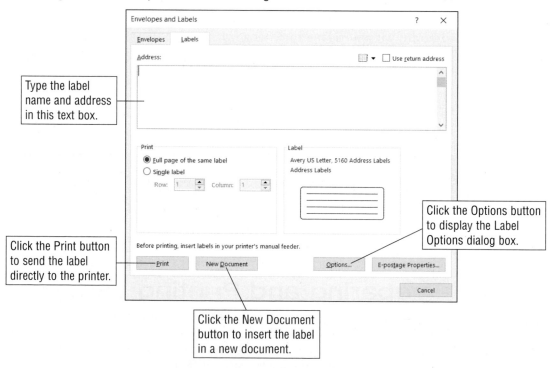

Type the label name and address in this text box.

Click the Print button to send the label directly to the printer.

Click the New Document button to insert the label in a new document.

Click the Options button to display the Label Options dialog box.

Figure 6.10 Label Options Dialog Box

Choose the label product number from this list box.

Click the *Label vendors* option box arrow to display a list of available label vendors.

Activity 4a Creating Mailing Labels with Different Names and Addresses

1. At a blank document, click the Mailings tab.
2. Click the Labels button in the Create group.
3. At the Envelopes and Labels dialog box with the Labels tab selected, click the Options button.
4. At the Label Options dialog box, click the *Label vendors* option box arrow and then click *Avery US Letter* at the drop-down list. (You may need to scroll down the list to see this option.)
5. Scroll down the *Product number* list box and then click *5160 Address Labels*.
6. Click OK or press the Enter key.
7. At the Envelopes and Labels dialog box, click the New Document button.
8. At the document screen, type the first name and address shown in Figure 6.11 in the first label.
9. Press the Tab key two times to move the insertion point to the next label and then type the second name and address shown in Figure 6.11.
10. Continue in this manner until all the names and addresses shown in Figure 6.11 have been typed. (After typing the third name and address, you only need to press the Tab key once to move the insertion point to the first label in the second row.)
11. Save the document and name it **6-Labels**.
12. Print and then close **6-Labels**.
13. Close the blank document without saving changes.

Check Your Work

Figure 6.11 Activity 4a

DAVID LOWRY	MARCELLA SANTOS	KEVIN DORSEY
12033 S 152 ST	394 APPLE BLOSSOM DR	26302 PRAIRIE DR
HOUSTON TX 77340	FRIENDSWOOD TX 77533	HOUSTON TX 77316
AL AND DONNA SASAKI	JACKIE RHYNER	MARK AND TINA ELLIS
1392 PIONEER DR	29039 107 AVE E	607 FORD AVE
BAYTOWN TX 77903	HOUSTON TX 77302	HOUSTON TX 77307

Tutorial

Creating Mailing
Labels with the
Same Name and
Address and an
Image

Creating Mailing Labels with the Same Name and Address

To create labels with the same name and address on each label, open a document containing the name and address, click the Mailings tab, and then click the Labels button. At the Envelopes and Labels dialog box, make sure the desired label vendor and product number are selected and then click the New Document button. Another method for creating labels with the same name and address is to display the Envelopes and Labels dialog box with the Labels tab selected, type the name and address in the *Address* text box, and then click the New Document button.

Creating Mailing Labels with an Image

Labels can be created with a graphic image, such as a company's logo and address and/or slogan. To create labels with an image, insert the image in a document, select the image, click the Mailings tab. and then click the Labels button. At the Envelopes and Labels dialog box, make sure the correct vendor and product number are selected and then click the New Document button.

Activity 4b Creating Mailing Labels with the Same Name and Address and an Image   Part 2 of 2

1. Open **LAProgram** and create mailing labels with the delivery address. Begin by clicking the Mailings tab.
2. Click the Labels button in the Create group.
3. At the Envelopes and Labels dialog box with the Labels tab selected, make sure the delivery address is shown properly in the *Address* text box, as shown at the right.
4. Make sure *Avery US Letter, 5160 Address Labels* displays in the *Label* section; if not, refer to Steps 3 through 6 of Activity 4a to select the label type.
5. Click the New Document button.
6. Save the mailing label document and name it **6-LAProgram**.
7. Print and then close **6-LAProgram**.
8. Close **LAProgram**.
9. At a blank document, insert an image by completing the following steps:
   a. Click the Insert tab and then click the Pictures button in the Illustrations group.
   b. At the Insert Picture dialog box, make sure your WL1C6 folder is active and then double-click the **BGCLabels** image file.
10. With the image selected in the document, click the Mailings tab and then click the Labels button.
11. At the Envelopes and Labels dialog box, make sure *Avery US Letter, 5160 Address Labels* displays in the *Label* section and then click the New Document button.
12. Save the document and name it **6-BGCLabels**.
13. Print and then close **6-BGCLabels**.
14. Close the document containing the image without saving changes.

Check Your Work

Activity 5 **Create a Business Letter Using a Template** **1 Part**

You will use a letter template provided by Word to create a business letter.

 Tutorial

Creating a
Document Using a
Template

Creating a Document Using a Template

Word includes a number of document templates that are formatted for specific uses. Each Word document is based on a template document and the Normal template is the default. Choose from other available Word templates to create a variety of documents with special formatting, such as letters, calendars, and certificates.

View available templates by clicking the File tab and then clicking the *New* option. Thumbnails of various templates display in the New backstage area, as shown in Figure 6.12. Open one of the templates by double-clicking it. This opens a new document based on the template.

In addition to the templates that are shown at the New backstage area, templates can be downloaded from the internet. To do this, click in the search text box, type the search text or category, and then press the Enter key. Templates that match the search text or category display in the New backstage area. Click the template and then click the Create button or double-click the template. This downloads the template and opens a document based on it. Placeholders or content controls may appear in the document as suggested locations for personalized text. Click the placeholder or content control and then type text to personalize the document.

If a template is used on a regular basis, consider pinning it to the New backstage area. To do this, search for the template, hover the mouse pointer over it, and then click the left-pointing push pin (Pin to list) to the right of the template name. To unpin a template, click the down-pointing push pin (Unpin from list).

Quick Steps

Create Document Using Template
1. Click File tab.
2. Click *New* option.
3. Click template.
OR
1. Click File tab.
2. Click *New* option.
3. Click in search text box.
4. Type search text.
5. Press Enter.
6. Double-click template.

Figure 6.12 New Backstage Area

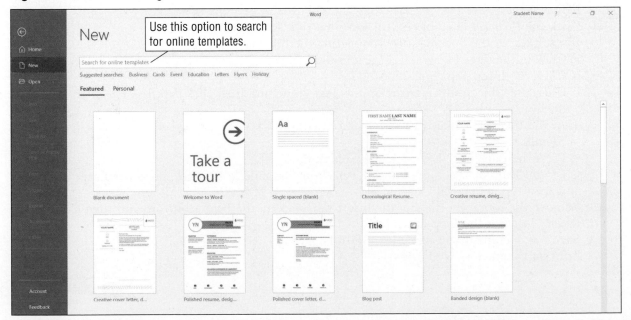

1. Click the File tab and then click the *New* option.
2. At the New backstage area, click in the search text box, type letter, and then press the Enter key.
3. When templates display that match *letter*, notice the *Category* list box at the right side of the New backstage area.
4. Click the *Business* option in the *Category* list box. (This displays only business letter templates.)
5. Search for a specific letter template by typing business letter simple design in the search text box and then pressing the Enter key.
6. Double-click the *Business letter (simple design)* template. (If this template is not available, open **BusinessLetter** from your WL1C6 folder.)

7. When the business letter document displays on the screen, click the *Company Name* content control and then type Sorenson Funds. (Clicking anywhere in the *Company Name* content control selects the entire control.)
8. Click the *Date* content control and then type the current date.
9. Click the *Street Address City, ST ZIP Code* content control. Type Ms. Jennifer Gonzalez, press the Enter key, type 12990 Boyd Street, press the Enter key, and then type Baltimore, MD 20375.
10. Click the *Recipient* content control and then type Ms. Gonzalez.
11. Insert a file in the document by completing the following steps:
    a. Click in the three paragraphs of text in the body of the letter and then press the Delete key.
    b. Click the Insert tab.
    c. Click the Object button arrow in the Text group and then click *Text from File* at the drop-down list.
    d. At the Insert File dialog box, navigate to your WL1C6 folder and then double-click **SFunds**.
    e. Press the Backspace key to delete a blank line.
12. Click the *Your Name* content control, type your first and last names, press the Enter key, and then type Financial Consultant.
13. Remove the footer by clicking the Insert tab, clicking the Footer button, and then clicking *Remove Footer* at the drop-down list.
14. Save the document and name it **6-SFunds**.
15. Print and then close **6-SFunds**.

> **Check Your Work**

Activity 6 Save Documents in Different File Formats　　　　　2 Parts

You will save an apartment lease agreement document in different file formats, including Word 97-2003 and plain text. You will also save a company document as a PDF file and then edit the file in Word.

Tutorial

Saving in a
Different Format

Quick Steps

Save in Different
Format at Save As
Dialog Box
1. Press F12 to display
   Save As dialog box.
2. Type document
   name.
3. Click *Save as type*
   option box.
4. Click format.
5. Click Save button.

Saving in a Different Format

When a document is saved, it is saved as a Word document with the file extension *.docx*. If the document is to be shared with someone who is using a different word processing program or a different version of Word, consider saving the document in another format. Save a document in a different file format by clicking the File tab and then clicking the *Export* option. At the Export backstage area, click the *Change File Type* option. Available file types display as shown in Figure 6.13. Save the Word document with the default file format, in a previous version of Word, in the OpenDocument Text format, or as a template. The OpenDocument Text format is an XML-based file format free from licensing and restrictions. It was designed to make word processing, spreadsheet, and presentation files easier to share across applications.

If a document is being sent to a user who does not have access to Microsoft Word, consider saving the document in plain text or rich text file format. Use the *Plain Text* option to save the document with all the formatting stripped, which is good for universal file exchange. Use the *Rich Text Format* option to save the document and preserve most of the formatting, including bold, italic, underline, bullets, and fonts. With the *Single File Web Page* option, a document can be saved as a single page web document. Double-click the *Save as Another File Type* option and the Save As dialog box opens. Use the *Save as type* option box to specify the file format.

In addition to displaying the Save As dialog box through the Export backstage area, the dialog box can be displayed by clicking the File tab, clicking the *Save As* option, and then clicking the *Browse* option. (Pressing the F12 function key will also display the Save As dialog box.) Click the *Save as type* option box at the Save As dialog box and a drop-down list displays containing all the available file formats for saving a document. Click the specific format and then click the Save button.

Figure 6.13 Export Backstage Area with the *Change File Type* Option Selected

Click the *Change File Type* option to display options for saving a file in a different format.

Click the file type and then click the Save As button.

Activity 6a Saving in Different File Formats

1. Open **AptLease** and then save it in Word 97-2003 format by completing the following steps:
   a. Click the File tab and then click the *Export* option.
   b. At the Export backstage area, click the *Change File Type* option.
   c. Click the *Word 97-2003 Document* option in the *Document File Types* section.
   d. Click the Save As button.

e. At the Save As dialog box with the *Save as type* option changed to *Word 97-2003 Document*, type 6-AptLease-Word97-2003 in the *File name* text box and then press the Enter key.

1e

2. At the document, notice *Compatibility Mode* after the document name.
3. Click the Design tab and notice that the Themes, Colors, and Fonts buttons are dimmed. (This is because the themes features were not available in Word 97 through 2003.)
4. Close **6-AptLease-Word97-2003**.
5. Open **AptLease**.
6. Save the document in plain text format at the Save As dialog box by completing the following steps:
   a. Press the F12 function key to display the Save As dialog box.
   b. At the Save As dialog box, type 6-AptLease-PlainTxt in the *File name* text box.
   c. Click the *Save as type* option box.
   d. Click *Plain Text* at the drop-down list.
   e. Click the Save button.
   f. At the File Conversion dialog box, click OK.

6c

6d

7. Close **6-AptLease-PlainTxt**.
8. Display the Open dialog box and, if necessary, display all the files. To do this, click the file type button at the right of the *File name* text box and then click *All Files* at the drop-down list.

8

9. Double-click **6-AptLease-PlainTxt**. At the File Conversion dialog box, click OK. (Notice that the formatting has been removed from the document.)
10. Close **6-AptLease-PlainTxt**.

Check Your Work

Tutorial

Saving and Opening a Document as a PDF File

Quick Steps

Save in PDF/XPS Format
1. Click File tab.
2. Click *Export* option.
3. Click Create PDF/XPS button.
4. At Publish as PDF or XPS dialog box, specify PDF or XPS format.
5. Click Publish button.

A Word document can be saved as a PDF file or in the XPS file format. PDF stands for *portable document format* and is a file format that preserves fonts, formatting, and images in a printer-friendly version that looks the same on most computers. A person who receives a Word file saved as a PDF file does not need to have the Word application on his or her computer to open, read, and print the file. Exchanging PDF files is a popular method for collaborating, since this file type has cross-platform compatibility, allowing users to open PDF files on both Macintosh and Windows-based computers, as well as different brands of tablets and smartphones. The XML paper specification (XPS) format, which was developed by Microsoft, is a fixed-layout format with all the formatting preserved (similar to PDF).

To save a document as a PDF file or in XPS format, click the File tab, click the *Export* option, and then click the Create PDF/XPS button. This displays the Publish as PDF or XPS dialog box with the *PDF* option selected in the *Save as type* option box. To save the document in XPS format, click the *Save as type* option box and then click *XPS Document* at the drop-down list. At the Save As dialog box, type a name in the *File name* text box and then click the Publish button.

A PDF file will open in Adobe Acrobat Reader, Microsoft Edge, and Word. (A PDF file may also open in other available web browsers such as Google Chrome.) An XPS file will open in Internet Explorer and XPS Viewer. One method for opening a PDF or XPS file is to open File Explorer, navigate to the folder containing the file, right-click the file, and then point to *Open with*. This displays a side menu with the programs that can be used to open the file. A PDF file can be opened and edited in Word but an XPS file cannot.

Activity 6b Saving as a PDF File and Editing a PDF File in Word   Part 2 of 2

1. Open **NSS** and then save the document as a PDF file by completing the following steps:
   a. Click the File tab and then click the *Export* option.
   b. At the Export backstage area, click the Create PDF/XPS button.
   c. At the Publish as PDF or XPS dialog box, make sure that *PDF* is selected in the *Save as type* option box and that the *Open file after publishing* check box contains a check mark. After confirming both selections, click the Publish button.

2. Scroll through the document in Adobe Acrobat Reader and then close Adobe Acrobat Reader by clicking the Close button in the upper right corner of the window.
3. Close **NSS**.
4. In Word, open the **NSS** PDF file you saved to your WL1C6 folder. At the message telling you that Word will convert the file to an editable Word document, click OK.
5. Notice that the formatting of the text is slightly different from the original formatting and that the graphic has been moved to the second page. Edit the file by completing the following steps:
   a. Click the Design tab and then click the *Lines (Distinctive)* style set.
   b. Delete the text *We are* in the text below the first heading and replace it with Northland Security Systems is.
6. Save the file with Save As and name it **6-NSS**. (The file will be saved as a Word file.)
7. Print and then close **6-NSS**.
8. Make a screen capture of the Open dialog box and then paste it in a Word document and print the document by completing the following steps:
   a. Display the Open dialog box.
   b. Press and hold down the Alt key, press the Print Screen button on your keyboard, and then release the Alt key.
   c. Close the Open dialog box and close the Open backstage area.
   d. Press Ctrl + N to open a blank document.
   e. Click the Paste button.
   f. Print the document by pressing Ctrl + P and then clicking the Print button.
9. Close the document without saving it

Check Your Work

Activity 7 Save and Open a Document Based on a Template   2 Parts

You will open a summons document, save it as a template, use it to create a summons, and then find and replace text within the document. You will also save the summons document as a template in your WL1C6 folder and then use File Explorer to locate the template and open a new document based on it.

Tutorial

Saving and Using
a Template

Saving a Template

If the content of a document will be used in many other documents, consider saving the document as a template. Save a template by changing the *Save as type* option at the Save As dialog box to *Word Template*.

Saving a Template in the Custom Office Templates Folder

When the *Save as type* option is changed to a Word template, Word will save the document as a template in the Custom Office Templates folder. To use the template, click the New tab and then click the *Personal* option. This displays all custom templates. Clicking a template will open a new document based on that template.

Activity 7a Saving and Opening a Document Based on a Template   Part 1 of 2

1. Open **Summons** and then save it as a template in the Custom Office Templates folder by completing the following steps:
   a. Press the F12 function key to display the Save As dialog box.
   b. At the Save As dialog box, click the *Save as type* option box and then click *Word Template* at the drop-down list. (When the *Save as type* option is changed to *Word Template*, Word automatically makes Custom Office Templates the active folder.)
   c. Select the name in the *File name* text box, type your last name followed by Summons, and then press the Enter key.

2. Close the summons template.

3. Open a document based on the summons template by completing the following steps:
   a. Click the File tab and then click the *New* option.
   b. At the New backstage area, click the *Personal* option.
   c. Click the summons template that is preceded by your last name.

4. With the summons document open, find and replace text as follows:
   a. Find *NAME1* and replace all occurrences with *AMY GARCIA*.
   b. Find *NAME2* and replace all occurrences with *NEIL CARLIN*.
   c. Find *NUMBER* and replace with *C-98002*.
5. Save the document in your WL1C6 folder and name it **6-SummonsGarcia**.
6. Print and then close **6-SummonsGarcia**.
7. Delete the summons template from the hard drive by completing the following steps:
   a. Press Ctrl + F12 to display the Open dialog box.
   b. At the Open dialog box, click the *Documents* folder in the Navigation pane.
   c. Double-click the **Custom Office Templates** folder in the Content pane.
   d. Click the summons template that begins with your last name.
   e. Click the Organize button and then click *Delete* at the drop-down list.

8. Close the Open dialog box.

Check Your Work

Opening a Template Using File Explorer

In Word, opening a document based on a template is accomplished through the New backstage area with the *Personal* option selected. If a template is saved in a location other than the Custom Office Templates folder, File Explorer can be used to open a document based on the template. To do this, click the File Explorer icon on the taskbar, navigate to the folder containing the template, and then double-click the template. This will open a new document based on the template.

1. Open **Summons** and then save it as a template in your WL1C6 folder by completing the following steps:
   a. Click the File tab and then click the *Export* option.
   b. At the Export backstage area, click the *Change File Type* option.
   c. Click the *Template* option in the *Document File Types* section.
   d. Click the Save As button.

   e. At the Save As dialog box with *Word Template* in the *Save as type* option box, type 6-SummonsTemplate in the *File name* text box.
   f. Navigate to your WL1C6 folder and then click the Save button.
2. Close the summons template.
3. Open a document based on the summons template using File Explorer by completing the following steps:
   a. Click the File Explorer icon on the taskbar. (The taskbar displays along the bottom of the screen.)
   b. Navigate to your WL1C6 folder and then double-click *6-SummonsTemplate*.
4. With the summons document open, find and replace text as follows:
   a. Find *NAME1* and replace all occurrences with *CASEY NYE*.
   b. Find *NAME2* and replace all occurrences with *SANDRA IVERS*.
   c. Find *NUMBER* and replace with *C-99743*.
5. Save the document in your WL1C6 folder and name it **6-SummonsNye**.
6. Print and then close **6-SummonsNye**.

 Check Your Work

Chapter Summary

- Change the document view with buttons in the view area on the Status bar or with options in the Views group on the View tab.

- Print Layout is the default view but this can be changed to other views, such as Draft view, Web Layout view and Read Mode view.

- Draft view displays the document in a format for efficient editing and formatting. Change to Web Layout view to display a document as it would appear online. Read Mode view displays a document in a format for easy viewing and reading.

- The File, Tools, and View tabs display in Read Mode view. Click the File tab to display the Backstage area, the Tools tab to display a drop-down list of options for finding and searching for specific text in a document or the internet, and the View tab for changing column width and page layout, reading text in the document, and customizing reading.

- In addition to Read Mode view, options for reading a document are available on the Immersive Learning Tools tab. Display this tab by clicking the Learning Tools button in the Immersive group on the View tab. Use buttons on the Immersive Learning Tools tab to change column width, page color, focus, text spacing, and display syllable breaks in words. Click the Read Aloud button to hear a reading of the document and to control the reading with buttons on the playback toolbar.

- Use the Side to Side button in the Page Movement group on the View tab to change page movement in a document from the default of vertical to side to side, where two pages are shown at one time. On a screen without touch screen capabilities, scroll through the side to side pages using the horizontal scroll bar or the mouse wheel. Click the Vertical button on the View tab to return to the default page movement.

- Use the Zoom slider bar or buttons in the Zoom group on the View tab to change the display percentage.

- Use options at the Ribbon Display Options button drop-down list to specify if the Quick Access Toolbar, ribbon, and Status bar should be visible or hidden.

- Save space on the screen by hiding white space at the top and bottom of pages. Hide white space using the Hide White Space icon, which appears when the mouse pointer is positioned at the top or bottom edge of a page. Redisplay white space using the Show White Space icon, which appears when the mouse pointer is positioned on the thin gray line separating pages.

- Move among open documents by hovering the mouse pointer over the Word button on the taskbar and then clicking the thumbnail of the document or by clicking the View tab, clicking the Switch Windows button in the Window group, and then clicking the document name.

- View portions of all open documents by clicking the View tab and then clicking the Arrange All button in the Window group.

- Use the Minimize, Restore, and Maximize buttons in the upper right corner of the active window to reduce or increase the size of the window.

- Divide a window into two panes by clicking the View tab and then clicking the Split button in the Window group.

- View the contents of two open documents side by side by clicking the View tab and then clicking the View Side by Side button in the Window group.

- Open a new window containing the same document by clicking the View tab and then clicking the New Window button in the Window group.

- Insert a document into the open document by clicking the Insert tab, clicking the Object button arrow, and then clicking *Text from File* at the drop-down list. At the Insert File dialog box, double-click the document.

- Preview a document at the Print backstage area. Scroll through the pages in the document with the Next Page and the Previous Page buttons, which are below the preview page. Use the Zoom slider bar to increase or decrease the display size of the preview page.

- Use options at the Print backstage area to customize the print job by changing the page orientation, size, and margins; specify how many pages to print on one page; indicate the number of copies and whether to collate the pages; and specify the printer.

- Prepare and print an envelope at the Envelopes and Labels dialog box with the Envelopes tab selected.

- If the Envelopes and Labels dialog box is opened in a document containing a name and address (with each line ending with a press of the Enter key), that information is automatically inserted in the *Delivery address* text box in the dialog box.

- Use Word's labels feature to print text on mailing labels, file labels, and other types of labels. Create labels at the Envelopes and Labels dialog box with the Labels tab selected.

- Available templates are shown in the New backstage area. Double-click a template to open a document based on it. Search for templates online by typing the search text or category in the search text box and then pressing the Enter key.

- Click the *Change File Type* option at the Export backstage area and options display for saving the document in a different file format. Documents can also be saved in different file formats with the *Save as type* option box at the Save As dialog box.

- Save a document as a PDF file or in XPS format at the Publish as PDF or XPS dialog box. Display this dialog box by clicking the *Create PDF/XPS Document* option at the Export backstage area and then clicking the Create PDF/XPS button. A PDF file can be opened and edited in Word.

- Change the *Save as type* option at the Save As dialog box to *Word Template* and the Custom Office Templates folder becomes the active folder. A template saved in this folder is available at the New backstage area with the *Personal* option selected. Open a document based on a template at the New backstage area with the *Personal* option selected.

- If a template is saved in a location other than the Custom Office Templates folder, File Explorer can be used to open a document based on the template.

Commands Review

FEATURE	RIBBON TAB, GROUP/OPTION	BUTTON, OPTION	KEYBOARD SHORTCUT
arrange documents	View, Window		
Draft view	View, Views		
Envelopes and Labels dialog box with Envelopes tab selected	Mailings, Create		
Envelopes and Labels dialog box with Labels tab selected	Mailings, Create		
Export backstage area	File, *Export*		
Insert File dialog box	Insert, Text	, *Text from File*	
learning tools	View, Immersive		
maximize document			Ctrl + F10
minimize document			
New backstage area	File, *New*		
new window	View, Window		
Print backstage area	File, *Print*		Ctrl + P
Read Mode view	View, Views		
restore document to previous size			
side to side page movement	View, Page Movement		
split window	View, Window		Alt + Ctrl + S
switch windows	View, Window		
synchronous scrolling	View, Window		
vertical page movement	View, Page Movement		
view documents side by side	View, Window		
Web Layout view	View, Views		

Microsoft®

Word

Creating Tables

Performance Objectives

Upon successful completion of Chapter 7, you will be able to:

1 Create a table

2 Change the table design

3 Select cells in a table

4 Change the table layout

5 Convert text to a table and a table to text

6 Draw a table

7 Insert a Quick Table

8 Perform calculations on data in a table

9 Insert an Excel spreadsheet

Use the Tables feature in Word to organize data in tables with any number of columns and rows. The data can consist of text, values, and/or mathematical formulas. Presenting information in a table can show patterns and relationships and help with data comprehension.

This chapter will introduce the steps for creating a table in Word using the Table button drop-down grid and options at the Insert Table dialog box. You will also learn to draw a table in a document and apply formatting to tables using buttons and options on the Table Tools Design and Table Tools Layout tabs. Finally, you will learn to perform calculations in a table and practice inserting an Excel spreadsheet into a Word document to display text and numerical data.

Data Files

Before beginning chapter work, copy the WL1C7 folder to your storage medium and then make WL1C7 the active folder.

The online course includes additional training and assessment resources.

You will create a table containing contact information and another containing information on employee benefit plans offered by a company. You will then change the design and layout of each table.

Tutorial

Creating a Table

Table

Quick Steps

Create Table
1. Click Insert tab.
2. Click Table button.
3. Point to create number of columns and rows.
4. Click mouse button.
OR
1. Click Insert tab.
2. Click Table button.
3. Click *Insert Table*.
4. Specify number of columns and rows.
5. Click OK.

Hint You can create a table within a table, creating a *nested* table.

Creating a Table

Tables are grids containing boxes of information called *cells*. Each cell is the intersection between a row and a column. A cell can contain text, characters, numbers, data, graphics, or formulas. Insert a table into a document by clicking the Insert tab, and then clicking the Table button in the Tables group. Move the mouse pointer down and to the right in the drop-down grid to select the number of rows and columns to include in the table. A table can also be created with options at the Insert Table dialog box. Display this dialog box by clicking the Table button in the Tables group on the Insert tab and then clicking *Insert Table* at the drop-down list.

Figure 7.1 shows an example of a table with four columns and four rows. Various parts of the table are identified in the figure. These include the gridlines, move table column markers, table move handle, and resize handle. In a table, nonprinting characters identify the ends of cells and the ends of rows. To view these characters, click the Show/Hide ¶ button in the Paragraph group on the Home tab. The end-of-cell marker appears inside each cell and the end-of-row marker appears at the end of each row of cells. These markers are identified in Figure 7.1.

Columns in a table are generally referred to using the letters A-Z while rows are numbered. When a table is inserted in a document, the insertion point is positioned in the first cell in the upper left corner of the table. This is referred to as cell A1, as it is located in column A, row 1. Cell B1 is to the right of A1, and cell A2 is directly below it.

When the insertion point is positioned in a cell in the table, move table column markers display on the horizontal ruler. These markers represent the ends of columns and can be moved to change the widths of columns. Figure 7.1 identifies move table column markers.

Figure 7.1 Table with Nonprinting Characters Displayed

Entering Text in Cells

Hint Pressing the Tab key in a table moves the insertion point to the next cell. Pressing Ctrl + Tab moves the insertion point to the next tab within a cell.

With the insertion point positioned in a cell, type or edit text. Point and click with the mouse to move the insertion point from cell to cell, or press the Tab key to move to the next cell and Shift + Tab to move to the preceding cell.

Text typed in a cell automatically wraps to the next line to fit the width of the column. The Enter key can also be pressed to move to the next line within a cell. The cell expands vertically to accommodate the text, and all cells in that row also expand. Pressing the Tab key in a table causes the insertion point to move to the next cell in the table. To move the insertion point to a tab within a cell, press Ctrl + Tab. If the insertion point is in the last cell of the table, pressing the Tab key adds another row to the table. Insert a page break within a table by pressing Ctrl + Enter. The page break is inserted between rows, not within a row.

Moving the Insertion Point within a Table

To use the mouse to move the insertion point to a different cell within the table, click in the specific cell. To use the keyboard to move the insertion point to a different cell within the table, refer to the information shown in Table 7.1.

Table 7.1 Insertion Point Movement within a Table Using the Keyboard

To move the insertion point	Press
to next cell	Tab
to preceding cell	Shift + Tab
forward one character	Right Arrow key
backward one character	Left Arrow key
to previous row	Up Arrow key
to next row	Down Arrow key
to first cell in row	Alt + Home
to last cell in row	Alt + End
to top cell in column	Alt + Page Up
to bottom cell in column	Alt + Page Down

1. At a blank document, turn on bold formatting and then type the title CONTACT INFORMATION, as shown in Figure 7.2.
2. Turn off bold formatting and then press the Enter key.
3. Create the table shown in Figure 7.2 by completing the following steps:
   a. Click the Insert tab.
   b. Click the Table button in the Tables group.
   c. Move the mouse pointer down and to the right in the drop-down grid until the label above the grid displays as *3x5 Table* and then click the left mouse button.

4. Type the text in the cells as indicated in Figure 7.2. Press the Tab key to move to the next cell and press Shift + Tab to move to the preceding cell. (If you accidentally press the Enter key within a cell, immediately press the Backspace key. Do not press the Tab key after typing the text in the last cell. If you do, another row is inserted in the table. If this happens, immediately click the Undo button on the Quick Access Toolbar.)
5. Save the table and name it **7-Tables**.

Check Your Work

Figure 7.2 Activity 1a

CONTACT INFORMATION

Maggie Rivera	First Trust Bank	(203) 555-3440
Les Cromwell	Madison Trust	(602) 555-4900
Cecilia Nordyke	American Financial	(509) 555-3995
Regina Stahl	United Fidelity	(301) 555-1201
Justin White	Key One Savings	(360) 555-8963

Using the Insert Table Dialog Box

A table can also be created with options at the Insert Table dialog box, shown in Figure 7.3. To display this dialog box, click the Insert tab, click the Table button in the Tables group, and then click *Insert Table*. At the Insert Table dialog box, enter the number of columns and rows and then click OK.

Figure 7.3 Insert Table Dialog Box

Use these measurement boxes to specify the numbers of columns and rows.

Activity 1b Creating a Table with the Insert Table Dialog Box

Part 2 of 8

1. With **7-Tables** open, press Ctrl + End to move the insertion point below the table.
2. Press the Enter key two times.
3. Turn on bold formatting and then type the title OPTIONAL PLAN PREMIUM RATES, as shown in Figure 7.4.
4. Turn off bold formatting and then press the Enter key.
5. Click the Insert tab, click the Table button in the Tables group, and then click *Insert Table* at the drop-down list.
6. At the Insert Table dialog box, type 3 in the *Number of columns* measurement box. (The insertion point is automatically positioned in this measurement box.)
7. Press the Tab key (this moves the insertion point to the *Number of rows* measurement box) and then type 5.
8. Click OK.
9. Type the text in the cells as indicated in Figure 7.4. Press the Tab key to move to the next cell and press Shift + Tab to move to the preceding cell. To indent the text in cells B2 through B5 and cells C2 through C5, press Ctrl + Tab to move the insertion point to a tab within a cell and then type the text.
10. Save **7-Tables**.

Check Your Work

Figure 7.4 Activity 1b

OPTIONAL PLAN PREMIUM RATES

Waiting Period	Basic Plan Employees	Plan 2021 Employees
60 days	0.67%	0.79%
90 days	0.49%	0.59%
120 days	0.30%	0.35%
180 days	0.23%	0.26%

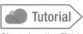

Tutorial

Changing the Table Design

Changing the Table Design

When a table is inserted in a document, the Table Tools Design tab is active. This tab contains a number of options for enhancing the appearance of the table, as shown in Figure 7.5. With options in the Table Styles group, apply a predesigned style that adds color and border lines to a table and shading to cells. Customize the formatting with options in the Table Style Options group. For example, click the *Total Row* check box to insert a total row in the table. Apply a predesigned table style with options in the Table Styles group.

Border Styles

Border Painter

Use options in the Borders group to change the look of cell borders in a table. Click the Border Styles button to display a drop-down list of available styles. Use other buttons in the Borders group to change the line style, width, and color and to add or remove borders. Apply the same border style to other cells with the Border Painter button.

Figure 7.5 Table Tools Design Tab

Activity 1c Applying Table Styles

1. With **7-Tables** open, click in any cell in the top table.
2. Apply a table style by completing the following steps:
   a. Make sure the Table Tools Design tab is active.
   b. Click the More Table Styles button in the table styles gallery in the Table Styles group.
   c. Click the *Grid Table 5 Dark - Accent 5* table style (sixth column, fifth row in the *Grid Tables* section).

3. After looking at the table, you realize that the first row is not a header row and the first column should not be formatted differently from the other columns. To format the first row and the first column in the same manner as the other rows and columns, click the *Header Row* check box and the *First Column* check box in the Table Style Options group to remove the check marks.

4. Click in any cell in the bottom table and then apply the List Table 6 Colorful - Accent 5 table style (sixth column, sixth row in the *List Tables* section).

5. Add color borders to the top table by completing the following steps:
   a. Click in any cell in the top table.
   b. Click the Pen Color button arrow in the Borders group on the Table Tools Design tab and then click the *Orange, Accent 2, Darker 50%* color option (sixth column, last row in the *Theme Colors* section).
   c. Click the *Line Weight* option box arrow in the Borders group and then click *1 ½ pt* in the drop-down list. (When you choose a line weight, the Border Painter button is automatically activated.)

   d. Using the mouse (the mouse pointer appears as a pen), drag along all four sides of the table. (As you drag with the mouse, a thick brown line is inserted. If you make a mistake or the line does not appear as you intended, click the Undo button and then continue drawing along each side of the table.)

6. Click the Border Styles button arrow and then click the *Double solid lines, 1/2 pt, Accent 2* option (third column, third row in the *Theme Borders* section).

7. Drag along all four sides of the bottom table.
8. Click the Border Painter button to turn off the feature.
9. Save **7-Tables**.

Check Your Work

Selecting Cells

Data within a table can be formatted in several ways. For example, the alignment of text within cells or rows can be changed, rows or columns can be moved or copied, and character formatting, such as bold, italic, and underlining, can be applied to text. To make changes to a cell, row, or column, first select the cells.

Selecting in a Table with the Mouse

Use the mouse pointer to select a cell, row, or column or to select an entire table. Table 7.2 describes methods for selecting in a table with the mouse. To select a cell, position the mouse pointer in the *cell selection bar*, an invisible strip just inside the left edge of a cell. The pointer turns into a small black arrow pointing up and to the right. Click to select the cell. Each row in a table contains a *row selection bar*, which is the space just outside the left edge of the table. Position the mouse pointer in the row selection bar and the mouse pointer turns into a white arrow that points up and to the right. Click to select the row.

Table 7.2 Selecting in a Table with the Mouse

To select this	Do this
cell	Position the mouse pointer in the cell selection bar at the left edge of the cell until it turns into a small black arrow that points up and to the right and then click the left mouse button.
row	Position the mouse pointer in the row selection bar at the left edge of the table until it turns into an arrow that points up and to the right and then click the left mouse button.
column	Position the mouse pointer on the uppermost horizontal gridline of the table in the appropriate column until it turns into a small black arrow that points down and then click the left mouse button.
adjacent cells	Position the mouse pointer in the first cell to be selected, click and hold down the left mouse button, drag the mouse pointer to the last cell to be selected, and then release the mouse button.
all cells in a table	Click the table move handle or position the mouse pointer in the row selection bar for the first row at the left edge of the table until it turns into an arrow that points up and to the right, click and hold down the left mouse button, drag down to select all the rows in the table, and then release the left mouse button.
text within a cell	Position the mouse pointer at the beginning of the text, click and hold down the left mouse button, and then drag the mouse across the text. (When a cell is selected, its background color changes to gray. When the text within a cell is selected, only those lines containing text are selected.)

Selecting in a Table with the Keyboard

In addition to the mouse, the keyboard can be used to select specific cells within a table. Table 7.3 shows the commands for selecting specific elements of a table.

To select only the text within a cell, rather than the entire cell, position the insertion point in front of text in a cell and then press the F8 function key to turn on the Extend mode. Move the insertion point with an arrow key to select one character at a time, being careful not to select the entire cell. When a cell is selected, its background color changes to gray. When the text within a cell is selected, only those lines containing text are selected.

Table 7.3 Selecting in a Table with the Keyboard

To select	Press
next cell's contents	Tab
preceding cell's contents	Shift + Tab
entire table	Alt + 5 (on numeric keypad with Num Lock off)
adjacent cells	Press and hold down the Shift key and then press an arrow key repeatedly.
column	Position the insertion point in the top cell of the column, press and hold down the Shift key, and then press and hold down the Down Arrow key until the column is selected.

Activity 1d Selecting, Moving, and Formatting Cells in a Table

Part 4 of 8

1. With **7-Tables** open, move two rows in the top table by completing the following steps:
   a. Position the mouse pointer in the row selection bar at the left edge of the row containing the name *Cecilia Nordyke*, click and hold down the left mouse button, and then drag down to select two rows (the *Cecilia Nordyke* row and the *Regina Stahl* row).
   b. Click the Home tab and then click the Cut button in the Clipboard group.
   c. Move the insertion point so it is positioned at the beginning of the name *Les Cromwell* and then click the Paste button in the Clipboard group.

2. Move the third column in the bottom table by completing the following steps:
   a. Position the mouse pointer on the top border of the third column in the bottom table until the pointer turns into a short black arrow that points down and then click the left mouse button. (This selects the entire column.)
   b. Click the Cut button.
   c. With the insertion point positioned at the beginning of the text *Basic Plan Employees*, click the Paste button. (Moving the column removed the right border.)
   d. Insert the right border by clicking the Table Tools Design tab, clicking the Border Styles button arrow, and then clicking the *Double solid lines, 1/2 pt, Accent 2* option at the drop-down list (third column, third row in the *Theme Borders* section).
   e. Drag along the right border of the bottom table.
   f. Click the Border Painter button to turn off the feature.

3. Apply shading to a row by completing the following steps:
   a. Position the mouse pointer in the row selection bar at the left edge of the first row in the bottom table until the pointer turns into an arrow that points up and to the right and then click the left mouse button. (This selects the entire first row of the bottom table.)
   b. Click the Shading button arrow in the Table Styles group on the Table Tools Design tab and then click the *Orange, Accent 2, Lighter 80%* color option (sixth column, second row in the *Theme Colors* section).

4. Apply a border line to the right sides of two columns by completing the following steps:
   a. Position the mouse pointer on the top border of the first column in the bottom table until the pointer turns into a short black arrow that points down and then click the left mouse button.

   b. Click the *Line Style* option box arrow and then click the top line option (a single line).
   c. Click the Borders button arrow and then click *Right Border* at the drop-down list.
   d. Select the second column in the bottom table.
   e. Click the Borders button arrow and then click *Right Border* at the drop-down list.
5. Apply italic formatting to a column by completing the following steps:
   a. Click in the first cell of the first row in the top table.
   b. Press and hold down the Shift key and then press the Down Arrow key four times. (This should select all the cells in the first column.)
   c. Press Ctrl + I.
   d. Click in any cell in the table to deselect the column.
6. Save **7-Tables**.

> **Check Your Work**

 > **Tutorial**

Changing the Table Layout

Changing the Table Layout

To further customize a table, consider changing the layout by inserting or deleting columns and rows and specifying how text should align in cells. Change the table layout with options at the Table Tools Layout tab, shown in Figure 7.6. Use options and buttons on the tab to select specific cells, delete and insert rows and columns, merge and split cells, specify cell height and width, sort data in cells, and insert formulas.

Selecting with the Select Button

Along with selecting cells with the keyboard and mouse, specific cells can be selected with the Select button in the Table group on the Table Tools Layout tab.

Figure 7.6 Table Tools Layout Tab

Select

Position the insertion point in the specific cell, column, or row and then click the Select button. At the drop-down list, specify what is to be selected: the entire table or a column, row, or cell.

Viewing Gridlines

Hint Some table layout options are available at a shortcut menu that can be viewed by right-clicking in a table.

By default, the cells in a table are bordered by a grid of thin black horizontal and vertical lines. These borders can be modified or removed using options in the Table Tools Design tab, as described on page 196. If the design of a table is changed so that there are no visible borders, it can be difficult to see the boundaries of each cell when entering data. In this case, turn on the display of nonprinting gridlines to be used as a reference when working with the table. These gridlines appear as dashed lines on the screen, but they will not print. Turn on or off the display of nonprinting dashed gridlines with the View Gridlines button in the Table group on the Table Tools Layout tab.

 View Gridlines

Inserting and Deleting Rows and Columns

Insert or delete a row or a column with buttons in the Rows & Columns group on the Table Tools Layout tab. Click a button in the group to insert the row or column above, below, to the left, or to the right. To delete a cell, a row, a column, or the entire table, click the Delete button and then click the option identifying what is to be deleted. The shortcut menu can also be used to insert or delete a row or column. To use the shortcut menu to insert a row or column, right-click in a cell, point to the *Insert* option, and then click an insert option at the side menu. To delete a row or column, right-click in a cell and then click the *Delete Cells* option. This displays the Delete Cells dialog box with options for deleting cells, a row, or a column.

In addition to using options on the Table Tools Layout tab, rows or columns can be inserted using an Insert Control. Display the Insert Control for a row by positioning the mouse pointer just outside the left border of the table at the left edge of the row border. When the Insert Control displays (a plus symbol in a circle and a border line), click the control and a row is inserted below the Insert Control border line. To insert a column, position the mouse pointer above the column border line until the Insert Control displays and then click the control. This inserts a new column immediately left of the Insert Control border line.

Insert Above

Insert Below

Insert Left

Insert Right

Delete

Activity 1e **Selecting, Inserting, and Deleting Columns and Rows**   Part 5 of 8

1. Make sure **7-Tables** is open.
2. The table style applied to the bottom table removed row border gridlines. If you do not see dashed row border gridlines in the bottom table, turn on the display of nonprinting gridlines by positioning your insertion point in the table, clicking the Table Tools Layout tab, and then clicking the View Gridlines button in the Table group. (The button should appear with a gray background, indicating it is active.)
3. Select a column and apply formatting by completing the following steps:
   a. Click in any cell in the first column in the top table.
   b. Make sure the Table Tools Layout tab is active, click the Select button in the Table group, and then click *Select Column* at the drop-down list.

3b

   c. With the first column selected, press Ctrl + I to remove italic formatting and then press Ctrl + B to apply bold formatting.

4. Select a row and apply formatting by completing the following steps:
   a. Click in any cell in the first row in the bottom table.
   b. Click the Select button in the Table group and then click *Select Row* at the drop-down list.
   c. With the first row selected in the bottom table, press Ctrl + I to apply italic formatting.

5. Insert a new row in the bottom table and type text in the new cells by completing the following steps:
   a. Click in the cell containing the text *60 days*.
   b. Click the Insert Above button in the Rows & Columns group.
   c. Type 30 days in the first cell of the new row. Press the Tab key, press Ctrl + Tab, and then type 0.85% in the second cell of the new row. Press the Tab key, press Ctrl + Tab, and then type 0.81% in the third cell of the new row.

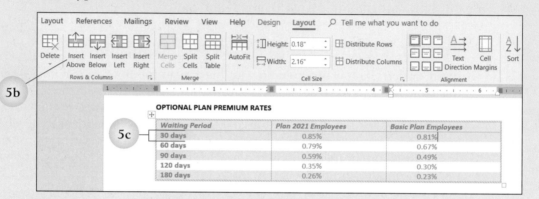

OPTIONAL PLAN PREMIUM RATES

Waiting Period	Plan 2021 Employees	Basic Plan Employees
30 days	0.85%	0.81%
60 days	0.79%	0.67%
90 days	0.59%	0.49%
120 days	0.35%	0.30%
180 days	0.26%	0.23%

6. Insert two new rows in the top table by completing the following steps:
   a. Select the two rows of cells that begin with the names *Cecilia Nordyke* and *Regina Stahl*.
   b. Click the Insert Below button in the Rows & Columns group.
   c. Click in any cell of the top table to deselect the new rows.

7. Insert a new row in the top table by positioning the mouse pointer at the left edge of the table next to the border line below *Regina Stahl* until the Insert Control displays and then clicking the Insert Control.

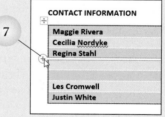

CONTACT INFORMATION

Maggie Rivera	
Cecilia Nordyke	
Regina Stahl	
Les Cromwell	
Justin White	

8. Type the following text in the new cells:

Teresa Getty	Meridian Bank	(503) 555-9800
Michael Vazquez	New Horizon Bank	(702) 555-2435
Samantha Roth	Cascade Mutual	(206) 555-6788

CONTACT INFORMATION

Maggie Rivera	First Trust Bank	(203) 555-3440
Cecilia Nordyke	American Financial	(509) 555-3995
Regina Stahl	United Fidelity	(301) 555-1201
Teresa Getty	Meridian Bank	(503) 555-9800
Michael Vazquez	New Horizon Bank	(702) 555-2435
Samantha Roth	Cascade Mutual	(206) 555-6788
Les Cromwell	Madison Trust	(602) 555-4900
Justin White	Key One Savings	(360) 555-8963

9. Delete a row by completing the following steps:
   a. Click in the cell containing the name *Les Cromwell*.
   b. Click the Delete button in the Rows & Columns group and then click *Delete Rows* at the drop-down list.

9b

10. Insert a new column in the top table by positioning the mouse pointer immediately above the border line between the first and second columns until the Insert Control displays and then clicking the Insert Control.

10

CONTACT INFORMATION

| Maggie Rivera | First Trust Bank |
| Cecilia Nordyke | American Financial |

11. Type the following text in the new cells:

B1 – Vice President
B2 = Loan Officer
B3 = Account Manager
B4 = Branch Manager
B5 = President
B6 = Vice President
B7 = Regional Manager

12. Save **7-Tables**.

11

CONTACT INFORMATION

Maggie Rivera	Vice President	First Tru:
Cecilia Nordyke	Loan Officer	America
Regina Stahl	Account Manager	United F
Teresa Getty	Branch Manager	Meridian
Michael Vazquez	President	New Ho
Samantha Roth	Vice President	Cascade
Justin White	Regional Manager	Key One

Check Your Work

Merging and Splitting Cells and Tables

Merge Cells

Split Cells

Split Table

Click the Merge Cells button in the Merge group on the Table Tools Layout tab to merge selected cells and click the Split Cells button to split the currently active cell. Click the Split Cells button and the Split Cells dialog box displays with options for specifying the number of columns or rows into which the active cell should be split. To split one table into two tables, position the insertion point in a cell in the row that will be the first row in the new table and then click the Split Table button.

1. With **7-Tables** open, insert a new row and merge cells in the row by completing the following steps:
   a. Click in the cell containing the text *Waiting Period* (in the bottom table).
   b. Click the Insert Above button in the Rows & Columns group on the Table Tools Layout tab.
   c. With all the cells in the new row selected, click the Merge Cells button in the Merge group.
   d. Type OPTIONAL PLAN PREMIUM RATES and then press Ctrl + E to center-align the text in the cell. (The text you type will be bold and italicized.)

2. Select and then delete the text *OPTIONAL PLAN PREMIUM RATES* above the bottom table.
3. Insert rows and text in the top table and merge cells by completing the following steps:
   a. Click in the cell containing the text *Maggie Rivera*.
   b. Click the Table Tools Layout tab.
   c. Click the Insert Above button two times. (This inserts two rows at the top of the table.)
   d. With the cells in the top row selected, click the Merge Cells button.
   e. Type CONTACT INFORMATION, NORTH and then press Ctrl + E to center-align the text in the cell.
   f. Type the following text in the four cells in the new second row.

        Name   Title   Company   Telephone

4. Apply heading formatting to the new top row by completing the following steps:
   a. Click the Table Tools Design tab.
   b. Click the *Header Row* check box in the Table Style Options group to insert a check mark.
5. Select and then delete the text *CONTACT INFORMATION* above the top table.
6. Split a cell by completing the following steps:
   a. Click in the cell containing the telephone number *(301) 555-1201*.
   b. Click the Table Tools Layout tab.
   c. Click the Split Cells button in the Merge group.
   d. At the Split Cells dialog box, click OK. (The telephone number will wrap to a new line. You will change this in the next activity.)
   e. Click in the new cell.

f. Type x453 in the new cell. If AutoCorrect automatically capitalizes the *x*, hover the mouse pointer over the *X* until the AutoCorrect Options button displays. Click the AutoCorrect Options button and then click *Undo Automatic Capitalization* or click *Stop Auto-capitalizing First Letter of Table Cells.*

6f

7. Split the cell containing the telephone number *(206) 555-6788* and then type x2310 in the new cell. (If necessary, make the *x* lowercase.)

8. Split the top table into two tables by completing the following steps:
   a. Click in the cell containing the name *Teresa Getty.*
   b. Click the Split Table button in the Merge group.
   c. Click in the cell containing the name *Teresa Getty* (in the first row of the new table).
   d. Click the Insert Above button in the Rows & Columns group on the Table Tools Layout tab.
   e. With the new row selected, click the Merge Cells button.
   f. Type CONTACT INFORMATION, SOUTH in the new row and then press Ctrl + E to center-align the text.

9. Save and then print **7-Tables**.

10. Delete the middle table by completing the following steps:
    a. Click in any cell in the middle table.
    b. Click the Table Tools Layout tab.
    c. Click the Delete button in the Rows & Columns group and then click *Delete Table* at the drop-down list.

11. Draw a dark orange border at the bottom of the top table by completing the following steps:
    a. Click in any cell in the top table and then click the Table Tools Design tab.
    b. Click the *Line Weight* option box arrow in the Borders group and then click *1 ½ pt* at the drop-down list. (This activates the Border Painter button.)
    c. Click the Pen Color button and then click the *Orange, Accent 2, Darker, 50%* color option (sixth column, bottom row in the *Theme Colors* section).
    d. Using the mouse, drag along the bottom border of the top table.
    e. Click the Border Painter button to turn off the feature.

12. Save **7-Tables**.

Check Your Work

Tutorial

Customizing Cell Size

Customizing Cells in a Table

When a table is created, the column widths are equal and the row heights are equal. Both can be customized with buttons in the Cell Size group on the Table Tools Layout tab. Use the *Table Row Height* measurement box to increase or decrease the heights of rows and use the *Table Column Width* measurement box to increase or decrease the widths of columns. The Distribute Rows button will make all the selected rows the same height and the Distribute Columns button will make all the selected columns the same width.

Distribute Rows

Distribute Columns

Column width can also be changed using the move table column markers on the horizontal ruler or using the table gridlines. To change column width using the horizontal ruler, position the mouse pointer on a move table column marker until it turns into a left-and-right-pointing arrow and then drag the marker on the horizontal ruler to the specific position. Press and hold down the Shift key while dragging a table column marker and the horizontal ruler remains stationary while the table column marker moves. Press and hold down the Alt key while dragging a table column marker and measurements display on the horizontal ruler. To change column width using gridlines, position the mouse pointer on the gridline separating columns until the insertion point turns into a left-and-right-pointing arrow with a vertical double-line in the middle and then drag the gridline to the new position. Press and hold down the Alt key while dragging the gridline and column measurements display on the horizontal ruler.

Adjust row height in a manner similar to adjusting column width. Drag the adjust table row marker on the vertical ruler or drag the gridline separating rows. Press and hold down the Alt key while dragging the adjust table row marker or the row gridline and measurements display on the vertical ruler.

AutoFit   Use the AutoFit button in the Cell Size group to make the column widths in a table automatically fit the contents. To do this, position the insertion point in any cell in the table, click the AutoFit button in the Cell Size group, and then click *AutoFit Contents* at the drop-down list.

Activity 1g   Changing Column Width and Row Height

1. With **7-Tables** open, change the width of the first column in the top table by completing the following steps:
   a. Click in the cell containing the name *Maggie Rivera*.
   b. Position the mouse pointer on the Move Table Column marker just right of the 1.5-inch mark on the horizontal ruler until the pointer turns into a left-and-right-pointing arrow.
   c. Press and hold down the Shift key and then click and hold down the left mouse button.
   d. Drag the marker to the 1.25-inch mark, release the mouse button, and then release the Shift key.

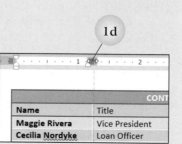

2. Complete steps similar to those in Step 1 to drag the move table column marker just right of the 3-inch mark on the horizontal ruler to the 2.75-inch mark. (Make sure the text *Account Manager* in the second column does not wrap to the next line. If it does, slightly increase the width of the column.)
3. Change the width of the third column in the top table by completing the following steps:
   a. Position the mouse pointer on the gridline separating the third and fourth columns until the pointer turns into a left-and-right-pointing arrow with a vertical double-line in the middle.
   b. Press and hold down the Alt key, click and hold down the left mouse button, drag the gridline to the left until the measurement for the third column on the horizontal ruler displays as *1.31˝*, and then release the mouse button followed by the Alt key.

4. Position the mouse pointer on the gridline that separates the telephone number *(301) 555-1201* from the extension *x453* and then drag the gridline to the 5.25-inch mark on the horizontal ruler. (Make sure the phone number does not wrap down to the next line.)
5. Drag the right border of the top table to the 5.75-inch mark on the horizontal ruler.

6. Automatically fit the columns in the bottom table by completing the following steps:
   a. Click in any cell in the bottom table.
   b. Click the AutoFit button in the Cell Size group on the Table Tools Layout tab and then click *AutoFit Contents* at the drop-down list.

7. Increase the height of the first row in the bottom table by completing the following steps:
   a. Make sure the insertion point is positioned in one of the cells in the bottom table.
   b. Position the mouse pointer on the top adjust table row marker on the vertical ruler.
   c. Press and hold down the Alt key and then click and hold down the left mouse button.
   d. Drag the Adjust Table Row marker down until the first row measurement on the vertical ruler displays as *0.39"*, release the mouse button, and then release the Alt key.

8. Increase the height of the first row in the top table by completing the following steps:
   a. Click in any cell in the top table.
   b. Position the mouse pointer on the gridline at the bottom of the top row until the mouse pointer turns into an up-and-down-pointing arrow with a vertical double-line in the middle.
   c. Click and hold down the left mouse button and then press and hold down the Alt key.
   d. Drag the gridline down until the first row measurement on the vertical ruler displays as *0.39"*, release the mouse button, and then release the Alt key.

9. Save **7-Tables**.

> Check Your Work

Changing Cell Alignment

The Alignment group on the Table Tools Layout tab contains a number of buttons for specifying the horizontal and vertical alignment of text in cells. Each button contains a visual representation of the alignment. Hover the mouse pointer over a button to display a ScreenTip with the button name and description.

Repeating a Header Row

Quick Steps

Repeat Header Row
1. Click in header row or select rows.
2. Click Table Tools Layout tab.
3. Click Repeat Header Rows button.

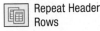
Repeat Header Rows

If a table continues over two or more pages, consider adding the header row at the beginning of each page for easier reference while reading. To repeat a header row, click in the first row (header row) and then click the Repeat Header Rows button in the Data group on the Table Tools Layout tab. To repeat more than one header row, select the rows and then click the Repeat Header Rows button.

1. With **7-Tables** open, click in the top cell in the top table (the cell containing the title *CONTACT INFORMATION, NORTH*).
2. Click the Align Center button in the Alignment group on the Table Tools Layout tab.
3. Format and align the text in the second row in the top table by completing the following steps:

   a. Select the second row.
   b. Press Ctrl + B to turn off bold formatting for the entry in the first cell and then press Ctrl + B again to turn on bold formatting for all the entries in the second row.
   c. Click the Align Top Center button in the Alignment group.
4. Click in the top cell in the bottom table and then click the Align Center button in the Alignment group.
5. Press Ctrl + End to move the insertion point to the end of the document, press the Enter key four times, and then insert a table into the current document by completing the following steps:
   a. Click the Insert tab.
   b. Click the Object button arrow in the Text group and then click *Text from File* at the drop-down list.
   c. At the Insert File dialog box, navigate to your WL1C7 folder and then double-click the **ContactsWest** document.
6. Repeat the header row by completing the following steps:
   a. Select the first two rows in the table you just inserted.
   b. Click the Table Tools Layout tab.
   c. Click the Repeat Header Rows button in the Data group.
7. Save, print, and then close **7-Tables**.

> Check Your Work

Activity 2 Create and Format Tables with Employee Information   6 Parts

You will create and format a table containing information on the names and departments of employees of Tri-State Products, two tables containing additional information on employees, and a calendar quick table.

Changing Cell Margin Measurements

🔲 Cell Margins

By default, the cells in a table contain specific margin measurements. The top and bottom margins in a cell have a default measurement of 0 inch and the left and right margins have a default measurement of 0.08 inch. Change these default measurements with options at the Table Options dialog box, shown in Figure 7.7. Display this dialog box by clicking the Cell Margins button in the Alignment group on the Table Tools Layout tab. Use the measurement boxes in the *Default cell margins* section to change the top, bottom, left, and/or right cell margin measurements.

Figure 7.7 Table Options Dialog Box

Use the measurement boxes in this section to increase and/or decrease the margin measurements in cells.

Changes to cell margins will affect all the cells in a table. To change the cell margin measurements for one cell or selected cells, position the insertion point in the cell or select the cells and then click the Properties button in the Table group on the Table Tools Layout tab (or click the Cell Size group dialog box launcher). At the Table Properties dialog box, click the Cell tab and then the Options button in the lower right corner of the dialog box. This displays the Cell Options dialog box, shown in Figure 7.8.

Before setting the new cell margin measurements, remove the check mark from the *Same as the whole table* check box. With the check mark removed, the cell margin options become available. Specify the new cell margin measurements and then click OK to close the dialog box.

Properties

Figure 7.8 Cell Options Dialog Box

Remove the check mark from this check box and the cell margin measurement boxes become available.

Activity 2a Changing Cell Margin Measurements   Part 1 of 6

1. Open **TSPTables** and then save it with the name **7-TSPTables**.
2. Change the top and bottom cell margin measurements for all the cells in the table by completing the following steps:
   a. Position the insertion point in any cell in the table and then click the Table Tools Layout tab.
   b. Click the Cell Margins button in the Alignment group.

c. At the Table Options dialog box, change the *Top* and *Bottom* measurements to 0.05 inch.

d. Click OK to close the Table Options dialog box.

3. Change the top and bottom cell margin measurements for the first row of cells by completing the following steps:

a. Select the first row of cells (the cells containing *Name* and *Department*).

b. Click the Properties button in the Table group.

c. At the Table Properties dialog box, click the Cell tab.

d. Click the Options button in the lower right corner of the dialog box.

e. At the Cell Options dialog box, click the *Same as the whole table* check box to remove the check mark.

f. Change the *Top* and *Bottom* measurements to 0.1 inch.

g. Click OK to close the Cell Options dialog box.

h. Click OK to close the Table Properties dialog box.

4. Change the left cell margin measurement for specific cells by completing the following steps:

a. Select all the rows in the table *except* the top row.

b. Click the Cell Size group dialog box launcher.

c. At the Table Properties dialog box, make sure the Cell tab is active.

d. Click the Options button.

e. At the Cell Options dialog box, remove the check mark from the *Same as the whole table* check box.

f. Change the *Left* measurement to 0.3 inch.

g. Click OK to close the Cell Options dialog box.

h. Click OK to close the Table Properties dialog box.

5. Save **7-TSPTables**.

Check Your Work

Changing Text Direction in a Cell

Text Direction

Change the direction of text in a cell using the Text Direction button in the Alignment group on the Table Tools Layout tab. Each time the Text Direction button is clicked, the text in the cell rotates 90 degrees.

Changing Table Alignment and Dimensions

By default, a table aligns at the left margin. Change this alignment with options at the Table Properties dialog box with the Table tab selected, as shown in Figure 7.9. To change the alignment, click the specific alignment option in the *Alignment* section of the dialog box. Change table dimensions by clicking the

Preferred width check box to insert a check mark. This makes active both the width measurement box and the *Measure in* option box. Type a width measurement in the measurement box and specify whether the measurement type is inches or a percentage with the *Measurement in* option box.

Figure 7.9 Table Properties Dialog Box with the Table Tab Selected

Specify the horizontal alignment of the table with options in this section.

Change the table width by inserting a check mark in the *Preferred width* check box and then specifying the table width and measurement type.

1. With **7-TSPTables** open, insert a new column and change text direction by completing the following steps:
   a. Click in any cell in the first column.
   b. Click the Insert Left button in the Rows & Columns group on the Table Tools Layout tab.
   c. With the cells in the new column selected, click the Merge Cells button in the Merge group.
   d. Type Tri-State Products.
   e. Click the Align Center button in the Alignment group.
   f. Click two times on the Text Direction button in the Alignment group.

   g. With *Tri-State Products* selected, click the Home tab and then increase the font size to 16 points.
2. Automatically fit the contents by completing the following steps:
   a. Click in any cell in the table.
   b. Click the Table Tools Layout tab.
   c. Click the AutoFit button in the Cell Size group and then click *AutoFit Contents* at the drop-down list.

3. Change the table width and alignment by completing the following steps:

   a. Click the Properties button in the Table group on the Table Tools Layout tab.

   b. At the Table Properties dialog box, click the Table tab.

   c. Click the *Preferred width* check box to insert a check mark.

   d. Select the measurement in the measurement box and then type 4.5.

   e. Click the *Center* option in the *Alignment* section.

   f. Click OK.

4. Select the two cells containing the text *Name* and *Department* and then click the Align Center button in the Alignment group.

5. Save **7-TSPTables**.

Check Your Work

Changing Table Size with the Resize Handle

Quick Steps

Move Table
1. Position mouse pointer on table move handle until pointer displays with four-headed arrow attached.
2. Click and hold down left mouse button.
3. Drag table to new location.
4. Release mouse button.

Hover the mouse pointer over a table and a resize handle displays in the lower right corner. The resize handle displays as a small white square. Drag this resize handle to increase and/or decrease the size and proportion of the table.

Moving a Table

Position the mouse pointer in a table and a table move handle displays in the upper left corner. Use this handle to move the table within the document. To move a table, position the mouse pointer on the table move handle until the pointer displays with a four-headed arrow attached, click and hold down the left mouse button, drag the table to the new location, and then release the mouse button.

Activity 2c Resizing and Moving Tables   Part 3 of 6

1. With **7-TSPTables** open, insert a table into the current document by completing the following steps:

   a. Press Ctrl + End to move the insertion point to the end of the document and then press the Enter key.

   b. Click the Insert tab.

   c. Click the Object button arrow in the Text group and then click *Text from File* at the drop-down list.

   d. At the Insert File dialog box, navigate to your WL1C7 folder and then double-click the **TSPEmps** document.

2. Automatically fit the bottom table by completing the following steps:

   a. Click in any cell in the bottom table.

   b. Click the Table Tools Layout tab.

   c. Click the AutoFit button in the Cell Size group and then click *AutoFit Contents* at the drop-down list.

3. Format the bottom table by completing the following steps:
   a. Click the Table Tools Design tab.
   b. Click the More Table Styles button in the table styles gallery, scroll down the gallery, and then click the *List Table 4 - Accent 6* table style (last column, fourth row in the *List Tables* section).
   c. Click the *First Column* check box in the Table Style Options group to remove the check mark.
   d. Select the first and second rows, click the Table Tools Layout tab, and then click the Align Center button in the Alignment group.
   e. Select the second row and then press Ctrl + B to apply bold formatting.

4. Size the bottom table by completing the following steps:
   a. Position the mouse pointer on the resize handle in the lower right corner of the bottom table.
   b. Click and hold down the left mouse button, drag down and to the right until the width and height of the table increase approximately 1 inch, and then release the mouse button.

5. Move the bottom table by completing the following steps:
   a. Move the mouse pointer over the bottom table and then position the mouse pointer on the table move handle that appears just outside the upper left corner of the table until the pointer displays with a four-headed arrow attached.
   b. Click and hold down the left mouse button, drag the table so it is positioned equally between the left and right margins, and then release the mouse button.

3b

TRI-STATE PRODUCTS		
Name	**Employee #**	**Department**
Whitaker, Christine	1432-323-09	Financial Services
Higgins, Dennis	1230-933-21	Public Relations
Coffey, Richard	1321-843-22	Research and Development
Lee, Yong	1411-322-76	Human Resources
Fleishmann, Jim	1246-432-90	Public Relations
Schaffer, Mitchell	1388-340-44	Purchasing
Porter, Robbie	1122-361-38	Public Relations
Buchanan, Lillian	1432-857-87	Research and Development
Kensington, Jacob	1112-473-31	Human Resources

4a-4b

5a-5b

TRI-STATE PRODUCTS		
Name	**Employee #**	**Department**
Whitaker, Christine	1432-323-09	Financial Services
Higgins, Dennis	1230-933-21	Public Relations

6. Select the cells in the column below the heading *Employee #* and then click the Align Top Center button in the Alignment group.
7. Save **7-TSPTables**.

Check Your Work

Converting Text to a Table and a Table to Text

Create a table and then enter text in the cells or create the text and then convert it to a table. Converting text to a table provides formatting and layout options available on the Table Tools Design tab and the Table Tools Layout tab. When typing the text to be converted to a table, separate units of information using separator characters, such as commas or tabs. These characters identify where the text is divided into columns. To convert text, select the text, click the Insert tab, click the Table button in the Tables group, and then click *Convert Text to Table* at the drop-down list. At the Convert Text to Table dialog box, specify the separator and then click OK.

Convert a table to text by positioning the insertion point in any cell of the table, clicking the Table Tools Layout tab, and then clicking the Convert to Text button in the Data group. At the Convert Table To dialog box, specify the separator and then click OK.

Activity 2d Converting Text to a Table

1. With **7-TSPTables** open, press Ctrl + End to move the insertion point to the end of the document. (If the insertion point does not display below the second table, press the Enter key until the insertion point displays there.)
2. Insert the document named **TSPExecs** into the current document.
3. Convert the text to a table by completing the following steps:
   a. Select the text you just inserted.
   b. Make sure the Insert tab is active.
   c. Click the Table button in the Tables group and then click *Convert Text to Table* at the drop-down list.
   d. At the Convert Text to Table dialog box, type 2 in the *Number of columns* measurement box.
   e. Click the *AutoFit to contents* option in the *AutoFit behavior* section.
   f. Click the *Commas* option in the *Separate text at* section.
   g. Click OK.

4. Select and merge the cells in the top row (the row containing the title *TRI-STATE PRODUCTS*) and then center-align the text in the merged cell.
5. Apply the List Table 4 - Accent 6 style (last column, fourth row in the *List Tables* section) and remove the check mark from the *First Column* check box in the Table Style Options group on the Table Tools Design tab.
6. Drag the table so it is centered below the table above it.
7. Apply the List Table 4 - Accent 6 style to the top table. Increase the widths of the columns so the text *Tri-State Products* is visible and the text in the second and third columns displays on one line.
8. Drag the table so it is centered above the middle table. Make sure the three tables fit on one page.

9. Click in the middle table and then convert the table to text by completing the following steps:

   a. Click the Table Tools Layout tab and then click the Convert to Text button in the Data group.

   b. At the Convert Table To dialog box, make sure *Tabs* is selected and then click OK.

10. Print **7-TSPTables**.

11. Click the Undo button to return the text to a table.

12. Save **7-TSPTables**.

Check Your Work

Drawing a Table

In Activity 1, options in the Borders group on the Table Tools Design tab were used to draw borders around an existing table. These options can also be used to draw an entire table. To draw a table, click the Insert tab, click the Table button in the Tables group, and then click *Draw Table* at the drop-down list. Or click the Draw Table button in the Draw group on the Table Tools Layout tab; this turns the mouse pointer into a pen. Drag the pen pointer in the document to create the table. To correct an error when drawing a table, click the Eraser button in the Draw group on the Table Tools Layout tab (which changes the mouse pointer to an eraser) and then drag over any border lines to be erased. Clicking the Undo button will also undo the most recent action. To turn off the draw feature, click the Draw Table button in the Draw group or press the Esc key on the keyboard.

Eraser

Activity 2e Drawing and Formatting a Table

Part 5 of 6

1. With **7-TSPTables** open, select and then delete three rows in the middle table from the row that begins with the name *Lee, Yong* through the row that begins with the name *Schaffer, Mitchell*.

2. Move the insertion point to the end of the document (outside any table) and then press the Enter key. (Make sure the insertion point is positioned below the third table.)

3. Click the Insert tab, click the Table button, and then click the *Draw Table* option at the drop-down list. (This turns the insertion point into a pen.)

4. Using the mouse, drag in the document (below the bottom table) to create the table shown at the right, drawing the outside border first. If you make a mistake, click the Undo button. You can also click the Eraser button in the Draw group on the Table Tools Layout tab and drag over a border line to erase it. Click the Draw Table button in the Draw group to turn off the draw feature.

5. After drawing the table, type Tri-State Products in the top cell, Washington Division in the cell at the left, Oregon Division in the middle bottom cell, and California Division in the cell at the right.

6. Apply the Grid Table 4 - Accent 6 table style (last column, fourth row in the *Grid Tables* section).

7. Select the table, change the font size to 12 points, apply bold formatting, and then center-align the text in the cells using the Align Center button in the Alignment group.
8. Make any adjustments needed to the border lines so the text in each cell is on one line.
9. Drag the table so it is centered and positioned below the bottom table.
10. Save **7-TSPTables**.

Check Your Work >

 Tutorial >

Inserting a Quick Table

Inserting a Quick Table

Word includes a Quick Tables feature for inserting predesigned tables in a document. To insert a quick table, click the Insert tab, click the Table button in the Tables group, point to *Quick Tables*, and then click a table at the side menu. Additional formatting can be applied to a quick table with options on the Table Tools Design tab and the Table Tools Layout tab.

Activity 2f Inserting a Quick Table   Part 6 of 6

1. With **7-TSPTables** open, press Ctrl + End to move the insertion point to the end of the document and then press Ctrl + Enter to insert a page break.
2. Insert a quick table by clicking the Insert tab, clicking the Table button, pointing to *Quick Tables*, and then clicking the *Calendar 3* option at the side menu.

3. Edit the text in each cell so the calendar reflects the current month. (If the bottom row is empty, select and then delete the last and second to last rows.)
4. Select the entire table by clicking the Table Tools Layout tab, clicking the Select button in the Table group, and then clicking the *Select Table* option. With the table selected, change the font to Copperplate Gothic Light.
5. Drag the table so it is centered between the left and right margins.
6. Save, print, and then close **7-TSPTables**.

Check Your Work >

You will insert formulas in a Tri-State Products sales table to calculate total sales, average sales, and top sales.

Tutorial

Performing
Calculations in
a Table

Performing Calculations in a Table

Use the Formula button in the Data group on the Table Tools Layout tab to insert formulas that perform calculations on data in a table. The numbers in cells can be added, subtracted, multiplied, and divided. Other calculations can be performed, such as determining averages, counting items, and identifying minimum and maximum values. For more complex calculations, consider using an Excel worksheet.

fx Formula

Quick Steps

**Insert Formula
in Table**
1. Click in cell.
2. Click Table Tools
   Layout tab.
3. Click Formula button.
4. Type formula in
   Formula dialog box.
5. Click OK.

To perform a calculation on the data in a table, position the insertion point in the cell where the result of the calculation is to be inserted and then click the Formula button in the Data group on the Table Tools Layout tab. This displays the Formula dialog box, as shown in Figure 7.10. At this dialog box, accept the default formula in the *Formula* text box or type a calculation and then click OK.

Four basic operators are available for writing a formula, including the plus symbol (+) for addition, the minus symbol (–) for subtraction, the asterisk (*) for multiplication, and the forward slash (/) for division. If a calculation contains two or more operators, Word performs the operations from left to right. To change the order of operations, put parentheses around the part of the calculation to be performed first.

In the default formula, the SUM part of the formula is called a *function*. Word also provides other functions for inserting formulas. These functions are available in the *Paste function* option box in the Formula dialog box. For example, use the AVERAGE function to average numbers in cells.

Specify the numbering format with the *Number format* option box in the Formula dialog box. For example, when calculating amounts of money, specify the number of digits that should follow the decimal point.

Hint Use the
Update Field keyboard
shortcut, F9, to update
the selected field.

If changes are made to a formula, the result of the formula needs to be updated. To do this, right-click the formula result and then click *Update Field* at the shortcut menu. Another method is to click the formula result and then press the F9 function key, which is the Update Field keyboard shortcut. To update the results of all the formulas in a table, select the entire table and then press the F9 function key.

Figure 7.10 Formula Dialog Box

1. Open **TSPSalesTable** and then save it with the name **7-TSPSalesTable**.
2. Insert a formula in the table by completing the following steps:
    a. Click in cell B9. (Cell B9 is the empty cell immediately below the cell containing the amount *$375,630.*)
    b. Click the Table Tools Layout tab.
    c. Click the Formula button in the Data group.
    d. At the Formula dialog box, make sure *=SUM(ABOVE)* appears in the *Formula* text box.
    e. Click the *Number format* option box arrow and then click *#,##0* at the drop-down list (the top option in the list).
    f. Click OK to close the Formula dialog box.

    g. In the table, type a dollar symbol ($) before the number just inserted in cell B9.
3. Complete steps similar to those in Steps 2c through 2g to insert a formula in cell C9. (Cell C9 is the empty cell immediately below the cell containing the amount *$399,120.*)
4. Insert a formula that calculates the average of amounts by completing the following steps:
    a. Click in cell B10. (Cell B10 is the empty cell immediately right of the cell containing the word *Average.*)
    b. Click the Formula button in the Data group.
    c. At the Formula dialog box, delete the formula in the *Formula* text box *except* for the equals (=) sign.
    d. With the insertion point positioned immediately right of the equals sign, click the *Paste function* option box arrow and then click *AVERAGE* at the drop-down list.
    e. With the insertion point positioned between the left and right parentheses, type B2:B8. (When typing cell designations in a formula, you can type either uppercase or lowercase letters.)
    f. Click the *Number format* option box arrow and then click *#,##0* at the drop-down list (the top option in the list).
    g. Click OK to close the Formula dialog box.
    h. Type a dollar symbol ($) before the number just inserted in cell B10.

5. Complete steps similar to those in Steps 4b through 4h to insert a formula in cell C10 that calculates the average of the amounts in cells C2 through C8.

6. Insert a formula that calculates the maximum number by completing the following steps:
   a. Click in cell B11. (Cell B11 is the empty cell immediately right of the cell containing the words *Top Sales*.)
   b. Click the Formula button in the Data group.
   c. At the Formula dialog box, delete the formula in the *Formula* text box *except* for the equals sign.
   d. With the insertion point positioned immediately right of the equals sign, click the *Paste function* option box arrow and then click *MAX* at the drop-down list. (You will need to scroll down the list to locate the *MAX* option.)
   e. With the insertion point positioned between the left and right parentheses, type B2:B8.
   f. Click the *Number format* option box arrow and then click *#,##0* at the drop-down list.
   g. Click OK to close the Formula dialog box.
   h. Type a dollar symbol ($) before the number just inserted in cell B11.

7. Complete steps similar to those in Steps 6b through 6h to insert the maximum number in cell C11.
8. Save and then print **7-TSPSalesTable**.
9. Change the amount in cell B2 from *$543,241* to *$765,700*.
10. Recalculate all the formulas in the table by completing the following steps:
    a. Make sure the Table Tools Layout tab is active and then click the Select button in the Table group.
    b. Click the *Select Table* option.
    c. Press the F9 function key.
11. Save, print, and then close **7-TSPSalesTable**.

Check Your Work

Activity 4 Insert an Excel Worksheet   1 Part

You will insert an Excel worksheet in a blank document, decrease the number of rows and columns in the worksheet, insert data from a Word document, and calculate data in the worksheet.

Tutorial

Inserting an Excel Spreadsheet

Inserting an Excel Spreadsheet

An Excel spreadsheet (usually referred to as a *worksheet*) can be inserted into a Word document, which provides some Excel functions for modifying and formatting the data. To insert an Excel worksheet, click the Insert tab, click the Table button in the Tables group, and then click the *Excel Spreadsheet* option at the drop-down list. This inserts a worksheet in the document with seven columns and ten rows visible. Increase or decrease the number of visible cells by dragging the sizing handles around the worksheet. Use buttons on the Excel ribbon tabs to format the worksheet. Click outside the worksheet and the Excel ribbon tabs are removed. Double-click the table to redisplay the Excel ribbon tabs.

1. Open **SalesIncrease**.
2. Press Ctrl + N to open a blank document.
3. Insert an Excel spreadsheet into the blank document by clicking the Insert tab, clicking the Table button in the Tables group, and then clicking *Excel Spreadsheet* at the drop-down list.

4. Decrease the size of the worksheet by completing the following steps:
   a. Position the mouse pointer on the sizing handle (small black square) in the lower right corner of the worksheet until the pointer displays as a black, diagonal, two-headed arrow.
   b. Click and hold down the left mouse button, drag up and to the left, and then release the mouse button. Continue dragging the sizing handles until columns A, B, and C and rows 1 through 7 are visible.
5. Copy a table into the Excel worksheet by completing the following steps:
   a. Position the mouse pointer on the Word button on the taskbar and then click the *SalesIncrease* thumbnail.
   b. Position the mouse pointer over the table and then click the table move handle (small square containing a four-headed arrow) in the upper left corner of the table. (This selects all the cells in the table.)
   c. Click the Copy button in the Clipboard group on the Home tab.
   d. Close **SalesIncrease**.
   e. With the first cell in the worksheet active, click the Paste button in the Clipboard group.
6. Format the worksheet and insert a formula by completing the following steps:

   a. Increase the width of the second column by positioning the mouse pointer on the column boundary between columns B and C and double-clicking the left mouse button.
   b. Click in cell C3, type the formula =B3*1.02, and then press the Enter key.
7. Copy the formula in cell C3 to the range C4:C7 by completing the following steps:
   a. Position the mouse pointer (white plus symbol) in cell C3, click and hold down the left mouse button, drag into cell C7, and then release the mouse button.

   b. Click the Fill button in the Editing group on the Home tab and then click *Down* at the drop-down list.
8. Click outside the worksheet to remove the Excel ribbon tabs.
9. Save the document and name it **7-Worksheet**.
10. Print and then close **7-Worksheet**.

Check Your Work

Chapter Summary

- Use the Tables feature to create columns and rows of information. Create a table with the Table button in the Tables group on the Insert tab or with options at the Insert Table dialog box.

- A cell is the intersection between a row and a column. The lines that form the cells of the table are called *gridlines*.

- Press the Tab key to move the insertion point to the next cell or press Shift + Tab to move the insertion point to the preceding cell.

- Press Ctrl + Tab to move the insertion point to a tab within a cell.

- Move the insertion point to cells in a table using the mouse by clicking in a cell or using the keyboard commands shown in Table 7.1.

- Change the table design with options and buttons on the Table Tools Design tab.

- Refer to Table 7.2 for a list of mouse commands for selecting specific cells in a table and Table 7.3 for a list of keyboard commands for selecting specific cells in a table.

- Change the layout of a table with options and buttons on the Table Tools Layout tab.

- Select a table, column, row, or cell using the Select button in the Table group on the Table Tools Layout tab.

- Turn on and off the display of gridlines by clicking the View Gridlines button in the Table group on the Table Tools Layout tab.

- Insert and delete columns and rows with buttons in the Rows & Columns group on the Table Tools Layout tab.

- Merge selected cells with the Merge Cells button and split cells with the Split Cells button, both in the Merge group on the Table Tools Layout tab.

- Change the column width and row height using the height and width measurement boxes in the Cell Size group on the Table Tools Layout tab; by dragging move table column markers on the horizontal ruler, adjust table row markers on the vertical ruler, or gridlines in the table; or using the AutoFit button in the Cell Size group.

- Change the alignment of text in cells with buttons in the Alignment group on the Table Tools Layout tab.

- If a table spans two pages or more, a header row can be inserted at the beginning of each page. To do this, click in the header row or select the header rows and then click the Repeat Header Rows button in the Data group on the Table Tools Layout tab.

- Change cell margins with options in the Table Options dialog box.

- Change text direction in a cell with the Text Direction button in the Alignment group on the Table Tools Layout tab.

- Change the table dimensions and alignment with options at the Table Properties dialog box with the Table tab selected.

- Use the resize handle to change the size of the table and the table move handle to move the table.

- Convert text to a table with the *Convert Text to Table* option at the Table button drop-down list. Convert a table to text with the Convert to Text button in the Data group on the Table Tools Layout tab.

- Draw a table in a document by clicking the Insert tab, clicking the Table button in the Tables group, and then clicking *Draw Table* at the drop-down list. Using the mouse, drag in the document to create the table.
- Quick tables are predesigned tables that can be inserted in a document by clicking the Insert tab, clicking the Table button in the Tables group, pointing to *Quick Tables*, and then clicking a table at the side menu.
- Perform calculations on data in a table by clicking the Formula button in the Data group on the Table Tools Layout tab and then specifying the formula and number format at the Formula dialog box.
- Insert an Excel spreadsheet (worksheet) into a Word document to provide Excel functions by clicking the Insert tab, clicking the Table button in the Tables group, and then clicking *Excel Spreadsheet* at the drop-down list.

Commands Review

FEATURE	RIBBON TAB, GROUP	BUTTON, OPTION
AutoFit table contents	Table Tools Layout, Cell Size	, *AutoFit Contents*
cell alignment	Table Tools Layout, Alignment	
convert table to text	Table Tools Layout, Data	
convert text to table	Insert, Tables	, *Convert Text to Table*
delete column	Table Tools Layout, Rows & Columns	, *Delete Columns*
delete row	Table Tools Layout, Rows & Columns	, *Delete Rows*
distribute columns	Table Tools Layout, Cell Size	
distribute rows	Table Tools Layout, Cell Size	
draw table	Insert, Tables	, *Draw Table*
Formula dialog box	Table Tools Layout, Data	fx
insert column left	Table Tools Layout, Rows & Columns	
insert column right	Table Tools Layout, Rows & Columns	
Insert Excel spreadsheet	Insert, Tables	, *Excel Spreadsheet*
insert row above	Table Tools Layout, Rows & Columns	
insert row below	Table Tools Layout, Rows & Columns	
Insert Table dialog box	Insert, Tables	, *Insert Table*
merge cells	Table Tools Layout, Merge	

FEATURE	RIBBON TAB, GROUP	BUTTON, OPTION
Quick Table	Insert, Tables	, *Quick Tables*
repeat header row	Table Tools Layout, Data	
Split Cells dialog box	Table Tools Layout, Merge	
table	Insert, Tables	
Table Options dialog box	Table Tools Layout, Alignment	
text direction	Table Tools Layout, Alignment	
view gridlines	Table Tools Layout, Table	

Microsoft®

Word

Applying and Customizing Formatting

Performance Objectives

Upon successful completion of Chapter 8, you will be able to:

1 Create and insert custom numbers and bullets

2 Create and insert multilevel list formatting

3 Specify AutoCorrect exceptions

4 Add and delete AutoCorrect text

5 Use the AutoCorrect Options button

6 Customize AutoFormatting

7 Create custom theme colors and theme fonts

8 Save, apply, edit, and delete a custom theme

9 Reset the template theme

Word offers a number of features to apply and customize formatting and to help streamline the formatting of a document. In this chapter, you will learn how to define and insert custom numbers and bullets and to format text in a multilevel list. You will use Word's AutoCorrect and Autoformatting features and customize them for your convenience when creating documents. The Microsoft Office suite offers design themes that provide consistent formatting and help create documents with a professional and polished look. This chapter provides instruction on how to customize a theme by modifying the color and fonts and applying theme effects.

 Data Files

Before beginning chapter work, copy the WL1C8 folder to your storage medium and then make WL1C8 the active folder.

The online course includes additional training and assessment resources.

You will open an agenda document, apply formatting that includes number formatting, and then define and apply custom numbering.

Inserting and Creating Custom Numbers and Bullets

 Numbering

Number paragraphs or insert bullets before paragraphs using buttons in the Paragraph group on the Home tab. Use the Numbering button to insert numbers before specific paragraphs and use the Bullets button to insert bullets. To insert custom numbering or bullets, click the button arrow and then choose from the drop-down gallery that displays.

Bullets

Inserting Custom Numbers

Insert numbers as text is typed or select text and then apply a numbering format. Type *1.* and then press the spacebar and Word indents the number approximately 0.25 inch. Type text after the number and then press the Enter key and Word indents all the lines in the paragraph 0.5 inch from the left margin (called a *hanging indent*). At the beginning of the next paragraph, Word inserts the number *2* followed by a period 0.25 inch from the left margin. Continue typing items and Word numbers successive paragraphs in the list. To number existing paragraphs of text, select the paragraphs and then click the Numbering button in the Paragraph group on the Home tab.

💡 *Hint* If the automatic numbering or bulleting feature is on, press Shift + Enter to insert a line break without inserting a number or bullet.

Click the Numbering button in the Paragraph group and arabic numbers (1., 2., 3., etc.) are inserted in the document. This default numbering can be changed by clicking the Numbering button arrow and then clicking an option at the drop-down gallery.

To change list levels, click the Numbering button arrow, point to the *Change List Level* option at the bottom of the drop-down gallery, and then click a list level at the side menu. Set the numbering value with options at the Set Numbering Value dialog box, shown in Figure 8.1. Display this dialog box by clicking the Numbering button arrow and then clicking the *Set Numbering Value* option at the bottom of the drop-down gallery.

Figure 8.1 Set Numbering Value Dialog Box

1. Open **FDAgenda** and then save it with the name **8-FDAgenda**.
2. Restart the list numbering at 1 by completing the following steps:
   a. Select the numbered paragraphs.
   b. Click the Numbering button arrow in the Paragraph group on the Home tab and then click *Set Numbering Value* at the drop-down gallery.
   c. At the Set Numbering Value dialog box, select the number in the *Set value to* measurement box, type 1, and then press the Enter key.

3. Change the paragraph numbers to letters by completing the following steps:
   a. With the numbered paragraphs selected, click the Numbering button arrow.
   b. At the Numbering drop-down gallery, click the option that uses capital letters (second column, second row in the *Numbering Library* section [this location may vary]).

4. Add text by positioning the insertion point immediately right of the text *Introductions*, pressing the Enter key, and then typing Organizational Overview.

5. Demote the lettered list by completing the following steps:
   a. Select the lettered paragraphs.
   b. Click the Numbering button arrow, point to the *Change List Level* option, and then click the *a.* option at the side menu (*Level 2*).

5b

6. With the paragraphs still selected, promote the list by clicking the Decrease Indent button in the Paragraph group on the Home tab. (The lowercase letters change back to capital letters.)

7. Move the insertion point to the end of the document and then type The meeting will stop for lunch, which is catered and will be held in the main conference center from 12:15 to 1:30 p.m.

8. Press the Enter key and then click the Numbering button.

9. Click the AutoCorrect Options button next to the *A.* inserted in the document and then click *Continue Numbering* at the drop-down list. (This changes the letter from *A.* to *H.*)

9

10. Type Future Goals, press the Enter key, type Proposals, press the Enter key, and then type Adjournment.

11. Press the Enter key and *K.* is inserted in the document. Turn off the numbering formatting by clicking the Numbering button arrow and then clicking the *None* option at the drop-down gallery.

11

12. Save and then print **8-FDAgenda**.
13. Select and then delete the paragraph of text in the middle of the list (the paragraph that begins *The meeting will stop*). (All the lettered items should be listed consecutively and the same amount of space should appear between them.)
14. Save **8-FDAgenda**.

Check Your Work

Creating Custom Numbering Formats

Along with default and custom numbers, custom numbering formats can be created with options at the Define New Number Format dialog box, shown in Figure 8.2. Display this dialog box by clicking the Numbering button arrow and then clicking *Define New Number Format* at the drop-down gallery. Use options at the dialog box to specify the number style, font, and alignment. Preview the formatting in the *Preview* section.

Any number format created at the Define New Number Format dialog box is automatically included in the *Numbering Library* section of the Numbering button drop-down gallery. Remove a number format from the drop-down gallery by right-clicking the format and then clicking *Remove* at the shortcut menu.

Figure 8.2 Define New Number Format Dialog Box

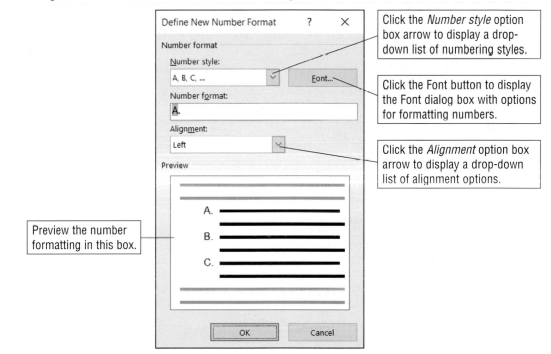

Click the *Number style* option box arrow to display a drop-down list of numbering styles.

Click the Font button to display the Font dialog box with options for formatting numbers.

Click the *Alignment* option box arrow to display a drop-down list of alignment options.

Preview the number formatting in this box.

Activity 1b Creating a Numbering Format

Part 2 of 2

1. With **8-FDAgenda** open, define a new numbering format by completing the following steps:
   a. With the insertion point positioned anywhere in the numbered paragraphs, click the Numbering button arrow in the Paragraph group on the Home tab.
   b. Click *Define New Number Format* at the drop-down list.
   c. At the Define New Number Format dialog box, click the *Number style* option box arrow and then click the *I, II, III, …* option.
   d. Click the Font button at the right of the *Number style* list box.

e. At the Font dialog box, scroll down the *Font* list box and then click *Calibri*.
f. Click *Bold* in the *Font style* list box.

g. Click OK to close the Font dialog box.
h. Click the *Alignment* option box arrow and then click *Right* at the drop-down list.
i. Click OK to close the Define New Number Format dialog box. (This applies the new formatting to the numbered paragraphs in the document.)
2. Insert a file into the current document by completing the following steps:
   a. Press Ctrl + End to move the insertion point to the end of the document and then press the Enter key two times.
   b. Click the Insert tab.
   c. Click the Object button arrow in the Text group and then click *Text from File* at the drop-down list.

d. At the Insert File dialog box, navigate to your WL1C8 folder and then double-click the **PDAgenda** document.
3. Select the text below the title *PRODUCTION DEPARTMENT AGENDA*, click the Home tab, click the Numbering button arrow, and then click the roman numeral style created in Step 1.
4. Remove from the Numbering Library the numbering format you created by completing the following steps:
   a. Click the Numbering button arrow.
   b. In the *Numbering Library* section, right-click the roman numeral numbering format that you created.
   c. Click *Remove* at the shortcut menu.
5. Save, print, and then close **8-FDAgenda**.

Check Your Work

Activity 2 Apply Custom Bullets to a Travel Document   **1 Part**

You will open a travel document and then define and insert custom picture and symbol bullets.

Creating Custom Bullets

Click the Bullets button in the Paragraph group and a round bullet is inserted in the document. Insert custom bullets by clicking the Bullets button arrow and then clicking a bullet type at the drop-down gallery. This drop-down gallery displays the most recently used bullets along with an option for defining a new bullet.

Click the *Define New Bullet* option and the Define New Bullet dialog box displays, as shown in Figure 8.3. Use options at the dialog box to choose a symbol or picture bullet, change the font size of the bullet, and specify the alignment of the bullet. When creating a custom bullet, consider matching the theme or mood of the document to maintain a consistent look or creating a picture bullet to add visual interest.

A custom bullet created at the Define New Bullet dialog box is automatically included in the *Bullet Library* section of the Bullets button drop-down gallery. Remove a custom bullet from the drop-down gallery by right-clicking the bullet and then clicking *Remove* at the shortcut menu.

As with the level of a numbered list, the level of a bulleted list can be changed. To do this, click the item or select the items to be changed, click the Bullets button arrow, and then point to *Change List Level*. At the side menu of bullet options that displays, click a bullet. To insert a line break in the list while the automatic bullets feature is on without inserting a bullet, press Shift + Enter. (A line break can also be inserted in a numbered list without inserting a number by pressing Shift + Enter.)

Figure 8.3 Define New Bullet Dialog Box

Choose a symbol bullet by clicking the Symbol button and then clicking a symbol at the Symbol dialog box.

Click the *Alignment* option box arrow to display a drop-down list of alignment options.

Preview the bullet formatting in this box.

Apply font formatting to a bullet by clicking the Font button and then applying formatting at the Font dialog box.

Use a picture as a bullet by clicking the Picture button and then searching for and inserting a picture from the Insert Pictures window.

1. Open **TTSHawaii** and then save it with the name **8-TTSHawaii**.
2. Define and insert a picture bullet by completing the following steps:
   a. Select the four paragraphs of text below the heading *Rainy Day Activities*.
   b. Click the Bullets button arrow in the Paragraph group on the Home tab and then click *Define New Bullet* at the drop-down gallery.

   c. At the Define New Bullet dialog box, click the Picture button.
   d. At the Insert Pictures window, click the *Browse* option at the right of the *From a file* option, navigate to your WL1C8 folder, and then double-click the **Flower** image file.
   e. Click OK to close the Define New Bullet dialog box. (The new bullet is applied to the selected paragraphs.)
3. Define and insert a symbol bullet by completing the following steps:
   a. Select the six paragraphs below the heading *Kauai Sights*.
   b. Click the Bullets button arrow and then click *Define New Bullet* at the drop-down gallery.
   c. At the Define New Bullet dialog box, click the Symbol button.
   d. At the Symbol dialog box, click the *Font* option box arrow, scroll down the drop-down list, and then click *Wingdings*.

   e. Click the flower symbol shown at the right (character code 124).
   f. Click OK to close the Symbol dialog box.
   g. At the Define New Bullet dialog box, click the Font button.
   h. At the Font dialog box, click *11* in the *Size* list box.
   i. Click the *Font color* option box arrow and then click the *Light Blue, Background 2, Darker 25%* color option (third column, third row in the *Theme Colors* section).
   j. Click OK to close the Font dialog box and then click OK to close the Define New Bullet dialog box.
4. Remove the two bullets you defined from the *Bullet Library* section of the Bullets button drop-down gallery by completing the following steps:
   a. Click the Bullets button arrow.
   b. Right-click the flower picture bullet in the *Bullet Library* section and then click *Remove* at the shortcut menu.
   c. Click the Bullets button arrow.
   d. Right-click the flower symbol bullet in the *Bullet Library* section and then click *Remove* at the shortcut menu.
5. Save, print, and then close **8-TTSHawaii**.

Check Your Work

Activity 3 Apply Multilevel List Numbering to a Job Search Document

2 Parts

You will open a document containing a list of job search terms, apply multilevel list numbering to the text, and then define and apply a new multilevel list numbering style.

Tutorial

Applying Multilevel
List Formatting

Multilevel
List

Quick Steps

**Insert Multilevel List
Formatting**
1. Click Multilevel List
   button.
2. Click style at drop-
   down gallery.

Applying Multilevel List Formatting

Use the Multilevel List button in the Paragraph group on the Home tab to specify the type of list formatting for paragraphs of text at the left margin, first tab, second tab, and so on. To apply predesigned multilevel list formatting to text in a document, click the Multilevel List button and then click a list style at the drop-down list.

Some options at the Multilevel List button drop-down list have labels such as *Heading 1, Heading 2,* and so on after the numbers. Click one of these options and Word inserts the numbering and applies the heading styles to the text.

Activity 3a Inserting Multilevel List Formatting

Part 1 of 2

1. Open **JSList** and then save it with the name **8-JSList(3a)**.
2. Select the paragraphs of text below the title and then apply multilevel list formatting by completing the following steps:
   a. Click the Multilevel List button in the Paragraph group on the Home tab.
   b. At the drop-down list, click the middle option in the top row of the *List Library* section.

   c. Deselect the text.
3. Save, print, and then close **8-JSList(3a)**.

Check Your Work

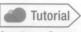

Quick Steps

Define Multilevel List
1. Click Multilevel List button.
2. Click *Define New Multilevel List.*
3. Choose level, list format, and/or position.
4. Click OK.

♀Hint When defining a multilevel list, you can mix numbers and bullets in the same list.

Creating a Custom Multilevel List

The Multilevel List button drop-down list contains predesigned level formatting options. If the drop-down list does not contain the type of list formatting required, create custom list formatting. To do this, click the Multilevel List button and then click the *Define New Multilevel List* option. This displays the Define new Multilevel list dialog box, shown in Figure 8.4. At this dialog box, click a level in the *Click level to modify* list box and then specify the level format, style, position, and alignment.

Typing a Multilevel List

Select text and then apply a multilevel list or apply the list and then type the text. When typing the text, press the Tab key to move to the next level or press Shift + Tab to move to the previous level.

Figure 8.4 Define New Multilevel List Dialog Box

Click a level to modify in this list box.

Specify the list format, style, position, and alignment for the selected level.

Define new Multilevel list

Click level to modify:

1)

  a)
   i)
    (1)
     (a)
      (i)
       1.
        a.
         i.

Number format

Enter formatting for number:

1)

Font...

Number style for this level:

1, 2, 3, ...

Include level number from:

Position

Number alignment: Left

Aligned at: 0"

Text indent at: 0.25"

Set for All Levels...

More >>

OK

Cancel

1. Open **JSList** and then save it with the name **8-JSList(3b)**.
2. Select the paragraphs of text below the title.
3. Click the Multilevel List button in the Paragraph group on the Home tab.
4. Click the *Define New Multilevel List* option at the drop-down list.
5. At the Define new Multilevel list dialog box, make sure *1* is selected in the *Click level to modify* list box.
6. Click the *Number style for this level* option box arrow and then click *A, B, C, …* at the drop-down list.
7. Click in the *Enter formatting for number* text box, delete any text after *A*, and then type a period. (See image at the right.)
8. Click the *Aligned at* measurement box up arrow until *0.3"* displays in the measurement box.
9. Click the *Text indent at* measurement box up arrow until *0.6"* displays in the measurement box.
10. Click *2* in the *Click level to modify* list box.
11. Click the *Number style for this level* option box arrow and then click *1, 2, 3, …* at the drop-down list.
12. Click in the *Enter formatting for number* text box, delete any text after the *1*, and then type a period.
13. Click the *Aligned at* measurement box up arrow until *0.6"* displays in the measurement box.
14. Click the *Text indent at* measurement box up arrow until *0.9"* displays in the measurement box.

15. Click *3* in the *Click level to modify* list box.
16. Click the *Number style for this level* option box arrow and then click *a, b, c, …* at the drop-down list.
17. Make sure that *a)* appears in the *Enter formatting for number* text box. (If not, delete any text after the *a* and then type a right parenthesis.)
18. Click the *Aligned at* measurement box up arrow until *0.9"* displays in the measurement box.
19. Click the *Text indent at* measurement box up arrow until *1.2"* displays in the measurement box.
20. Click OK to close the dialog box. (This applies the new multilevel list numbering to the selected text.)
21. Deselect the text.
22. Save, print, and then close **8-JSList(3b)**.

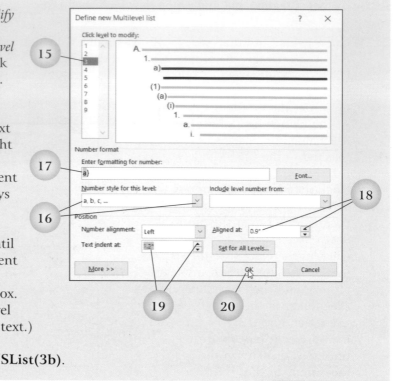

Check Your Work

Activity 4 **Create a Travel Document Using AutoCorrect**   **4 Parts**

You will create several AutoCorrect entries, open a letterhead document, and then use the AutoCorrect entries to type text in the document.

 Tutorial

Customizing AutoCorrect

Quick Steps

Display AutoCorrect Exceptions Dialog Box
1. Click File tab.
2. Click *Options*.
3. Click *Proofing*.
4. Click AutoCorrect Options button.
5. Click AutoCorrect tab.
6. Click Exceptions button.

Customizing AutoCorrect

Word's AutoCorrect feature corrects certain text automatically as it is typed. The types of corrections that can be made are specified with options at the AutoCorrect dialog box with the AutoCorrect tab selected, as shown in Figure 8.5.

Display this dialog box by clicking the File tab, clicking *Options*, clicking *Proofing* in the left panel, clicking the AutoCorrect Options button, and then clicking the AutoCorrect tab. At the dialog box, turn AutoCorrect features on or off by inserting or removing check marks from the check boxes. In addition, specify AutoCorrect exceptions, replace frequently misspelled words with the correctly spelled words, add frequently used words, and specify keys to quickly insert the words in a document.

Figure 8.5 AutoCorrect Dialog Box with the AutoCorrect Tab Selected

Remove the check marks from the check boxes identifying corrections that should not be made by AutoCorrect.

Click this button to display the AutoCorrect Exceptions dialog box.

Type the text shown in the first column of this list box in a document and then press the spacebar and the text is replaced by the symbol or text shown in the second column.

Specifying AutoCorrect Exceptions

The check box options at the AutoCorrect dialog box with the AutoCorrect tab selected identify the types of corrections made by AutoCorrect. Specify which corrections should not be made with options at the AutoCorrect Exceptions dialog box, shown in Figure 8.6. Display this dialog box by clicking the Exceptions button at the AutoCorrect dialog box with the AutoCorrect tab selected.

AutoCorrect usually capitalizes a word that comes after a period, since a period usually ends a sentence. This automatic capitalization may be incorrect in some cases, as when the period is used in an abbreviation. Exceptions to this general practice are shown in the AutoCorrect Exceptions dialog box with the First Letter tab selected. Many exceptions already display in the dialog box but additional exceptions can be added by typing each exception in the *Don't capitalize after* text box and then clicking the Add button.

Figure 8.6 AutoCorrect Exceptions Dialog Box

Click this tab to display a list box to add exceptions to correcting two initial capital letters in a word.

Click this tab to display a list box to add any other exceptions to corrections.

Add capitalization exceptions to this list box.

By default, AutoCorrect corrects the use of two initial capital letters in a word. If AutoCorrect should not correct these instances, display the AutoCorrect Exceptions dialog box with the INitial CAps tab selected and then type the exception text in the *Don't correct* text box. At the AutoCorrect Exceptions dialog box with the Other Corrections tab selected, type the text that should not be corrected in the *Don't correct* text box. Delete an exception from the dialog box with any of the tabs selected by clicking the text in the list box and then clicking the Delete button.

 Tutorial

Adding and
Deleting an
AutoCorrect Entry

Adding and Deleting an AutoCorrect Entry

Commonly misspelled words and/or typographical errors can be added to AutoCorrect. For example, if a user consistently types *relavent* instead of *relevant*, *relavent* can be added to the AutoCorrect dialog box with the AutoCorrect tab selected with the direction to correct it to *relevant*. The AutoCorrect dialog box also contains a few symbols that can be inserted in a document. For example, type *(c)* and AutoCorrect changes the text to © (copyright symbol). Type *(r)* and AutoCorrect changes the text to ® (registered trademark symbol). The symbols display at the beginning of the AutoCorrect dialog box list box.

Quick Steps

Add Word to AutoCorrect
1. Click File tab.
2. Click *Options*.
3. Click *Proofing*.
4. Click AutoCorrect Options button.
5. Click AutoCorrect tab.
6. Type misspelled or abbreviated word.
7. Press Tab.
8. Type correctly spelled or complete word.
9. Click Add button.
10. Click OK.

An abbreviation can be added to AutoCorrect that will insert the entire word (or words) in the document when it is typed. For example, in Activity 4a, the abbreviation *fav* will be added to AutoCorrect and *Family Adventure Vacations* will be inserted when *fav* is typed followed by a press of the spacebar or Enter key. The capitalization of the abbreviation can also be controlled. For example, in Activity 4a, the abbreviation *Na* will be added to AutoCorrect and *Namibia* will be inserted when *Na* is typed and *NAMIBIA* will be inserted when *NA* is typed.

AutoCorrect text can be deleted from the AutoCorrect dialog box. To do this, display the AutoCorrect dialog box with the AutoCorrect tab selected, click the word or words in the list box, and then click the Delete button.

Activity 4a Adding Text and Specifying Exceptions to AutoCorrect

Part 1 of 4

1. At a blank screen, click the File tab and then click *Options*.
2. At the Word Options dialog box, click *Proofing* in the left panel.
3. Click the AutoCorrect Options button in the *AutoCorrect options* section.
4. At the AutoCorrect dialog box with the AutoCorrect tab selected, add an exception to AutoCorrect by completing the following steps:
   a. Click the Exceptions button.
   b. At the AutoCorrect Exceptions dialog box, click the INitial CAps tab.
   c. Click in the *Don't correct* text box, type STudent, and then click the Add button.

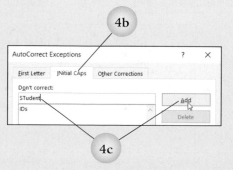

d. Click in the *Don't correct* text box, type STyle, and then click the Add button.
  e. Click OK.
5. At the AutoCorrect dialog box with the AutoCorrect tab selected, click in the *Replace* text box and then type fav.
6. Press the Tab key (which moves the insertion point to the *With* text box) and then type Family Adventure Vacations.
7. Click the Add button. (This adds *fav* and *Family Adventure Vacations* to AutoCorrect and also selects *fav* in the *Replace* text box.)

8. Type Na in the *Replace* text box. (The text *fav* is automatically removed when the typing of *Na* begins.)
9. Press the Tab key and then type Namibia.
10. Click the Add button.
11. With the insertion point positioned in the *Replace* text box, type vf.
12. Press the Tab key and then type Victoria Falls.
13. Click the Add button.
14. With the insertion point positioned in the *Replace* text box, type tts.
15. Press the Tab key and then type Terra Travel Services.
16. Click the Add button.
17. Click OK to close the AutoCorrect dialog box and then click OK to close the Word Options dialog box.
18. Open **TTSLtrhd** and then save it with the name **8-TTSAfrica**.
19. Type the text shown in Figure 8.7. Type the text exactly as shown (including applying bold formatting and centering *fav* at the beginning of the document). AutoCorrect will correct the words as they are typed.
20. Save **8-TTSAfrica**.

Check Your Work

Figure 8.7 Activity 4a

fav

Na and vf Adventure

tts is partnering with fav to provide adventurous and thrilling family vacations. Our first joint adventure is a holiday trip to Na. Na is one of the most fascinating holiday destinations in Africa and offers comfortable facilities, great food, cultural interaction, abundant wildlife, and a wide variety of activities to interest people of all ages.

During the 12-day trip, you and your family will travel across Na through national parks, enjoying the beautiful and exotic scenery and watching wildlife in natural habitats. You will cruise along the Kwando and Chobe rivers and spend time at the Okapuka Lodge located near Windhoek, the capital of Na.

If you or your family member is a college student, contact one of our college travel adventure consultants to learn more about the newest Student Travel package titled "STudent STyle" that offers a variety of student discounts, rebates, and free travel accessories for qualifying participants.

tts and fav are offering a 15 percent discount if you sign up for this once-in-a-lifetime trip to Na. This exciting adventure is limited to twenty people, so don't wait to sign up.

 Tutorial

Undoing an
AutoCorrect
Correction

 AutoCorrect
Options

Using the AutoCorrect Options Button

After AutoCorrect corrects a portion of text, hover the mouse pointer near the text and a small blue box displays below it. Move the mouse pointer to this blue box and the AutoCorrect Options button displays. Click this button to display a drop-down list with the options to change the text back to the original version, stop automatically correcting the specific text, and display the AutoCorrect dialog box.

If the AutoCorrect Options button does not display, turn on the feature. To do this, display the AutoCorrect dialog box with the AutoCorrect tab selected, click the *Show AutoCorrect Options buttons* check box to insert a check mark, and then click OK to close the dialog box.

Activity 4b Using the AutoCorrect Options Button
Part 2 of 4

1. With **8-TTSAfrica** open, select and then delete the last paragraph.
2. With the insertion point positioned on the blank line below the last paragraph of text (you may need to press the Enter key), type the following text. (AutoCorrect will automatically change *Ameria* to *America*, which you will change in the next step.) Through the sponsorship of Ameria Resorts, we are able to offer you a 15 percent discount for groups of twelve or more people.
3. Change the spelling of *America* back to *Ameria* by completing the following steps:
   a. Position the mouse pointer over *America* until a blue box displays below it.
   b. Position the mouse pointer on the blue box until the AutoCorrect Options button displays.

c. Click the AutoCorrect Options
button and then click the *Change
back to "Ameria"* option.
4. Save and then print **8-TTSAfrica**.

3c

Through the sponsorship of America Resorts, we are able to offer you a 15
of twelve or more people

↰ Change back to "Ameria"

Stop Automatically Correcting "Ameria"

✎ Control AutoCorrect Options...

Check Your Work

Inserting Symbols Automatically

AutoCorrect recognizes and replaces symbols as well as text. Several symbols
included in AutoCorrect are shown in the AutoCorrect dialog box and are listed
first in the *Replace* text box. Table 8.1 lists these symbols along with the characters
to insert them.

In addition to the symbols provided by Word, other symbols can be inserted
in the AutoCorrect dialog box with the AutoCorrect button in the Symbol dialog
box. To insert a symbol in the AutoCorrect dialog box, click the Insert tab, click
the Symbol button in the Symbols group, and then click *More Symbols* at the drop-
down list. At the Symbol dialog box, click the specific symbol and then click the
AutoCorrect button in the lower left corner of the dialog box. This displays the
AutoCorrect dialog box with the symbol inserted in the *With* text box and the
insertion point positioned in the *Replace* text box. Type the text that will insert the
symbol, click the Add button, and then click OK to close the AutoCorrect dialog
box. Click the Close button to close the Symbol dialog box.

Table 8.1 AutoCorrect Symbols Available at the AutoCorrect Dialog Box

Type	To insert
(c)	©
(r)	®
(tm)	™
...	. . .
:) or :-)	☺
:| or :-|	☺
:(or :-(	☹
-->	→
<--	←
==>	→
<==	←
<=>	⇔

1. With **8-TTSAfrica** open, move the insertion point so it is positioned immediately right of the last *s* in *Resorts* (located in the last paragraph) and then type (r). (This inserts the registered trademark symbol.)
2. Move the insertion point immediately left of the *1* in *15* and then type ==>. (This inserts the ➔ symbol.)
3. Move the insertion point immediately right of the *t* in *discount* and then type <==. (This inserts the ← symbol.)
4. Insert the pound (£) currency unit symbol in AutoCorrect by completing the following steps:
   a. Click the Insert tab.
   b. Click the Symbol button and then click *More Symbols* at the drop-down list.
   c. At the Symbol dialog box, make sure that *(normal text)* displays in the *Font* option box. If it does not, click the *Font* option box arrow and then click *(normal text)* at the drop-down list (first option in the list).
   d. Scroll through the list of symbols and then click the pound (£) currency unit symbol (located in approximately the sixth or seventh row; character code *00A3*).
   e. Click the AutoCorrect button in the lower left corner of the dialog box.
   f. At the AutoCorrect dialog box, type pcu in the *Replace* text box and then click the Add button.
   g. Click OK to close the AutoCorrect dialog box.

   h. Click the Close button to close the Symbol dialog box.
5. Press Ctrl + End to move the insertion point to the end of the document and then press the Enter key.
6. Type the text shown in Figure 8.8. (Press Shift + Enter or the Enter key as indicated in the figure.) Create the pound currency unit symbol by typing pcu and then pressing the spacebar. Press the Backspace key once and then type 2,999. (Complete similar steps when typing *£2,549 (UK)*.)
7. Save **8-TTSAfrica**.

▶ Check Your Work

Figure 8.8 Activity 4c

Individual price: *(press Shift+ Enter)*
$3,999 (US) *(press Shift+ Enter)*
£2,999 (UK) *(press Enter)*

Individual price for groups of twelve or more: *(press Shift+ Enter)*
$3,399 (US) *(press Shift+ Enter)*
£2,549 (UK)

Tutorial

Customizing
AutoFormatting

Customizing AutoFormatting

When typing text, Word provides options to automatically apply some formatting, such as changing a fraction to a fraction character (1/2 to ½), changing numbers to ordinals (1st to 1st), changing an internet or network path to a hyperlink (https://ppi-edu.net to https://ppi-edu.net), and applying bullets or numbers to text. The autoformatting options display in the AutoCorrect dialog box with the AutoFormat As You Type tab selected, as shown in Figure 8.9.

Display this dialog box by clicking the File tab and then clicking *Options*. At the Word Options dialog box, click *Proofing* in the left panel and then click the AutoCorrect Options button. At the AutoCorrect dialog box, click the AutoFormat As You Type tab. At the dialog box, remove the check marks from those options to be turned off and insert check marks for those options to be formatted automatically.

Figure 8.9 AutoCorrect Dialog Box with the AutoFormat As You Type Tab Selected

1. Make sure **8-TTSAfrica** is open.
2. Suppose that you need to add a couple of web addresses to a document and do not want the addresses automatically formatted as hyperlinks (since you are sending the document as hard copy rather than electronically). Turn off the autoformatting of web addresses by completing the following steps:
   a. Click the File tab and then click *Options*.
   b. At the Word Options dialog box, click *Proofing* in the left panel.
   c. Click the AutoCorrect Options button.
   d. At the AutoCorrect dialog box, click the AutoFormat As You Type tab.
   e. Click the *Internet and network paths with hyperlinks* check box to remove the check mark.

   f. Click OK to close the AutoCorrect dialog box.
   g. Click OK to close the Word Options dialog box.
3. Press Ctrl + End to move the insertion point to the end of the document, press the Enter key, and then type the text shown in Figure 8.10.
4. Turn on the autoformatting of web addresses that was turned off in Step 2 by completing Steps 2a through 2g (except in Step 2e, insert the check mark rather than remove it).
5. Delete *fav* from AutoCorrect by completing the following steps:
   a. Click the File tab and then click *Options*.
   b. At the Word Options dialog box, click *Proofing* in the left panel.
   c. Click the AutoCorrect Options button.
   d. At the AutoCorrect dialog box, click the AutoCorrect tab.
   e. Click in the *Replace* text box and then type fav. (This selects the entry in the list box.)
   f. Click the Delete button.
6. Complete steps similar to those in Steps 5e and 5f to delete the *Na*, *tts*, and *vf* AutoCorrect entries.

7. Delete the exceptions added to the AutoCorrect Exceptions dialog box by completing the following steps:
   a. At the AutoCorrect dialog box with the AutoCorrect tab selected, click the Exceptions button.
   b. At the AutoCorrect Exceptions dialog box, if necessary, click the INitial CAps tab.
   c. Click *STudent* in the list box and then click the Delete button.
   d. Click *STyle* in the list box and then click the Delete button.
   e. Click OK to close the AutoCorrect Exceptions dialog box.
8. Click OK to close the AutoCorrect dialog box.
9. Click OK to close the Word Options dialog box.
10. Save, print, and then close **3-TTSAfrica**.

Check Your Work

Figure 8.10 Activity 4d

For additional information on the Na adventure, as well as other exciting vacation specials, please visit our website at https://ppi-edu.net/terratravel or visit https://ppi-edu.net/famadv.

Activity 5 Apply Custom Themes to Company Documents   **5 Parts**

You will create custom theme colors and theme fonts and then apply theme effects. You will save the changes as a custom theme, apply the custom theme to a company services document and a company security document, and then delete the theme.

Customizing Themes

A document created in Word is based on the Normal template. This template provides a document with default layout, formatting, styles, and themes. The default template provides a number of built-in or predesigned themes. Some of these built-in themes have been used in previous chapters to apply colors, fonts, and effects to content in documents. The same built-in themes are available in Microsoft Word, Excel, Access, PowerPoint, and Outlook. Because the same themes are available across these programs, business files—such as documents, workbooks, databases, and presentations—can be branded with a consistent and professional appearance.

A theme is a combination of theme colors, theme fonts, and theme effects. Within a theme, any of these three elements can be changed with the additional buttons in the Document Formatting group on the Design tab. Apply one of the built-in themes or create a custom theme. A custom theme will display in the *Custom* section of the Themes button drop-down gallery. To create a custom theme, change the theme colors, theme fonts, and/or theme effects.

💡 **Hint** Every document created in Word has a theme applied to it.

Themes

 Colors

A Fonts

The Themes, Colors, and Fonts buttons in the Document Formatting group on the Design tab provide representations of the current theme. For example, the Themes button shows uppercase and lowercase *Aa* with colored squares below the letters. When the theme colors are changed, the changes are reflected in the small colored squares on the Themes button and the four squares on the Colors button. If the theme fonts are changed, the letters on the Themes button and the Fonts button reflect the change.

Tutorial

Creating Custom Theme Colors

Quick Steps

Create Custom Theme Colors
1. Click Design tab.
2. Click Colors button.
3. Click *Customize Colors*.
4. Type name for custom theme colors.
5. Change background, accent, and hyperlink colors.
6. Click Save button.

Creating Custom Theme Colors

To create custom theme colors, click the Design tab, click the Colors button, and then click *Customize Colors* at the drop-down gallery. This displays the Create New Theme Colors dialog box, similar to the one shown in Figure 8.11. Type a name for the custom theme colors in the *Name* text box and then change colors. Theme colors contain four text and background colors, six accent colors, and two hyperlink colors, as shown in the *Theme colors* section of the dialog box. Change a color in the list box by clicking the color button at the right of the color option and then clicking a color at the color palette.

After making all the changes to the colors, click the Save button. This saves the custom theme colors and also applies the color changes to the active document. Display the custom theme by clicking the Colors button. The custom theme will display at the top of the drop-down gallery in the *Custom* section.

Resetting Custom Theme Colors

If changes have been made to colors at the Create New Theme Colors dialog box, the colors can be reset by clicking the Reset button in the lower left corner of the dialog box. Clicking this button restores the colors to the default Office theme colors.

Figure 8.11 Create New Theme Colors Dialog Box

Type a name for the custom theme in the *Name* text box.

Click the Reset button to reset the colors back to the default.

Change a theme color by clicking the color button and then clicking a color at the drop-down palette.

Note: If you are running Word on a computer connected to a network in a public environment, such as a school, you may need to complete all five parts of Activity 5 during the same session. Network system software may delete your custom themes when you exit Word. Check with your instructor.

1. At a blank document, click the Design tab.
2. Click the Colors button in the Document Formatting group and then click *Customize Colors* at the drop-down gallery.
3. At the Create New Theme Colors dialog box, click the color button to the right of the *Text/Background - Light 1* option and then click the *Dark Red* option (first option in the *Standard Colors* section).

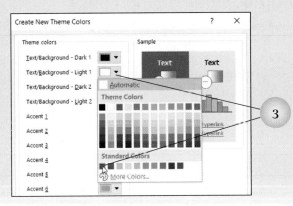

4. Click the color button to the right of the *Accent 1* option and then click the *Yellow* option (fourth option in the *Standard Colors* section).
5. You decide that you do not like the colors you have chosen and want to start over. To do this, click the Reset button in the lower left corner of the dialog box.
6. Click the color button to the right of the *Text/Background - Dark 2* option and then click the *Blue* option (eighth option in the *Standard Colors* section).
7. Change the color for the *Accent 1* option by completing the following steps:
   a. Click the color button to the right of the *Accent 1* option.
   b. Click the *More Colors* option below the color palette.
   c. At the Colors dialog box, click the Standard tab.
   d. Click the dark green color, as shown below.
   e. Click OK to close the dialog box.

8. Save the custom colors by completing the following steps:
   a. Select the current text in the *Name* text box.
   b. Type your first and last names (without a space between).
   c. Click the Save button.
9. Close the document without saving it.

| 8b | 8c |

Name: StudentName

Reset   Save   Cancel

 Tutorial

Creating Custom Theme Fonts

Creating Custom Theme Fonts

Quick Steps

Create Custom Theme Fonts

1. Click Design tab.
2. Click Fonts button.
3. Click *Customize Fonts*.
4. Choose fonts.
5. Type name for custom theme fonts.
6. Click Save button.

To create a custom theme font, click the Design tab, click the Fonts button, and then click *Customize Fonts* at the drop-down gallery. This displays the Create New Theme Fonts dialog box. At this dialog box, type a name for the custom fonts in the *Name* text box. Choose a font for headings and a font for body text and then click the Save button.

Activity 5b Creating Custom Theme Fonts

Part 2 of 5

1. At a blank document, click the Design tab.
2. Click the Fonts button in the Document Formatting group and then click the *Customize Fonts* option at the drop-down gallery.
3. At the Create New Theme Fonts dialog box, click the *Heading font* option box arrow, scroll up the drop-down list, and then click *Arial*.
4. Click the *Body font* option box arrow, scroll down the drop-down list, and then click *Cambria*.
5. Save the custom fonts by completing the following steps:
   a. Select the current text in the *Name* text box.
   b. Type your first and last names (without a space between).
   c. Click the Save button.

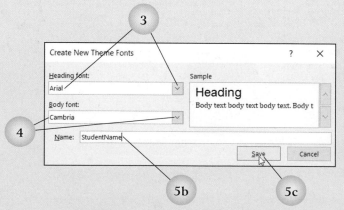

6. Close the document without saving it.

Applying Custom Theme Colors and Fonts

Apply custom theme colors to a document by clicking the Colors button in the Document Formatting group on the Design tab and then clicking the custom theme colors option at the top of the drop-down gallery in the *Custom* section. Complete similar steps to apply custom theme fonts.

Applying Theme Effects

The options in the Theme Effects button drop-down gallery apply sets of line and fill effects to the graphics in a document. Custom theme effects cannot be created but a theme effect can be applied to a document and the formatting can then be saved in a custom theme.

 Tutorial

Saving a Custom
Document Theme

Saving a Custom Document Theme

A custom document theme containing custom theme colors, fonts, and effects can be saved. To do this, create and apply custom theme colors, fonts, and theme effects to a document, click the Themes button on the Design tab, and then click *Save Current Theme* at the drop-down gallery. This displays the Save Current Theme dialog box, which has many of the same options as the Save As dialog box. Type a name for the custom document theme in the *File name* text box and then click the Save button.

Quick Steps

**Save Custom
Document Theme**
1. Click Design tab.
2. Click Themes button.
3. Click *Save Current Theme*.
4. Type name for theme.
5. Click Save button.

Activity 5c Applying Theme Effects and Saving a Custom Document Theme   Part 3 of 5

1. Open **NSSServices** and then save it with the name **8-NSSServices**.
2. Make the following changes to the document:
   a. Apply the Title style to the company name *Northland Security Systems*.
   b. Apply the Heading 1 style to the heading *Northland Security Systems Mission*.
   c. Apply the Heading 2 style to the remaining headings, *Security Services* and *Security Software*.
   d. Apply the Word 2010 style set (the last option in the expanded style set gallery on the Design tab).
3. Apply the custom theme colors you saved by completing the following steps:
   a. Click the Colors button in the Document Formatting group on the Design tab.
   b. Click the theme colors option with your name at the top of the drop-down gallery in the *Custom* group.

4. Apply the custom theme fonts you saved by clicking the Fonts button in the Document Formatting group and then clicking the custom theme font with your name.

5. Apply a theme effect by clicking the Effects button in the Document Formatting group and then clicking *Glossy* at the drop-down gallery (last option).

6. Make the following changes to the SmartArt graphic:
   a. Click the graphic to select it. (When the graphic is selected, a gray border displays around it.)
   b. Click the SmartArt Tools Design tab.
   c. Click the Change Colors button and then click *Colorful Range - Accent Colors 5 to 6* (last option in the *Colorful* section).
   d. Click the More SmartArt Styles button in the SmartArt Styles group and then click *Cartoon* (third option in the *3-D* section).
   e. Click outside the SmartArt graphic to deselect it.
7. Save the custom theme colors and fonts, as well as the Glossy theme effect, as a custom document theme by completing the following steps:
   a. Click the Design tab.
   b. Click the Themes button in the Document Formatting group.
   c. Click the *Save Current Theme* option at the bottom of the drop-down gallery.
   d. At the Save Current Theme dialog box, type your first and last names (without a space between) in the *File name* text box and then click the Save button.

7d

File name:	StudentName	
Save as type:	Office Theme	

∧ Hide Folders   Tools ▾   Save   Cancel

8. Save and then print **8-NSSServices**.

Check Your Work

Tutorial

Editing a Custom Theme

Quick Steps

Edit Custom Theme Colors or Fonts
1. Click Design tab.
2. Click Colors button or Fonts button.
3. Right-click custom theme colors or fonts.
4. Click *Edit.*
5. Make changes.
6. Click Save button.

Editing Custom Themes

Custom theme colors and theme fonts can be edited. To edit custom theme colors, click the Design tab and then click the Colors button in the Document Formatting group. At the drop-down gallery of custom and built-in theme colors, right-click the custom theme colors and then click *Edit* at the shortcut menu. This displays the Edit Theme Colors dialog box, which contains the same options as the Create New Theme Colors dialog box. Make changes to the theme colors and then click the Save button.

To edit custom theme fonts, click the Fonts button in the Document Formatting group on the Design tab, right-click the custom theme fonts, and then click *Edit* at the shortcut menu. This displays the Edit Theme Fonts dialog box, which contains the same options as the Create New Theme Fonts dialog box. Make changes to the theme fonts and then click the Save button.

Activity 5d Editing Custom Themes   Part 4 of 5

1. With **8-NSSServices** open, edit the theme colors by completing the following steps:
   a. If necessary, click the Design tab.
   b. Click the Colors button.
   c. Right-click the custom theme colors named with your first and last names.
   d. Click *Edit* at the shortcut menu.
   e. At the Edit Theme Colors dialog box, click the color button to the right of the *Text/ Background - Dark 2* option.
   f. Click the *More Colors* option below the color palette.
   g. At the Colors dialog box, click the Standard tab.
   h. Click the dark green color. (This is the same color you chose for *Accent 1* in Activity 5a.)
   i. Click OK to close the dialog box.
   j. Click the Save button.

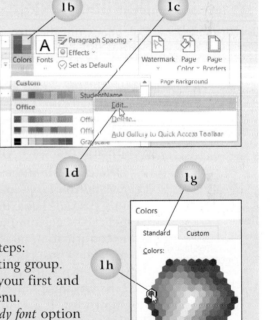

2. Edit the theme fonts by completing the following steps:
   a. Click the Fonts button in the Document Formatting group.
   b. Right-click the custom theme fonts named with your first and last names and then click *Edit* at the shortcut menu.
   c. At the Edit Theme Fonts dialog box, click the *Body font* option box arrow, scroll down the drop-down list, and then click *Constantia*.
   d. Click the Save button.
3. Apply a different theme effect by clicking the Effects button and then clicking *Extreme Shadow* at the drop-down gallery (second column, last row). (This applies a shadow behind each shape.)

4. Save the changes to the custom theme by completing the following steps:
   a. Click the Themes button and then click *Save Current Theme* at the drop-down gallery.
   b. At the Save Current Theme dialog box, click the theme named with your first and last names in the content pane.
   c. Click the Save button.
   d. At the message stating that the theme already exists and asking if you want to replace it, click Yes.
5. Save, print, and then close **8-NSSServices**.

 Check Your Work

Resetting a Template Theme

Quick Steps

Resetting Template Theme
1. Click Design tab.
2. Click Themes button.
3. Click *Reset to Theme from Template.*

If a built-in theme other than the Office default theme or a custom theme is applied to a document, the theme can be reset to the default by clicking the Themes button and then clicking the *Reset to Theme from Template* at the drop-down gallery. If the document is based on the default template provided by Word, clicking this option resets the theme to the Office default theme.

Tutorial

Deleting a Custom Theme

Deleting Custom Themes

Delete custom theme colors from the Colors button drop-down gallery, delete custom theme fonts from the Fonts drop-down gallery, and delete custom themes at the Themes button drop-down gallery or the Save Current Theme dialog box.

Quick Steps

Delete Custom Theme Colors or Fonts
1. Click Design tab.
2. Click Colors or Fonts button.
3. Right-click custom theme.
4. Click *Delete.*
5. Click Yes.

Delete a Custom Theme
1. Click Design tab.
2. Click Themes button.
3. Right-click custom theme.
4. Click *Delete.*
5. Click Yes.

To delete custom theme colors, click the Colors button, right-click the theme to be deleted, and then click *Delete* at the shortcut menu. At the confirmation message, click Yes. To delete custom theme fonts, click the Fonts button, right-click the theme to be deleted, and then click *Delete* at the shortcut menu. At the confirmation message, click Yes.

Delete a custom theme (including custom colors, fonts, and effects) at the Themes button drop-down gallery or the Save Current Theme dialog box. To delete a custom theme from the drop-down gallery, click the Themes button, right-click the custom theme, click *Delete* at the shortcut menu, and then click Yes at the confirmation message. To delete a custom theme from the Save Current Theme dialog box, click the Themes button and then click *Save Current Theme* at the drop-down gallery. At the dialog box, click the custom theme document name, click the Organize button on the dialog box toolbar, and then click *Delete* at the drop-down list. If a confirmation message displays, click Yes.

Changing Default Settings

If formatting is applied to a document—such as a specific style set, theme, and paragraph spacing—it can be saved as the default formatting. To do this, click the Set as Default button in the Document Formatting group on the Design tab. At the message asking if the current style set and theme should be set as the default and indicating that the settings will be applied to new documents, click Yes.

1. Open **NSSSecurity** and then save it with the name **8-NSSSecurity**.
2. Apply the Title style to the company name, apply the Heading 1 style to the two headings in the document, and then apply the Word 2010 style set.
3. Apply your custom theme by completing the following steps:
   a. If necessary, click the Design tab.
   b. Click the Themes button.
   c. Click the custom theme named with your first and last names at the top of the drop-down gallery in the *Custom* section.
4. Save and then print **8-NSSSecurity**.
5. Reset the theme to the Office default theme by clicking the Themes button and then clicking *Reset to Theme from Template* at the drop-down gallery.
6. Save and then close **8-NSSSecurity**.
7. Press Ctrl + N to display a new blank document.
8. Delete the custom theme colors by completing the following steps:
   a. Click the Design tab.
   b. Click the Colors button in the Document Formatting group.
   c. Right-click the custom theme colors named with your first and last names.
   d. Click *Delete* at the shortcut menu.

   e. At the message that displays asking if you want to delete the theme colors, click Yes.
9. Complete steps similar to those in Step 8 to delete the custom theme fonts named with your first and last names.
10. Delete the custom theme by completing the following steps:
    a. Click the Themes button.
    b. Right-click the custom theme named with your first and last names.
    c. Click *Delete* at the shortcut menu.
    d. At the message asking if you want to delete the theme, click Yes.
11. Close the document without saving it.

Check Your Work

Chapter Summary

- Use the Bullets button to insert bullets before specific paragraphs of text and use the Numbering button to insert numbers.

- Insert custom numbers by clicking the Numbering button arrow and then clicking an option at the drop-down gallery.

- Set the numbering value by clicking the Numbering button arrow and then clicking the *Set Numbering Value* option to display the dialog box.

- Define custom numbering formatting by clicking the Numbering button arrow and then clicking *Define New Number Format* to display the dialog box.

- Insert custom bullets by clicking the Bullets button arrow and then clicking an option at the drop-down gallery. Define new custom bullets by clicking the Bullets button arrow and then clicking *Define New Bullet* at the drop-down gallery to display the dialog box.

- Apply list formatting to multilevel paragraphs of text by clicking the Multilevel List button in the Paragraph group on the Home tab. Define new custom multilevel list formatting by clicking the Multilevel List button and then clicking *Define New Multilevel List* at the drop-down gallery to display the dialog box.

- When typing a multilevel list, press the Tab key to move to the next level and press Shift + Tab to move to the previous level.

- Words can be added to AutoCorrect at the AutoCorrect dialog box. Display this dialog box by clicking the File tab, clicking *Options*, clicking *Proofing*, clicking the AutoCorrect Options button, and then clicking the AutoCorrect tab.

- Specify exceptions to AutoCorrect by clicking the Exceptions button at the AutoCorrect dialog box with the AutoCorrect tab selected to display the dialog box.

- Use the AutoCorrect Options button, which displays when the mouse pointer is hovered over corrected text, to change corrected text back to the original spelling, stop automatically correcting specific text, or display the AutoCorrect dialog box.

- The AutoCorrect dialog box contains several symbols that can be inserted in a document by typing specific text or characters. To add more symbols, display the Symbol dialog box, click the specific symbol, and then click the AutoCorrect button.

- When typing text, control what Word formats automatically with options at the AutoCorrect dialog box with the AutoFormat As You Type tab selected.

- A Word document is based on the Normal template that provides a document with default layout, formatting, styles, and themes. The Normal template provides a number of predesigned themes, that are available in the Document Formatting group on the Design tab.

- A theme is a combination of theme colors, theme fonts, and theme effects. A custom theme can be created that includes custom theme colors, theme fonts, and/or theme effects.

- Create custom theme colors with options at the Create New Theme Colors dialog box. Display this dialog box by clicking the Colors button on the Design tab and then clicking *Customize Colors* at the drop-down gallery. Click the Reset button in the dialog box to return to the default Office theme colors.

- Create custom theme fonts with options at the Create New Theme Fonts dialog box. Display this dialog box by clicking the Fonts button on the Design tab and then clicking *Customize Fonts* at the drop-down gallery.
- A theme effect is a set of lines and fill effects that can be applied to a document. Custom theme effects cannot be created but a theme effect can be applied to a document and then saved in a custom theme.
- Save a custom theme by clicking the Themes button on the Design tab and then clicking *Save Current Theme* at the drop-down gallery to display the dialog box.
- Apply custom theme colors by clicking the Colors button in the Document Formatting group on the Design tab and then clicking the custom theme colors option at the top of the drop-down gallery. Complete similar steps to apply custom theme fonts.
- Edit custom theme colors by clicking the Design tab and then clicking the Colors button in the Document Formatting group. At the drop-down gallery, right-click the custom theme colors and then click *Edit* at the shortcut menu. This displays the Edit Theme Colors dialog box where changes can be made to the theme colors. Edit custom theme fonts in a similar manner.
- Click the *Reset to Theme from Template* option at the Themes button drop-down gallery to reset the theme to the Office default theme.
- Delete a custom theme at the Themes button drop-down gallery or at the Save Current Theme dialog box.
- Formatting applied to a document can be saved as the default formatting by clicking the Set as Default button in the Document Formatting group on the Design tab.

Commands Review

FEATURE	RIBBON TAB, GROUP/OPTION	BUTTON, OPTION
AutoCorrect dialog box	File, *Options*	*Proofing*, AutoCorrect Options
bullets	Home, Paragraph	
Create New Theme Colors dialog box	Design, Document Formatting	, *Customize Colors*
Create New Theme Fonts dialog box	Design, Document Formatting	, *Customize Fonts*
Define New Bullet dialog box	Home, Paragraph	, *Define New Bullet*
Define New Multilevel List dialog box	Home, Paragraph	, *Define New Multilevel List*
Define New Number Format dialog box	Home, Paragraph	, *Define New Number Format*
numbering	Home, Paragraph	
Save Current Theme dialog box	Design, Document Formatting	, *Save Current Theme*

Index

to last location in document, 16

with mouse, 14

moving within table using keyboard, 193

to specific line or page, 15

in table, when created, 192

Insert Table dialog box, 195

Italic button, 34

italic typeface, 33, 34–35

K

keyboard shortcuts

case of text, 36

closing Word, 9

copying and pasting, 80

cutting and pasting, 77

date and time, inserting, 128

deleting text, 17

display Reveal Formatting task pane, 56

font group buttons, 36–37

Help, 26

inserting page break, 90–91

line spacing, 55

moving insertion point, 15

in tables, 193

new document, 10

Open backstage area, 10

Open dialog box, 11

paragraph alignment, 46

in Read Mode view, 157

repeat last action, 53–54

selecting cells in table with, 199

selecting text, 18–19

spelling and grammar check, 22

L

Label Options dialog box, 177

labels, creating and printing, 175–178

Labels button, 176

landscape orientation, 86–87

Layout Options button, 130

leader tab, setting, 76

Learning Tools, 158–160

letter, template to create, 179–180

Line and Paragraph Spacing button, 54, 55

line drawing, 139

Line Focus button, 158

line spacing

automatic adjustments, 54

default, 33

default setting, 54

keyboard shortcut for changing, 55

Paragraph dialog box, 55

lists

bulleted, 65

creating numbered, 62–64

multilevel, 233–236

live preview feature, 33

M

mailing labels

with an image, 178

creating and printing, 175–178

Manual Hyphenation dialog box, 108

margins

changing cell margin measurements, 208–210

changing page margins, 86–89

default setting, 156

Margins button, 86

Margins button drop-down list, 86

Maximize button, 164

Merge Cells button, 203

merging, cells, 203–205

Minimize button, 164

Mini toolbar, 17

formatting text, 37

minus sign, 217

monospaced typeface, 32

mouse

dragging text with, 78

moving insertion point using, 14

scrolling in document, 14

selecting cells in table with, 198

selecting text with, 18

move table column marker, 192

moving

cells in table, 199–200

SmartArt graphic, 148–149

table, 212–213

multilevel list

creating custom, 234–235

inserting, 233

typing, 234

Multilevel List button, 233

Multiple Pages button, 161

multiplication formula, 217

N

naming, document, 8

Navigation pane, 113–114

New backstage area, 179–180

New Line command, 6

newspaper columns, 104

New Window button, 167

nonprinting characters, displaying, 103

No Spacing style, 42

numbering

automatic, 62–63

custom numbering formats, 229–230

inserting and removing page numbers, 93–94

inserting custom numbers, 226–228

lists, 62–63

paragraphs, 62–64

turning off, 62–64

Numbering button, 62–64, 226

O

Object button, 168

objects, enclosed object, 139

100% button, 161

One Page button, 161

OneDrive, 13
OneDrive for Business, 13
Online Pictures button, 129
Open dialog box, 10–11
OpenDocument Text format, 181
opening
	blank document, 4
	documents, 10–11
	multiple documents, 164–165
	from recent document list, 11
	Word, 4
option buttons, 6
organizational chart with SmartArt, 150–151
Orientation button, 86

P

page border, inserting and changing, 100–102
Page Break button, 90
page breaks, 90–91
Page Color button, 158
page numbers, inserting and removing, 93–94
page orientation, 86–87
pages
	display options
		changing display percentage, 161
		changing page movement, 160–161
		hiding/showing white space, 162–163
	formatting background
		changing page color, 99
		inserting and changing page border, 100–102
		inserting watermark, 99
	inserting
		blank page, 91–93
		cover page, 91–93
		page breaks, 90–91
		page numbers, 93–94
		predesigned headers and footers, 95–97

removing, page numbers, 93–94
setup changes
	margins, 86–89
	page orientation, 86–87
	paper size, 87–89
view, changing, 156–158
Page Setup dialog box
	margin changes, 88–89
	paper size changes, 88–89
	vertical alignment option box, 112–113
page size, 87, 88
Page Width button, 161
panes, dividing window into, 165–166
Paragraph dialog box, 48
	change line spacing in, 55
paragraphs
	alignment
		buttons and keyboard shortcuts, 46
		changing as you type, 46
		changing at dialog box, 48
		changing existing text, 46–47
		default, 45
	borders, 66–68
	bulleting, 65
	collecting and pasting with Clipboard, 82
	cutting, copying and pasting text, 77–82
	display paragraph symbol, 46
	indenting text in, 49–52
	numbering, 62–64
	setting and modifying tabs, 71–77
	sorting text in, 70–71
	spacing
		before and after, 52
		changing with Paragraph Spacing button, 44–45
Paragraph Spacing button, 43
Paste button, 77
Paste Options button, 79
PDF file, saving document as, 183–184

pictures. *See also* images
	inserting and customizing, 129–135
Pictures button, 129
pinning
	document, 11–12
	folder, 12
plain text, saving document as, 181, 183
Playback Toolbar, 158–159
plus sign, 217
points, 33
portrait orientation, 86–87
Position button, 130, 148
predesigned text box, 135–137
previewing, pages in document, 168–170
printing
	document, 8–9
	envelopes, 173–175
	labels, 175–178
	pages in document, 170–172
	previewing pages, 168–170
	Print backstage area, 8–9
	Quick Print button, 9
Print Layout view
	as default view, 156
	hiding/showing white space in, 162–163
Properties button, 209
proportional typeface, 6, 33
pull quote text box, 135–137

Q

Quick Access toolbar, 5
	inserting button on, 9
	New button, 10
	Quick Print button on, 9
	Save button, 13
	Undo and Redo button, 20–21
Quick Print button, 9
Quick Table, inserting, 216

R

readability, 104
	Learning Tools and, 158–160

Read Aloud button, 158–160
Read Mode view, 156–157
Recent Documents list
    opening document from, 11
    pinning and unpinning
        document to, 11–12
Redo button, 20–21
Remove Background button,
    132
Remove Split button, 165
Repeat command, 53–54
Repeat Header Rows button,
    207–208
Replace button, 113
Reset Picture button, 132
resize handle, 192, 212
resizing table, 212–213
Restore button, 164
restoring, windows, 164–165
Reveal Formatting task pane,
    56–57
ribbon, 5
Ribbon Display Options button,
    162
Rich Text Format (RTF), saving
    document as, 181
Rotate button, 130
rows
    changing height in table,
        206–207
    inserting and deleting in
        table, 201–203
row selection bar, 198
ruler
    displaying, 49
    horizontal, 5
        setting/modifying tabs on,
            71–74
        view, 71
    vertical, 5

S

sans serif typeface, 32–33
Save As dialog box, 7–8, 13
Save button, 7, 13
saving documents, 7–8
    in different formats, 181–184
    changes to, 13

in PDF/XPS format, 183–184
with Save As, 13
screen clipping, creating and
    formatting, 144–145
Screenshot button, 142
screenshots, inserting and
    formatting, 142–144
ScreenTip, 26
scrolling
    in documents, 14
    synchronous, 166
search
    finding and highlighting text,
        113–115
    specifying options, 116–118
section break
    continuous, 103–104
    inserting, 103–104
Select button, 201
Selection Mode, 18–19
serif typeface, 32–33
Set Numbering Value dialog
    box, 226–227
shading, 68–69
Shading button, 68
Sharepoint, 13
shapes
    copying, 139–140
    drawing, 139–140
Shapes button, 139
shortcuts. *See* keyboard
    shortcuts
Show/Hide ¶ button, 46, 90,
    103
Side to Side button, 160
Size button, 87
sizing
    images, 129–130
    tables, 212–213
SmartArt button, 146
SmartArt graphic
    arranging and moving,
        148–149
    Choose a SmartArt Graphic
        dialog box, 145
    creating organizational chart
        with, 150–151
    inserting and formatting,
        146–147

Smart Lookup option, 25
soft copy, 8
soft page break, 90
Sort button, 70
sorting, text in paragraphs, 70–71
Sort Text dialog box, 70–71
spacing
    changing before/after
        paragraphs, 52
    changing with Paragraph
        Spacing button,
        44–45
    line spacing changes, 54–55
special characters, inserting,
    126–127
spelling
    automatic spelling checker, 4
    spelling and grammar check,
        22–23
    Spelling task pane, 22
Split button, 165
Split Cells button, 203
Split Table button, 203
split window, 165–166
Status bar, 5
Strikethrough button, 36
styles
    applying, 42–43
    No Spacing style, 42
style set
    changing, 42–43
    customizing, 42–43
Subscript button, 36
subtraction formula, 217
suffixes, finding and replacing,
    118
SUM function, 217
superscript, AutoCorrect and, 4
Superscript button, 36
Switch Windows button, 164
Syllables button, 158
Symbol button, 126
Symbol dialog box, 126
symbols, inserting
    with AutoCorrect, 241–242
    with Symbol button, 126–
        127
Synchronous Scrolling button,
    166

T

table
  converting text to table, 214–215
  creating
    entering text in cells, 193
    Insert Table dialog box, 195
    moving cells in, 199–200
    moving insertion point within, 193
    with Quick Table, 216
    with Table button, 192, 194
  design changes, 196–197
  drawing, 215–216
  inserting formulas, 217–219
  layout changes
    alignment and dimensions, 210–211
    cell alignment, 207–208
    cell direction, 210, 211
    cell margin measurements, 208–210
    customizing cells size, 205–207
    inserting and deleting rows and columns, 201–203
    merging and splitting cells and tables, 203–205
    repeating header rows, 207–208
    resizing and moving, 212–213
    Table Tools Layout tab, 200
  parts of, 192
  performing calculations in, 217–219
  selecting cells
    with keyboard, 199
    with mouse, 198
    with Select button, 200–201
Table button, 192, 194
table move handle, 192
Table Options dialog box, 209

Tables Properties dialog box, 211
Table Tools Design tab, 196
Table Tools Layout tab, 200
tabs, 5
  alignment buttons, 71–72
  clearing, 74
  default setting, 71
  deleting, 74
  modifying
    on horizontal ruler, 71–74
    at Tabs dialog box, 74–76
  moving, 74
  setting, 72–74
  setting leader tab, 76
Tabs dialog box, 74–76
taskbar, 5
  Word button on, 164
Tell Me feature, 5
  Smart Lookup option, 25
  using, 25–26
template
  creating letter with, 179–180
  opening, with File Explorer, 186–187
  saving, in Custom Office Template folder, 185–186
text
  changing direction of, in cells, 210, 211
  Click and Type feature, 110–111
  collecting and pasting with Clipboard, 82
  converting to table, 214–215
  copying and pasting, 80
  cutting and pasting, 77–78
  deleting, 17, 77
  dragging with mouse, 78
  drop cap, 109–110
  editing, with find and replace, 113
  entering text in cells, 193
  finding and highlighting, 113–115
  formatting into columns, 104–107
  hyphenating words, 108–109

indenting in paragraphs, 49–52
  inserting, 17
  Paste Options button, 79
  pull quote text box, 135–137
  readability, 104
  selecting, 17–20
  sorting in paragraphs, 70–71
  symbols and special characters, 126–127
  undo and redo deletions, 20–21
  vertically aligning, 112–113
  vertically centering, 112–113
  WordArt, 141–142
text box
  drawing, 137
  inserting predesigned, 135–137
Text Box button, 135
Text Direction button, 210
Text Effects and Typography button, 36
Text Highlight Color button, 36
Text Spacing button, 158
Theme Colors button, 43
Theme Effects button, 43
Theme Fonts button, 43
themes
  applying, 43–45
  customizing
    applying theme effects, 249–250
    changing default setting, 252
    creating custom theme fonts, 248
    creating theme colors, 246–248
    deleting custom theme, 252
    editing themes, 251–252
    resetting custom theme color, 246
    resetting template theme, 252
    saving custom document theme, 249–250
  modifying, 44–45

Interior Photo Credits

Page GS-1, © lowball-jack/GettyImages, Courtesy of Paradigm Education Solutions; page *GS-2*, © irbis picture/Shutterstock.com; page *GS-3*, © th3fisa/Shutterstock.com; page *GS-4*, © goldyg/Shutterstock.com; page *GS-5*, © Pressmaster/Shutterstock.com.